SING FOR YOUR SUPPER

THE BROADWAY MUSICAL IN THE 1930S

The Broadway
Musical in the
1930s

ETHAN MORDDEN

SING FOR
YOUR SUPPER

palgrave
macmillan

SING FOR YOUR SUPPER
© Ethan Mordden, 2005.

Portions of Chapter Three first appeared in somewhat different form in
The New Yorker magazine on October 28, 1991.

First published in 2005 by
PALGRAVE MACMILLAN™
175 Fifth Avenue, New York, N.Y. 10010 and
Houndmills, Basingstoke, Hampshire, England RG21 6XS
Companies and representatives throughout the world.

PALGRAVE MACMILLAN is the global academic imprint of the Palgrave
Macmillan division of St. Martin's Press, LLC and of Palgrave Macmillan Ltd.
Macmillan® is a registered trademark in the United States, United Kingdom
and other countries. Palgrave is a registered trademark in the European
Union and other countries.

ISBN 0–312–23951–3

Design by Newgen Imaging Systems (P) Ltd., Chennai, India.

Printed in the United States of America.

To
Ian Marshall Fischer

Contents

ACKNOWLEDGMENTS

As the second of the series but the last to be completed, this volume should look back generally: to my classic editors, Sheldon Mayer at Oxford University Press and Michael Flamini here at Palgrave; to my Royal Mounted agent, Joe Spieler; to copyeditors Benjamin Dreyer and Jolanta Benal; to Palgrave's inspired jacket designer, David Baldeosingh Rotstein; to the production editor at Palgrave, Alan Bradshaw, racked uncomplainingly by the crazy little chord notations that so baffle the compositor; to the staff upstairs at Lincoln Center Library, which I think of as Vandamm City; to Ted Chapin of the Rodgers and Hammerstein Organization; to Richard Whitehouse in London, for the material on *Three Sisters*; and to my friend and colleague Ken Mandelbaum, not only for assistance in the sheer archeology of the musical but for his broad perspective on it. This is especially helpful if, like me, you believe the art has been locked in a spiral of degradation ever since *Babes in Toyland*. Until you have had a few conversations with Ken, you don't know the musical.

INTRODUCTION

This is the second volume in a decade-by-decade chronicle of the musical's Golden Age, and the last to be completed. That is because the 1930s is the most difficult decade in the set: the one that left the fewest remains behind for the archeologist, whether as filmed souvenirs of its performing styles or the simple survival of scripts and scores.

Two things struck me when I began writing this series, in 1995. One was that, except for fellow historians, no one had any grip on which musicals belong to which eras, or how the musical defined itself in each decade. The latter is particularly worthy of remark, because American art often answers to developments unique to specific decades. One thinks of the movies' 1910s (the bourgeois acculturation of moviegoing and the institution of the full-length feature), 1920s (the flowering of the silent), 1930s (the talkie); or pop music's 1920s ("jazz"), 1940s (swing), 1960s (rock and roll turns into the vastly more various rock).

The other thing was that all these confused opinions—about, say, the qualities of twenties musical comedy as opposed to fifties musical comedy—included the assumption that the musicals of the 1930s stood out in some very important way. The Great Depression, F.D.R, "Brother, Can You Spare a Dime?": this is rich material, right?

In fact, the 1930s was the least enterprising decade in the musical's Golden Age, roughly 1920 to 1980. The notion that the political atmosphere greatly affected the musical is incorrect. With some notable exceptions, the Depression did not politicize the musical's worldview. One finds far more "awareness" in the scripts of the Warner Bros. backstager at this time, not to mention the rest of that studio's output. Nor did the first truly great musical, Jerome Kern and Oscar Hammerstein's *Show Boat* (1927), inspire many other works with comparable serious content.

What the Depression did to the musical above all is demoralize both its capitalization structure and its profit potential. The money just vanished. Suddenly, those producers who could weasel up a budget had to concentrate on the most commercial projects, the sure things. That meant avoiding "difficult" subjects in favor of standard-make fun.

Some may cite *Of Thee I Sing* (1931) or *I'd Rather Be Right* (1937), daringly breakaway with their political commentary. These shows were in fact neither daring nor breakaway. They were, once again, musical comedy of traditional style in political settings. *Of Thee I Sing* was a babes-and-jokes show, albeit of unusually high satiric quality; and *I'd Rather Be Right* was a star turn.

There were daring breakaway shows, to be sure; the historian thinks at once of *Johnny Johnson* (1936) and *The Cradle Will Rock* (1937). But these titles are extremely exceptional. The decade of the 1930s consists mainly of Cole Porter and Rodgers and Hart scores cut into librettos by Herbert Fields or George Abbott, not to mention countless attempts to imitate them. The essential thirties musical is a twenties-style song-and-dance frolic with the tiniest hint of social commentary, Porter's *Anything Goes* (1934). And if the decade claims a theme song, it is not the somewhat atypical "Brother, Can You Spare a Dime?" but yet another Porter title, "Night and Day," a song hit of literally global impact.

Then, too, the onrushing development of American song, so energetic in the 1920s, slowed up in the 1930s. After the innovation of—just for instance—"Ol' Man River," a certain uniformity dulls the very sound of Broadway. It's all AABA structures, all generic ideas. The collapse of operetta—too expensive to thrive in the Depression—deprives us of the wonderful twenties invention of the "musical scene." Now, in the 1930s, the dialogue stops, the orchestra strikes up, and somebody sings a song. Then the dialogue starts up again. It gets familiar.

There were but two inventions in the 1930s, one technical and the other artistic. The latter comprises the development of choreography from decoration by hoofing zanies to illumination of theme by specialists in ballet and modern dance. There had of course been ballet in musicals long before the 1930s. The generally acknowledged "first" musical, *The Black Crook* (1866), was a melodrama pestered by a ballet troupe, and those ballet girls had never fallen out of fashion as the First Age gave way to the Second and Third. The historian, again, will think of *Sally*'s "Butterfly Ballet," right at the start of the Third Age, in 1920: Marilyn Miller thrills an imaginary *Ziegfeld Follies* with her "toe dancing" (as Broadway termed it then). Closer to the 1930s, ballet mistress Albertina Rasch and her ballet girls thrilled the real-life *Follies* in 1927, one of the great entries in the series.

So real dancing had always been on site. What was new, now, was its application—by George Balanchine, Charles Weidman, Madame Rasch, José Limón, and others—to the content of shows. Dance suddenly started to express what the book, music, and lyrics had no vocabulary for. The job description of the choreographer expanded.

The technical innovation of the 1930s was in the long run artistically significant: the revolving stage. This novelty frees the set designer of the ancient use of backdrop, wing pieces, and free-standing furniture on a stationary stage floor, substituting a circular cutout within that floor, ready to turn at any time. A set change in the old style consisted of a laborious replacement of everything; a set change on a revolve consists of a simple turn of the revolve, which brings another set into view.

The advantage is obvious: in the old style, shows had to be written to accommodate set changes with piffling scenes "in one" (i.e., before the downstage traveler curtain), clogging the narrative flow. The revolve's quick-change effect freed the musical of these hectoring interruptions: shows could now move from a given moment in the action to the next moment without having to make a rest stop along the way.

So musicals no longer had to be written around the stagehands. The revolve was introduced to Broadway during the 1920s, exploited most notably in 1929, in the Shuberts' sneaky copy of Max Reinhardt's Berlin production of *Die Fledermaus*, here called *A Wonderful Night*. Reinhardt used the revolve also in his staging of *Grand Hotel*—as did *Grand Hotel*'s producer-director in New York, Herman Shumlin, albeit in a new mounting, in 1930.

However, about seven months after *Grand Hotel* arrived on Broadway, the revue *The Band Wagon* introduced a surprise-within-a-surprise: the *double* revolve. This created striking stage pictures when the two mobile areas moved in opposite directions bearing dancers working in contrary motion as well.

We should note that the revolving stage became common but not standardized; and *The Band Wagon's* producer, Max Gordon, put legal constraints on imitative use of the double revolve. What matters is that design technology was actively seeking to liberate the musical of impedient physical conventions. (Other solutions were later brought into play, for instance projections instead of material decoration, or mechanized wagons to draw free-standing pieces on and off stage.)

Despite these revolutions in dance and design, I have to call the 1930s the decade that, in the musical, is praised the most for doing the least. As we'll see, there are some great events here, but mostly a lot of I Saw This Show Already. What sparks the time above all is the sheer smarts of those Cole Porter and Rodgers and Hart scores that everybody else is trying to turn out, too. We love the dancing that at last grows sensible of its responsibilities. Composers Harold Arlen and Kurt Weill come to town. The age glories in unique performers, from Bert Lahr to Dennis King, Vivienne Segal to Beatrice Lillie. *Porgy and Bess* centers the decade in 1935. There is much to cheer us—but less history than at any other time in the Golden Age.

I

A Lady Needs a Change: The State of the Art

Let's get our bearings by considering the different forms that a typical thirties show could take—in musical comedy, operetta or musical play, and revue. All of these genres were in rotation by 1900, but each developed in a particular direction during the 1920s.

For example, the most notable form of musical comedy was a type more or less invented—at least crystallized—by the producing partnership of Alex A. Aarons and Vinton Freedley in their first joint effort, *Lady, Be Good!* (1924). The format was built around the mating of star performers with star songwriters, in this case Fred and Adele Astaire and George and Ira Gershwin. I use "star" in the broadest sense, because these two teams, though well noticed, did not truly gain stardom till *Lady, Be Good!* itself.

Star performers in the musical are almost as old as the musical itself, perhaps best dated to the sudden prominence, in *Humpty Dumpty* (1868), of George L. Fox after some thirty-five years of obscurity. However, not till the 1920s was the notion of a "star score" even viable. First Age scores were hodgepodges. Then came Victor Herbert, but the lyrics lacked wit; and George M. Cohan's songs were drunk on genre. Not till P. G. Wodehouse arrived, in 1916, was a genuinely sharp lyric possible; and by then Kern and Berlin had begun their invention of American Song.

So now a star score was possible, especially because Cole Porter, the Gershwins, Rodgers and Hart, and DeSylva, Brown, and Henderson came along at about the same time. It is no coincidence that Aarons and Freedley (or Freedley alone) worked with all those named in this paragraph, and they would probably have got to Vincent Youmans as well if he hadn't become his own producer for most of his work from 1927 on.

Today, we know the importance of the director and choreographer in the making of musicals, not to mention the librettist. But twenties musical comedy—and its successor in the 1930s—counted on journeymen in these professions. There were a few ace directors, such as George M. Cohan. Most of the others were capably ordinary. Choreographers worked with the ensemble only, for solo dancers usually devised their own routines or assisted each other, as when Fred Astaire guided Marilyn Miller on her *Sunny* (1925) numbers.

As for the libretto, this, too, was at best functional. Our modern idea of the script that builds character, elaborates place and time, and even enlarges upon an idea—the kind of writing we find in *Wonderful Town* (1953) or *The Music Man* (1957)—is, as those parenthesized years remark, something that comes in after the Rodgers and Hammerstein revolution in the 1940s. Producers of the 1920s and 1930s didn't star librettists: they put up with them.

There was one other significant ingredient in the Aarons-Freedley show, this one difficult to pin down. It's something like imagination, or ingenuity, or surprise; and it's not clear whose job it was to supply it. But with so many shows resembling each other, a given work might prosper only if it offered something most other shows lacked. What to call this? Freshness? Zip? Delight?

Here's an instance: *Flying High* (1930), a show about aviation, begins with a book scene between two young women on a Manhattan rooftop. After a bit of identity establishment, telling us who is heroine and who sidekick, the heroine sings her Wanting Song, "I'll Know Him." And while the audience is applauding, the airmail pilot hero, as if answering her summons, floats into view in a parachute.

I hope the reader noticed that *Flying High* begins with a book scene; and we need to pause here for emphasis. The most persistent of the fac-toids beloved of certain writers in this field is that absolutely every single show before *Oklahoma!* began with a choral number: and this is simply not the case. Only in operetta and musical play was an initiating ensemble (or underscored pantomime) preferred. Musical comedy, less permeated by music, sometimes started with a little tootle from the orchestra to set atmosphere but then a dialogue scene—not a few spoken lines: a *scene*— before reaching the first number. The most famous example of this (because the work is so constantly in view) is the start of *Anything Goes*

(1934). Not only is there a book scene first of all but it is followed, much too early in the evening according to the musical-comedy handbook, by one of the show's major numbers, "I Get a Kick Out Of You."*

While very much in the Aarons-Freedley mode, *Flying High* was produced by George White, the ex-dancer who made fame with his annual revue, the *Scandals*. Every so often, White put on a book show; *Flying High* was built around Bert Lahr, who earned a flash stardom in an Aarons-Freedley show about boxing, *Hold Everything!* (1928). Lahr and Victor Moore were *Hold Everything!*'s main performing assets, and DeSylva, Brown, and Henderson were its songwriters. White decided to retain the latter set for the *Flying High* songs, along with John McGowan, who co-wrote *Hold Everything!*'s libretto with DeSylva. Their assignment was Mission Very Possible: to fit Lahr's specialty character into the aviation background, balancing the crazy Lahr stuff with the requisite Boy Meets Girl stuff.

The character that Lahr specialized in was the adorable fraud, notable not only as the washroom attendant–monarch of *DuBarry Was a Lady* (1939) or Volpone in *Foxy* (1964), but in his classic Cowardly Lion. *Flying High*'s top joke will be that Lahr, as plane mechanic Rusty Krause, breaks the record for time spent in the air because he doesn't know how to land the plane, and the story will have plenty of space for set-piece sketches, including Rusty's press conference after he finally gets down, and, earlier, a physical exam:

> DOCTOR: What's your name?
> RUSTY: Emil Krause.
> DOCTOR: Born?
> RUSTY: (doing a take) What do you think?

The examination's blackout jest, involving Lahr's confusing a jigger of whiskey with a urine sample, was the terror of the critics but had

---

* Keep in mind that, in those days before cast albums, a latecomer might thus have missed his one chance to hear Ethel Merman introduce a Cole Porter standard. As it happened, Merman recorded the number two weeks into *Anything Goes'* run, with a studio group more or less following the show's arrangements. Still, to stay on the safe side, Merman's final number, "Buddie, Beware," was soon replaced by a "Kick" reprise, to ensure that this essential Porter-Merman experience reach all ears.

audiences roaring. It was a shock laugh, really: the public's realization that, unlike the format that Aarons and Freedley had developed for the Astaires and the Gershwins in *Lady, Be Good!* six years earlier, thirties musical comedy intended to dare the taboos, shake the place up.

As he had done in *Hold Everything!*, Bert Lahr occupied the center of the entertainment but not that of the plot, which got rather fascinated with the sweetheart couple. Grace Brinkley played the heroine we met when *Flying High*'s curtain rose, and Oscar Shaw was her parachuting vis-à-vis, the true aviator of the piece. More interesting to readers today will be Lahr's opposite, Kate Smith, as Pansy Sparks. Smith made her contribution far more in radio than on stage or in film, because she was a big girl in a time that had no sympathy for such, though she became so beloved on the air that she was able to make a success in television in the 1950s. *Flying High* treated Smith with cruelty; Robert Littell of the *New York World* felt "embarrassed at the crude sort of fun for which she is the target."

Smith's main reason for being in *Flying High* was to sing the heck out of the music, for neither romantic lead was a strong vocalist and Lahr had only two numbers. Smith's big one was "Red Hot Chicago," a jazz anthem with a verse suggestive of a clarinet in heat, the whole devoted to the idea of Chicago as the nation's musical capital. So vital was Smith to the evening's musical presentation that after Brinkley and Shaw each got a shot at the torchy "Without Love," Smith was allotted its third rendition so that its melody might at last be savored.

Truth to tell, the Aarons-Freedley plan expects a better score than DeSylva, Brown, and Henderson gave producer White. The songs are good enough, with the functional choruses such as "Air Minded" and "Rusty's Up in the Air" and—typical especially of this songwriting trio— the risqué charm song. "Thank Your Father" mixes a fetching whimsy with its erotic intimations, and "Good For You—Bad For Me" includes a gem of a line in the verse, "Stop that Chevalier stuff!" And *Flying High* ended as the season's biggest musical hit, at 357 performances.

Still, it was not an outstanding show in any way, and like most others was in part a vaudeville. "Red Hot Chicago" all but blundered into the action, and a dance specialty was performed *twice*, by the acrobatic girl group the Gale Quadruplets and also by Pearl Osgood, who played Grace Brinkley's sidekick. Note, too, that while the founding title of this format, *Lady, Be Good!*, left behind one of the hardiest of standards in

"Fascinating Rhythm" and is generally extremely tuneful, *Flying High* didn't even throw off an ephemeral hit tune.

Cole Porter's *The New Yorkers* (1930) offered a much stronger sing, in a genre different from Aarons-Freedley. The latter style uses any old story at all, with the familiar mistaken identity, purloined jewels, farcical solutions to problems that are worse than the problems, and so on. With *The New Yorkers* we have stars and songs, but also a novel idea for the libretto, one to create unique events not seen in other shows. *Flying High* wasn't about aviation; it simply used aviation. But *The New Yorkers'* subject matter is as discussed as the first theme in a sonata-allegro development section.

The idea for the show came from *New Yorker* cartoonist Peter Arno, who not only helped plot the script, drafted ideas for the sets, and designed some of the costumes, but also drew the logo art. This featured three couples out on the town in full dress kit: a snooty older pair, distracted youngsters, and, at center, a renegade heiress with a crook in a fedora, grinning out of the side of his mouth as he draws his gun.

This mating of the rich and the lawless was *The New Yorkers'* concept: the corruption of urban life is found not at the bottom of the human scale but at the top, where money is morality. Billed as "a sociological musical satire," *The New Yorkers* followed the adventures of that renegade heiress (Hope Williams) as she pairs off with gangster Al Spanish (Charles King). The entire evening is cast as her dream; one character keeps getting shot dead and keeps reappearing. Still, the action is otherwise naturalistic rather than fantastical. Arno's plan was to show the places where the sophisticated cluster—a speakeasy, outside Reuben's restaurant, even Sing Sing prison—and fill it with adulterers and entertainers, bootleggers and V.I.P.s. As Arno saw it, they're all of a type, and Herbert Fields' book expanded on the racy satire he had been injecting into the musical since he began work, with Rodgers and Hart, in the mid-1920s:

There comes a time in every man's life when a woman needs fifty dollars.

or:

I don't think it's respectable to accept jewelry from a man—unless you're at least living with him.

or:

> There are only two kinds of girls. Those who do and those who say they
> don't.

The Boy Meets Girl of Hope Williams and Charles King is more liberated
than such things had been but half a dozen years before:

KING: Are you a wet?
WILLIAMS: I'm so wet that if you blow on me I'll ripple.

and Williams got a line that so typified the spirit of not only *The New
Yorkers* but thirties musical comedy generally that it has been quoted right
up to the present day (sometimes incorrectly lacking the preposition), a
definition of Park Avenue:

The street where bad women walk with good dogs.

Hope Williams was pertinently cast as the protagonist of Arno's
debunking spoof, for she had established a persona as the smart and idealistic Philip Barry heroine, having created Linda Seton in Barry's *Holiday*
just two years earlier. Thus, Arno and Fields could make a hash of the
high moral fibre of Barry's wealthy, who at worst are selfish or silly. In *The
New Yorkers*, the rich—like everyone else—are sociopaths.

The New Yorkers had more than Williams: it was lousy with stars.
Williams' parents were Richard Carle and Marie Cahill, the latter a long-
reigning diva making a bold career move after playing the wholesome
heroines of shows like *Sally in Our Alley* (1902), *The Boys and Betty*
(1908), and, struck by amnesia, *Judy Forgot* (1910). In *The New Yorkers*,
Cahill played the kind of mother who presents her daughter with a bejew-
eled machine gun as a wedding gift, and Cahill's solo (dropped during the
Philadelphia tryout) was an early version of the lascivious list song "The
Physician," later used in *Nymph Errant* (1933). Considering that Cahill
established *her* persona introducing "Under the Bamboo Tree"—the
number that Judy Garland and Margaret O'Brien perform in *Meet Me in
St. Louis*—*The New Yorkers* really was a breakaway, or perhaps simply
Cahill's observation that Cole Porter and Herbert Fields are what happens to Sally, Betty, and Judy twenty years later. It was Cahill's farewell,
too: she retired after the show's 168 performances and died in 1933.

Filling out the view was singer Frances Williams, dancer Ann Pennington, and, most important, the comedy team of Lou Clayton, Eddie Jackson, and Jimmy Durante. As bootlegger Jimmie Deegan, Durante was his usual whirlwind of malapropisms, righteous indignation at imagined slurs, and sudden non sequiturs. At one point, a bell went off somewhere, and Durante, with a child's innocence, said to the audience, "Mama, there's somebody in the candy store."* "He is a mug at heart" was Brooks Atkinson's report. "There is a huge, elemental joke in finding him removed from a mug's environment and smashing his dangerous way through a metropolitan musical show." Everyone loved especially the first-act finale, a number called "Wood!," during which Durante and his two pals dressed the stage with instances of the subject matter—wagons, pushcarts, barrels, canoes, tree stumps, a barber pole, and even instruments they grabbed from the orchestra players just before the curtain came down.

"Wood!" was not by Cole Porter. It and almost all of Durante's other numbers were specialties run up by Durante himself: "The Hot Patata," "Money!," and "Data!." Porter's job was to figure out what music suited society's loafers, cheats, and sinners, and he didn't have to take a wild guess. However, while his Broadway byline was already fourteen years old, *The New Yorkers* was only his second book score in any real sense. Barring the short-lived and all but unknown *See America First* (1916), which would appear to be little more than college-show material or its equivalent taken to Broadway, and the play with songs *Paris* (1928), Porter's shows before *The New Yorkers* were revues and *Fifty Million Frenchmen* (1929), a story piece set in Paris.

So this was Porter's first chance to style a précis of the culture he thrived in. There was no all-basic New York ensemble number to bring up the curtain, for *The New Yorkers* is another piece opening with a book scene. When the chorus finally did get its innings, with "Say It With Gin," Hope Williams had already fallen for Charles King in the pounding minor-key "Where Have You Been?" Amusingly, Porter wrote numbers for both New York homesickness and New York fatigue, in, respectively,

---

* Aficionados of obscure early Warner Bros. talkies may skip this footnote. You others: the family of the candy-store proprietor lived by tradition in an apartment behind or over the store. When a customer entered the commercial precincts, the street door activated a bell that could be heard in the living quarters.

Frances Williams' jaunty "Take Me Back To Manhattan" and the lovers' wistful "Let's Fly Away," with the typical Porter patter section referring to people and places of the era.

Oddly, the score's one standard was banned for some years from the radio play that ensures popularity, because of the wicked honesty that was as much a part of Porter as his flip sangfroid. This was "Love For Sale," one of Porter's most distinctive musical inventions. The verse, almost as spare as recitative, seems to set a scene visually, in the moon looking down on a woman on a near-deserted street. A prostitute, she moves into a lightly swinging chorus filled with mocking ironies till the release hits a bitter climax on the most sentimental of phrases—which later earned Porter one of his four Oscar nominations for Best Song—"true love." As the last A section soars to a grand high note on the dominant augmented seventh, Porter repeats the song's title on a curious melisma that falls and then rises in a woebegone sigh.

Kathryn Crawford introduced it in that scene in front of Reuben's, backed by a singing group billed as the Three Girl Friends. The same crit-ics who found Bert Lahr's *Flying High* physical comedy tasteless raised objections to "Love For Sale"; astonishingly, *The New Yorkers'* producer, E. Ray Goetz, simply changed the view to Harlem and reassigned the solo to Elizabeth (later Elisabeth) Welch, a black woman. Oh, *now* the song is tasteful? All prostitutes are black?

"Love For Sale" is more celebrated today than ever, but a *New Yorkers* item somewhat overlooked for decades has recently been catching up to it. This is "I Happen To Like New York." Even more unusual than "Love For Sale" in its musical construction, it is made on a chain of chords built out of a three-note cell repeated over and over, varied only by a transition into minor-key harmony during the release. Over this, the singer salutes the city in a vocal line with little variation, all melodic interest depend-ing on the sheer intensity of iteration. The effect is of the clanging of a great bell, muted in the release and then booming at the close in an ecstatic affirmation of one's identity as a citizen of the most original spot on the planet.

Comparable to *The New Yorkers*, and with another saucy Herbert Fields book, is Rodgers and Hart's *America's Sweetheart* (1931). Here the novel idea is Hollywood and its crazy concatenations of the idiotic and the creative, the basic and the inspired. A midwestern couple (Jack

Whiting, Harriette Lake [Ann Sothern]) is sundered when she makes good as a silent movie star; then the talkies defeat her while he prospers. Fields told the story well, but it was the satire that mattered, not the plot. "It lacks a star and a major comic," wrote John Anderson of the *Journal*. But that kind of show—*Irene* (1919), say, or *Sally* (1920)—was going antique. Coming into fashion was the libretto that focused on a place or an idea; and the score, now, could be as important as the performers in all but poster billing.

Anyway, in a show like *America's Sweetheart*, every lead character plays the comic. The big producer (John Sheehan), the French queen of the lot (Jeanne Aubert), and the secondary couple (Gus Shy, Inez Courtney) dug into the jokes in both script and score, as did the sweetheart pair. Shy's amorous entanglement with Aubert ends when "she found out how young I was and threw me off her sofa."

The score is all but unknown, except for the hit, "I've Got Five Dollars." The dashing "How About It?," whose lyric amusingly repeats the three title words immediately, in false accenting, was popular with dance bands, and the authors favored "We'll Be the Same" with extra playings during the show proper. Still, it's odd to see how many of the critics, preferring three or four titles in the fashion of the day, cited "Innocent Chorus Girls of Yesterday" and "Sweet Geraldine," because these two have never made it onto disc, even those anthology recordings of arcane show music.*

It's odd as well to see how many of the reviews complained of the racy tone. Brooks Atkinson's blurb is ready: "Much of the humor is foul." And "More dirt than humor," Charles Darnton agrees. "Dully dirty," says George Jean Nathan. Dorothy Parker notes in Hart's lyrics a "nastiness of flavor." *The New Yorkers* might have been expected to test limits because of its raffish characters. But musical comedy generally was abandoning the family-ready charm of the Cohan and Kern model.

---

* Until relatively recently, the lyrics to almost all the unpublished *America's Sweetheart* songs were lost, though much of the music survived. "Sweet Geraldine," an a cappella close-harmony girls' trio in which Tennessee rustics sing Harriette Lake's praises—thus to show how widespread is her fame without wasting a book scene on it—survived for decades only in part, and at this writing the trio's other number, "Tennessee Dan," appears not to have resurfaced with the rest of the score.

In 1995, a small Manhattan company gave a staged concert of *America's Sweetheart*, on piano but with Broadway-level talent, including Jarrod Emick and Darcie Roberts as Boy and Girl, Ed Dixon as the producer, and Alison Fraser as the French vamp. There was no dancing, leaving all the (now restored) songs to cut off on a tonic chord after the vocal just where, in 1931, choreographer Bobby Connolly would have set his people hoofing. Still, the public was at last able to revisit a tightly constructed piece loaded with the oddities of cinemaland. Broadway loved to spoof film the way Hollywood loved to spoof *its* worst competitor, radio; a studio conference room is described as the place "where they turn good plays into bad movies." Rodgers and Hart were at their casual best, not inspired but always tuneful and smart, even in that bane of convention, the second-act opening. Just as "Sweet Geraldine" was used synoptically to reveal that the heroine has made stardom, a number for the producer and his corps of directors, called simply "Opening," let us know that, during the intermission, the silents have ceded the screen to sound. Rodgers can get a melody out of little more than a rising scale, and Hart cuts right to the core of what's happening in a single couplet, linking "They sing! They dance! They speak!" with "You see! You hear! You thrill!" For a nifty irony, *America's Sweetheart* was the team's last Broadway show before their own Hollywood adventure, lasting four years and including what is arguably the masterpiece of the early movie musical, *Love Me Tonight* (1932).

The third type of early thirties musical comedy was the easiest to pull off: one simply added song and dance to a pre-existing comedy, adding in characters and opening up the scene plot where necessary. *No, No, Nanette* (1925) didn't even have to open up *My Lady Friends* (1919), retaining its principals and three-act design plan of interior, exterior, and the same interior again. *Whoopee* (1928), however, expanded the Arizona canyon and ranch house used in *The Nervous Wreck* (1923) into a western panorama filled with new characters. But then, *No, No, Nanette* was the work of pinchpenny producer H. H. Frazee, and *Whoopee* was a Ziegfeld show.

Mr. J. J. Shubert put on our next title, based on a Shubert Brothers property called *Up Pops the Devil*. A farce that had closed merely eight months before its musical version opened, it must have seemed extremely potential: a couple living the bohemian lifestyle in Greenwich Village (that is, without clerical blessing) trade gender identities. He'll stay home so he can write a novel, and she'll take a day job. According to *Up Pops the Devil*'s authors, Albert Hackett and Frances Goodrich, the fun lies in the distracting intrusions that animate the man's day and keep him from his writing, including household chores, a drunk who wants to make a long-distance phone call, the laundryman, and a flirtatious southern belle from upstairs.

With Shubert perennial Harold Atteridge writing the book and a score by Sammy Fain and Irving Kahal, the musical was opened up by the expedient of making the heroine's day job that of a dancer at Proxy's Music Hall.* This allowed the action to leave the apartment for a host of onstage numbers at Proxy's, complete with *The New Yorkers*' Frances Williams as a Proxy vocalist and the Albertina Rasch girls as Proxy's kickline. With *America's Sweetheart*'s Harriette Lake and *Flying High*'s Oscar Shaw as the primary couple and another *New Yorkers* alumna, Ann Pennington, as the southern vamp, Mr. J. J. Shubert had a lively attraction on his hands, even if the Ritz Brothers comedy trio left the cast on its very last tryout stop, at the Majestic in Brooklyn. The musical's title, a fine bit of sarcasm, was *Everybody's Welcome* (1931), and it had a modest success at 139 performances, just a week less than *Up Pops the Devil*'s 148.

However, the Proxy's numbers, having nothing to do with the plot, did not open up the play as much as interfere with it. Moreover, the Fain-Kahal songs typify the worst aspect of thirties musical comedy, generic posing that gives no taste of character. The couple's numbers, "All Wrapped Up in You," "Lease on My Heart," and "Even As You and I" (a reference to the Rudyard Kipling poem "The Vampire," very well known at the time and a fecund source of titles) are any couple's numbers. And Frances Williams' songs were those Proxy's songs, anyone's songs. True, one of them was "As Time Goes By," the tune Humphrey Bogart would request of Sam in *Casablanca*. And a vibrant finale found Williams and Ann Pennington taking over Proxy's stage for "Is Rhythm Necessary?," though it's odd to find Pennington suddenly turned into a Proxy's employee on some bland technicality.

* The reference is to the real life Roxy Theatre, a film-and-stage-show palace in whose rubble, decades after this, Gloria Swanson would pose in the famous photograph associated with the deeper concept and higher truth of the Sondheim musical *Follies* (1971).

We learn how ambiguous was the very concept of a thirties musical-comedy score in *Everybody's Welcome*'s use of interpolations—five in all, including "As Time Goes By," a contribution from Herman Hupfeld. This never mattered in revue, potpourri by nature; *New Faces of 1952*'s score, arguably the best in revue history, was as much assembled as written, by ten different people. In a story show, however, we want the characters defined not only in words but in how the music presents them. People like to say that most musicals before *Oklahoma!* are hard to revive because they aren't integrated. True enough: but the lack of character content *in the songs* is what really makes old shows unworthy of our attention. All too often, the beautiful music is empty.

Of course, it is the musical comedies that seem so insubstantial; operettas were not only integrated as a rule but tended to inspire their creators to specific delineations in character, time, place. Those who caught *The New Moon* at Encores! in 2003 will recall its narrative precision. Seventy-five years old, it was rusty and corny but it *played*.

The New Moon is a Sigmund Romberg show, and if Romberg hadn't composed it, Rudolf Friml would have, for these two were operetta's outstanding masters in its heyday, in the 1920s. To learn where operetta stands at the start of the 1930s, we need only consider how Romberg and Friml are doing in the decade's first year. And, lo, the boys are not doing all that well, in, respectively, *Nina Rosa* and *Luana*.

At 137 performances in the vast Majestic, *Nina Rosa* wasn't a failure, and it went on to enjoy one of those mysterious vogues that the French occasionally lavish on unworthy American art, in a nearly two-year stay at the yet vaster Théâtre du Chatelet. Nevertheless, the score is horribly conventional, with its been-there waltzes and marches and even the hero's fox-trot salute to the heroine (recalling "Rose-Marie" and *The New Moon*'s "Marianne"). Worse, *Nina Rosa*'s story is a dull retread.

The setting is Peru, where an American mining entrepreneur (Guy Robertson) is in danger of losing his life to the usual villains, especially the knife-happy Pablo (Leonard Ceeley), who aches for an Inca treasure that the gringos are about to discover. The comic is the hero's sidekick (Jack Sheehan, the movie mogul in *America's Sweetheart*), whose official valentine is the hero's sister (Marion Marchante).

By law, operetta comics don't engage in love plots. They're on hand for capering numbers, such as "(Won't you be) The Secret in My Life" and

"Pizarro Was a Very Narrow Man," and for one-liners. Announcing that he's writing a book on Peru, Sheehan says, "I must study the natives," while executing a zany walk to go bother the chorus girls. Or: "Peru—where all the world's a stage and women are leading men." The critics remarked favorably on the verisimilitude of a fight between Robertson and Ceeley that had them tumbling all over the place, and in another scene Ceeley had Robertson trussed up for whipping. Of course, they were rivals for Nina Rosa (Ethelind Terry, who first played this tale along the Rio Grande in the original *Rio Rita* [1927]).

The show looked great. One reason why operettas always took place Somewhere Else was to exploit locale with spectacle; and tiny Armida and the team of Cortez and Peggy were the native dance specialists. But there was still that droning score. Lyricist Irving Caesar, a musical-comedy journeyman, was miscast in this world of high romance, though even a routined expert might have started with "caballero," reached for "sombrero," then capped it with "bolero," as Caesar does. Anyway, Romberg always composed the music first, letting the lyricist fill in the notes. So we can't blame Caesar for "A Gaucho Love Song" (which, just to make things difficult for us, is also called "The Gaucho March"), because it's jammed with persnickety little triplets calling up such lines as "Oh, a roaring volcano is he." Luckily, the lyrics could never be heard, because even big baritone Ceeley couldn't spit them out fast enough. Apparently, the show's librettist, Otto Harbach, assisted Caesar on the lyrics. But *Nina Rosa* was lamed from the start by the dully derivative music, though Ethelind Terry and the ever ready Cortez and Peggy crossed the Atlantic to grace the London staging, punched up with some new numbers.

If *Nina Rosa* was underpowered but at least stylistically correct, *Luana* was incorrect because of its subject matter, Richard Walton Tully's hopelessly outdated play *The Bird of Paradise*. A vehicle for Laurette Taylor (and, on tour, Lenore Ulric) in 1912, the play is lowbrow tragedy about the romance between a white man and a local girl in Hawaii. Her fellow tribesmen get resentful and menacing, in the sort of narrative that one thought had died out with silent movies. In fact, Tully's play was not filmed till 1932 (with Dolores Del Rio and Joel McCrea), when RKO and director King Vidor could count on the camera to revel in the sheer geography of it all, as the young lovers date by going for swims and the unhappy heroine placates native rage by throwing herself into a volcano.

Had RKO released *Bird of Paradise* in 1929, *Luana* might never have happened—how can a stage work compete with that sensuous photography? But we're in 1930 at present, when the longtime Friml associate Arthur Hammerstein (the producer son of Oscar I and uncle of Oscar II) somehow saw possibilities for spectacle in Tully's property, if nothing else in a bathing-pool scene and the usual population explosion—*Luana* counted twenty-one principals and a chorus of seventy.

One difference between operetta and musical comedy—the essential one, in fact—lies in the music: because operetta's has breadth and point. A second difference lies in the settings: because operetta likes that Somewhere Else and musical comedies are usually set in New York, as, indeed, are three of the four musical comedies in this chapter. A third difference, almost invariably overlooked, lies in the casting: because operettas were never made on unique personalities in the Aarons-Freedley manner. There were excellent operetta people here and there, such as Mary Ellis and Dennis King, the original Rose-Marie and Jim. But they hardly commanded the fame of a Bert Lahr, even an Ann Pennington or Hope Williams.

Thus, *Luana*'s romantic leads, Ruth Altman and Joseph Macaulay, were virtual unknowns (though some buffs may recognize Altman as New York's original Madame Dubonnet in *The Boy Friend*). The sole other important role, a beachcomber wasting his life away, was entrusted to Robert Chisholm, a very strong baritone in constant demand but, again, a name of note only to playbill typesetters. The critics singled Chisholm out all the same for his stirring delivery of "Son of the Sun," a march with sequences of recitative.

It's a hideous number, dramatic but even more tuneless than everything in *Nina Rosa*. Some of *Luana*'s love songs are not bad, but it may be a problem when Rudolf Friml has to compose music for titles like "Hoku Loa," "By Welawela," and "Wanapoo Bay." Lyricist J. Keirn Brennan is no help; and, for that matter, librettist Howard Emmett Rogers unfortunately hewed to Tully, complete with the pidgin dialect. "Somehow it all sounds too absurd with music," said Richard Lockridge, in the *Sun*. Robert Littell of the *World* agreed: "Come, we go see *Luana*, song-dance show about Hawaii. Plentee grass skirt, plentee girlie swishee skirtee. Plentee nood girlie in swimming poolee. Plenty much Viennese waltz by Rudolf Friml; sound mighty strange in middle of Hawaii." Littell wrote his entire review thus, closing with "[Harry] Jans and [Harold] Whalen they Marines. They make jokee. They terrible. They kick girlie for make funee. They give me painee. . . . Me next boatee to Vienna. Aloha Vienna."

So musical comedy is sifting through its potential and not yet entirely integrated; and operetta is in trouble. It isn't so much the drying up of Romberg and Friml as the difficulty in paying operetta's bills in a Depression economy. Producer Hammerstein was so distressed by *Luana*'s two-and-a-half-week run that when his W. C. Fields musical comedy *Ballyhoo* (1930) failed to draw he went bankrupt and lost the theatre named for his father, a show palace only three years old (and today the place where David Letterman tapes).

One form did undergo positive transformation at this time, the revue. In the 1920s, revue came in all sizes and sorts, but the genre was dominated by the epic annuals reflecting the particular taste of Florenz Ziegfeld, George White, and Earl Carroll: the *Follies*, *Scandals*, and *Vanities*. Although Ziegfeld put on a *Follies* every single year from the founding of the line in 1907 through 1925, he then began skipping years, and the much younger *Scandals* (initiated in 1919) and *Vanities* (from 1923) also failed to materialize now and again. However, while only Carroll laid claim to revue's public in 1930, all three men put entries on view in 1931.

The *Follies* had started small, as a look back at the events of the preceding year. But over time, Ziegfeld twisted and pointed his project till, from about 1915 on, the big *Follies* format defined revue: huge casts led by five or six headliners; visual spectacle in the beautifully colored backdrops of Joseph Urban; compilation scores of second-division quality occasionally throwing off a favorite tune or two; and of course the showgirl parades.

The 1931 *Follies* upheld the style. Singers Harry Richman, Helen Morgan, and Ruth Etting, comic Jack Pearl, and hoofers Hal LeRoy and Mitzi Mayfair took the top spots, not only appearing for their specialty solos but collaborating in ensemble numbers, an integration of talent not always typical of Ziegfeld's format. Thus, a burlesque of *Grand Hotel* by Mark Hellinger offered Morgan as the ballerina, here called Polly Adlervitch (Adler being a notorious *bordeliste* of the day); Richman as her young swain, Baron Al Capone; Pearl as Cecil B. Goldwarner "of Hollywood"; and so on.

Yet more integrated talent delighted the panorama of a "then and now" look at Broadway nightlife. First came a recreation of Rector's restaurant, where Etting revived Nora Bayes' theme song, "Shine On Harvest Moon," Richman imitated Al Jolson in "You Made Me Love You," and Jack Pearl revitalized the moribund art of "Dutch" comedy, recalling one of the most prominent of its exponents, Sam Bernard. A jump forward in time took the audience to a kind of Rector's of 1931, a speakeasy, where Etting sang a number clearly modeled on her Rodgers and Hart hit "Ten Cents a Dance": "Cigarettes, Cigars." The lament of a cigarette girl,* it matched "Ten Cents" even unto the patter section on the quality of her customers, such as "hoboes and street gals with no beaux." It's a bold image from lyricist Mack Gordon (to Harry Revel's music), perhaps inspired by the "queer romance" mentioned in "Ten Cents a Dance." To finish off the Rector's sequence, a scenario worthy of a Busby Berkeley production number in a Warner Bros. backstager calls for a gangland shootout, with LeRoy dying in Etting's arms for the fade.

Dancers (Ford) Buck and (John W.) Bubbles and impressionist Albert Carroll had their moments before the curtain while the next gala set was being readied, and Helen Morgan enjoyed the characteristically Morganesque "Half-Caste Woman," a Noël Coward piece introduced in London earlier that year. The *Follies* had seldom encouraged the big dance number that became routine in twenties musical comedy; the *Follies*, one might say, tolerated the kickline. Perhaps Ziegfeld felt that all that activity interfered with the contemplation of beauty. Nevertheless, this year the Albertina Rasch girls, to the music of Mr. Rasch, Dmitri Tiomkin, danced the "Fandango-Bolero," "Tom Tom Dance" (for a jungle scene), and "Illusion in White." Further, Act One ended before a dazzling set of the city's brand-new Empire State Building for one of the last of the New Dance Sensations, "Do the New York." Pounding and syncopated like the town itself, the song's chorus topped its release with the improbable harmony of an augmented E Flat triad over D Flat Major, a loony shriek of a chord.

---

* No, not Carmen. Cigarette girls rambled through niteries wearing peddler trays of tobacco products. The invention of the cigarette machine erased the profession, though its adherents are ubiquitous in thirties movies.

It was really the *Scandals* that featured the big dance number, for White's was the art of jazz theatre, fast and sly and this week; there was always a bit of the antique about the *Follies*, with its posed tableaux and ragtime. And those showgirls in their glorified beauty . . . was this the ultimate completion of timeless carnal grace or a new way of reading the *Police Gazette*? White's showgirls couldn't just turn up wearing little more than an insanely elaborate hat; they had to earn their paycheck exercising talent.

White, too, hired Joseph Urban to design his revue in 1931, but otherwise the show emphasized White's favorite thing, new young stars who sang or danced. True, the comics were Willie and Eugene Howard, starting their fourth decade in show biz. They suggest a *Follies* credit, perhaps, though in fact the brothers never worked for Ziegfeld.* Besides, the big news in the 1931 *Scandals* was the vocal talent, Ethel Merman and Rudy Vallee, he in his Broadway debut and she in her first appearance after *her* debut, in *Girl Crazy* (1930). A most Whitean casting coup was the use of Ray Bolger for—yes, of course—dancing, but also to do Al Smith, "Walter Windshield," radio announcer Graham McNamee, and gender founder Adam in various sketches.

A third singer, Met baritone Everett Marshall, was on hand for what we now call "crossover" music, especially in a number clearly designed to pile Ossa upon "Ol' Man River." Entitled "That's Why Darkies Were Born," it's the logical outcome of decades of black stereotyping of all kinds: the Bert Williams lament at its core, a March of Time narrator giving it voice, and eight or nine folk plays' worth of destiny packed into its worldview. Today, such items are regarded as condescending; and Marshall sang it in blackface, which is worse. Still, if the intention is to create a burnt-cork "Vesti la giubba," the content is all the same a plea for racial tolerance.

Merman took no part in the sketches, or in anything other than Merman. In one of the boldest proclamations of expertise in revue history, she just stood and delivered "Life Is Just a Bowl of Cherries," "My Song" (with Vallee), and the racy list number "(Ladies and Gentlemen)

---

* Willie alone, aged fifteen, was a vocal prodigy rather than a comic when he turned up in Ziegfeld's Anna Held vehicle *The Little Duchess* (1901); and the brothers together did make it into a *Follies* in 1934, one of several mounted by another pair of brothers, the Shuberts, using the late Ziegfeld's name.

That's Love." Merman also got the eleven o'clock spot, to trot out whatever other numbers took her fancy.

The *Vanities* had long been the big revue with the least defined of formats, unless soggy music, dreary comedy, and third-division talent be the particulars of form. But then, the star of the 1931 *Vanities* was Carroll's brand-new four-and-a-half-million-dollar theatre at Seventh Avenue and Fiftieth Street. Named for himself, it was a gorgeous art nouveau monster of a place seating three thousand—not that much less than the Met. The amenities (such as a program-reading light at each seat) were many, yet the top was a then relatively modest $3.00, because the house's gross potential was so large.

Surely, this one time Carroll should have come up with something special to match the theatre; but the show was the same crude imitation of Ziegfeld. The uncelebrated vocalists Will Mahoney and Lillian Roth* and comic William Demarest headed the bill, and the support was all but anonymous. Carroll did make one strategic discovery in the eighteen-year-old Vincente Minnelli, who helped design both sets and costumes. Even so, this was the same old vaudeville. Big to match the auditorium, it presented fifty-seven different acts, sketches, and such, from the randy old routine about the coeds and the crazy dean to, in the new style, Gluck Sandor's modern dances "Masks and Hands" and "Chromium" (distinguished by trick metallic scenery); or from the airing of the newest Western musical instrument, the theremin, to the *passéiste* "Parasols on Parade," with the showgirls twirling about under Parasol Eugénie, Parasol Créole, Parasol Sans-Gêne. For a grand finale, Carroll offered a giant dance number set to Ravel's *Bolero*.

One piece of the show, at least, was the talk of the town: "the dinosaur," as everyone called it. Technical wizardry allowed Carroll to set before his public a forty-six-foot-tall terror lizard that spat fire and altered its facial expressions. Constructed by the man in charge of the Met's *Siegfried* Fafner, it took seven men to operate, one in each leg, one in the head, and two on lookout. The whole thing had to be very carefully manipulated, for besides looming out over the orchestra to the seventh or

---

* To be fair, Roth was a wonderful singer; but she was fresh from an unproductive stay at Paramount and wouldn't really be a figure of consequence—despite a Hollywood bio, *I'll Cry Tomorrow* (1955)—even after leading the ensemble cast of *I Can Get It For You Wholesale* some thirty years after the *Vanities*.

eighth row, the monster held dancer Lucille Page in its mouth. She made her entrance by freeing herself, coming down to the deck, and then oozing around in the Earl Carroll manner (that is, in whatever "business" Carroll recalled seeing Ziegfeld's Drucilla Strain, Hazel Forbes, Kay Laurell, and others pull off). John Mason Brown likened Carroll to "one of the Minsky Brothers dressed up in chromium," and Percy Hammond declared the *Vanities* "a debauch." Still, the annuals ran more on PR and the drawing power of the producer's name than on reviews, and this edition's 278 performances—at a gigantic house, remember—showed how strong big revue still was.

But I promised you a generical development, and it starts with *The Little Show* (1929). Historians praise it for the teaming up of Arthur Schwartz and Howard Dietz and for the institution of the "intimate" revue: meaning for sophisticated rather than mainstream theatregoers, and thus relying more on wit than on gesture and spectacle. *The Little Show* began a small series and inspired imitations—less little than smart—and the results can fairly be said to have reinvented revue, eventually sweeping away the Ziegfeld, White, and Carroll styles.*

However, what is most important about *The Little Show* and its progeny is neither Schwartz and Dietz nor its sophistication. What the new approach introduced was a complete integration of talent, so that the specialty stylists were dropped in favor of versatile performers. Intimate revue doesn't like impressionists who make no other contact with the audience. Intimate revue doesn't let Ethel Merman sing whatever she feels like singing. Before *The Little Show*, revues were assemblies of performing spots, bridging them with some interaction among cast members but too often observing the limits of vaudeville: a sequence of independent acts.

In the new thirties revue, one's act lasted from opening to finale; comics sang and dancers played in the sketches. Not only had to: wanted to.

---

* The *Scandals* held out fitfully into 1939, though White survived his series by three decades. The *Vanities* made it into 1940, eight years before Carroll's death in a plane crash. Ziegfeld passed on in 1932; not only the Shuberts, as mentioned, but others kept the *Follies* alive into 1957, one year after a *New Faces* dropped its first-act curtain on a devastating takeoff of the Ziegfeldian showgirl parade, "Isn't She Lovely?" Art imitates life because the best life *is* art: this *New Faces* was emceed by a drag queen imitating Tallulah Bankhead, while the star of the penultimate *Follies* when it tried out (and closed) in 1956 was . . . Tallulah Bankhead. The real one.

This was the heyday of Beatrice Lillie, Bob Hope, and Bobby Clark, who could, more or less, do everything—and doesn't that recall to us the Rodgers and Hart Theatre Guild revue *The Garrick Gaieties* (1925)? The *Little Show* songs and performers mean more to us than the *Gaieties'* one lasting title ("Manhattan") and unrenowned cast list. Yet the *Gaieties* remains one of the two or three most historical revue titles: because it, too, popularized a "new" team in Rodgers and Hart, and seemed to sweep Broadway with a fresh air.

Also like *The Little Show*, the *Gaieties* threw off second and third editions, the last *Gaieties* (1930) offering a wonderful first moment in its revised return engagement, when the curtain rose on four actors sitting in chairs around a table in exactly the pose that Glenn Anders, Lynn Fontanne, Tom Powers, and Earle Larimore had struck for the photograph of *Strange Interlude* that was reproduced constantly during the 1927–28 season. The *Gaieties* version, a takeoff on the austerity of the very concept of the Theatre Guild, offered James Norris dressed as Ferenc Molnar; Rosalind Russell in precisely the pose that Fontanne had struck but wearing a hat made of the Theatre Guild logo, a three-story house; Sterling Holloway as George Bernard Shaw; and Roger Stearns as Eugene O'Neill. It was an insouciant, carefree touch—youthful above all, whereas the *Follies*, *Scandals*, and *Vanities* were your father's revue.

There were, of course, other preceding "little shows" before the *Garrick Gaieties*, most prominently *The Greenwich Village Follies*, in eight editions from 1919 to 1928. Still, critics seemed to feel, in 1929, that only now had revue marked out a new map for itself. Perhaps this feeling lay in something as simple as a ballad called "Hammacher Schlemmer, I Love You." It may sound contrived to us today, but in the era of Robert Benchley and Alexander Woollcott this kind of precious twisty fun was the very summit of—wait for it—*sophistication*. So, too, was *The Little Show*'s most famous sketch, still cited today, George S. Kaufman's "The Still Alarm." It reads on the macabre side: two men in a tenth-floor hotel room learn that the building is on fire. They make no attempt to flee; on the contrary, they await the firemen, and treat the whole affair in the style, Kaufman directs, "of an English drawing-room comedy." And note, by the way, that singer-dancer Clifton Webb and monologuist Fred Allen, two of *The Little Show*'s three stars (the other being singer Libby

Holman), both played parts in the scene:

> SECOND GUEST [WEBB]: (to firemen) Well, I guess you boys want to get
> to work, don't you?
> FIRST FIREMAN [ALLEN]: Well, if you don't mind. We would like to spray
> around a little bit.

At the close, as the fire rages unchecked, the two guests have settled in
to hear one of the firefighters practice on his violin.

In fairness, the sketches of the new intimate revue did not break away
from tradition as much as the staging and music did. Possibly the most
influential episode in *The Little Show* was the presentation of "Moanin'
Low" as a dance of death between Holman and Webb. The pair played in
high-yaller blackface, reminding us that, as with *The New Yorkers'* "Love
For Sale," in this age Broadway liked to locate kinky romance in Harlem.
After singing the number, Holman awoke the sleeping Webb, the two
performed an erotic apache, and, at the close, he strangled her.

Wow. So this is what *The Little Show* achieved, in the long run: the
reinstatement of earlier experiments in the integrated revue of versatile
talents offering smarter writing, unencountered situations, and better
music. Though every top songwriter of the 1920s (except Vincent
Youmans) wrote at least one revue, and though Irving Berlin created his
own style of variety show in the four *Music Box Revues* in the mid-1920s,
it was not till the 1930s that producers of the form routinely commissioned an entire score from one songwriting source alone.

It didn't happen overnight. For *The Little Show*, Schwartz and Dietz
wrote only six numbers as a team. They hitched up with other writers for
the other numbers, and a few titles came from some other place—"Can't
We Be Friends" from Kay Swift and her banker husband, who wrote as
Paul James; "Or What Have You?" from Morris Hamilton and Grace
Henry. Still, these titles fit effortlessly in with the Schwartz and Dietz "I'll
Guess I'll Have To Change My Plan" and "I've Made a Habit Of You" or
even Dietz's "Moanin' Low" lyric, to Ralph Rainger's music. Whether trying
out flip satire on courtship rituals in "Habit," blithely ruing that the Girl
whom Boy Met is married in "Plan" ("Why did I buy those blue pajamas,"
he laments, "before the big affair began?"), or going into heavy torch in

"Moanin' Low," the score holds together for its innovative harmony and playful rhymes. Like Rodgers and Hart in 1925, Schwartz and Dietz announce a new voice in town.

There's another parallel with the *Garrick Gaieties*. Like the earlier show, which started as a special Sunday attraction that got held over for an open run, *The Little Show* began on "let's see" Sundays at the Selwyn Theatre, produced by Tom Weatherly and James B. Pond. William Anthony Brady Jr. and Dwight Deere Wiman joined Weatherly in taking *The Little Show* to the Music Box, where it enjoyed ten months of delighted houses. After the bloated clichés of the big annuals, here was, indeed, a cute little pot of joy cooked up by eighteen players and "The Little Show Girls." The song sheets bore a drawing of an elegant couple gazing upon a scene suggesting the nineteenth-century melodrama *Tempest and Sunshine* (from the Cotton Blossom's repertory), as the villain points the unmarried mother and her baby out into the cruel world.

What irony! *The Little Show* was not the oldest but the latest thing in show biz, so protean that its second edition, under the same management, did away with an essential of its own form, the three stars of the first edition. Something about Holman's smoky voice, Webb's elegance, and Allen's deadpan sarcasm veritably *defined* sophistication—yet *The Second Little Show* (1930) had no stars, a smaller cast, more Schwartz and Dietz and interpolations, and some Little Show Boys to Meet those Little Show Girls. Is this too trim even for a trim format? Jay C. Flippen puffed on a cigar while telling corny jokes such as the one about the Scotchman who asked his girl friend if she was free tonight; and the one song that landed was Herman Hupfeld's "Sing Something Simple," which was banged out loud and fast and over and over till the public cheered out of sheer helplessness.

For *The Third Little Show*, Wiman and Weatherly brought back the headliners, this time Beatrice Lillie and Ernest Truex, billing the piece as "The Aristocrat of All Revues." Schwartz and Dietz went missing, leaving a grabbag of contributions and, worse, rather a number of solo specialties instead of the ensemble playing that the first of the series had made indispensable. Lillie's solos, at least, were choice, especially the campy "There Are Fairies at the Bottom of Our Garden" and, in its stage debut, Noël Coward's "Mad Dogs and Englishmen," made into a production number with Lillie in a rickshaw amid a swarm of natives. Walter O'Keefe got the

Herman Hupfeld novelty, this time the adorably idiotic "When Yuba Plays the Rumba on the Tuba." But it was Lillie who helped herself to a real treat in a takeoff of Ruth Draper, famed for creating a stageful of atmosphere through the meticulous variety of her characters. Dressed in Draper's apologetic shawl, Lillie cut right to the paradox of it all: "In this little sketch, ladies and gentlemen," she began, "I want you to imagine far too much."

The Second Little Show was a failure and *The Third* a minor success. But meanwhile first-time producer Max Gordon had learned one secret of the new revue: bring back *The Little Show*'s three stars with a mostly Schwartz and Dietz score. Then why not add in ballerina Tamara Geva and choreographer Albertina Rasch in fealty to the growing movement in arty dance? The result was what *The Second Little Show* probably should have been in the first place, given that the new revue's intimacy inhered less in size than in a "familiar" address of its public: less *small* than knowing, facetious, and chic.

Three's A Crowd (1930) was the title—in honor of the reunion of Holman, Webb, and Allen—and by now, one year into the decade, the thirties renovation of the revue form was more or less complete and simply waiting to collect its masterpieces. But *Three's A Crowd*'s opening was almost defiantly traditional: the usual bedroom adultery sketch, a twenties staple. How many times were audiences supposed to laugh when the husband leaned over to ask the lover, hiding under the bed, what he wanted for breakfast? This seemed a jejune note for *Three's A Crowd* to strike. But wait: Fred Allen suddenly walked onstage before a minute had passed, calling for stagehands to carry off that tired old bed and promising the public an evening of fresh enjoyment.

Ironically, there *was* an adultery sketch in the show, though not of the bedroom type. In "The Private Life of a Roxy Usher," Clifton Webb treated his wife and her lover to the finesse of a man who is in effect the social director of a vast theatre. Then, "In Marbled Halls" found Webb disturbed in his bath by stranger Tamara Geva. She has blundered in; the doorknob falls off; they're trapped together:

GEVA: Where does that window lead to?
WEBB: Lexington Avenue. But look out for the first step. We're on the eighth floor.

Somehow or other the bathtub plug is pulled, and, as the water runs out, Geva sneaks a peek at Webb's privates:

GEVA: Well, if it isn't Harry Smith! Fancy meeting you here!

The score was again a parade of contributions, including "Body and Soul," another mournful ballad for Libby Holman. But now Webb followed the vocal dancing with Geva, in whiteface, and he didn't kill her. Holman sang also the show's most lasting title, "Something To Remember You By," to departing sailor Fred MacMurray, the two of them surrounded by his buddies in their red-and-white-striped shirts and blue pants and coats on a French quai. A cute dance number, "All the King's Horses," took off from Margaret Lee's vocal, likening her heart to Humpty Dumpty, with the dancing girls in beards and dressed as playing cards. Geva's solo spot was "Talkative Toes." And each one of these songs was by a different team, to a total of eight different men in various combinations.

"What this country needs is cruelty to the writers of sketches," wrote Ross Lockridge, actually about *The Third Little Show*. "It is a sad commentary on the craft, but almost any writer will scamp his job if you give him a chance." This difficulty haunted revue virtually throughout its history. The music is easy, because there are plenty of good songwriters. Then, too, the freedom of the revue structure attracted the top staging talents. Hassard Short, one of the few directors at this time who had a reputation outside the theatre community, had been in charge of one of the *Greenwich Village Follies* and all four of the *Music Box Revues*; he also directed *Three's A Crowd*.

So the problem was the sketches—and it's not that writers were, as Lockridge suggests, "scamping." It's that sustaining a good idea at heavy grip for five to eight minutes is all but impossible. Fred Allen's high spot in *Three's A Crowd* found him as a rear admiral returning from the Antarctic. With his faithful crew standing behind him in their parkas (including MacMurray again, and also one gent in tropical garb but with a short woolen scarf around his neck), Allen gave a slide show of the trip, taking in his aircraft, his living quarters, some locals, and the South Pole. Every slide showed nothing but snow.

That's not really funny, is it? One easy out was the burlesque, bouncing off an existing entity with which most if not all of the public is familiar—the kind of thing that today's *Forbidden Broadway* does so well. However, when Max Gordon decided to follow *Three's A Crowd* with the same creative staff and yet more stars; *and* when the sketches, by George S. Kaufman and Howard Dietz, seemed all first-rate rather than scamped; *and* when Schwartz and Dietz produced the best assortment of numbers yet without a single interpolation, the first masterpiece was attained. This was *The Band Wagon* (1931), which starred Fred and Adele Astaire, Helen Broderick, Frank Morgan, and Tilly Losch. Hassard Short directed, with choreography by Albertina Rasch and settings by Albert R. Johnson.

Johnson's may be the most important name on the staging staff. The others are better remembered, but it was Johnson* who created the aforementioned double revolve that empowered so much of *The Band Wagon's* unique presentation. Its production numbers seemed a very physics of dance, amazing the performers taking hold of them, scattering then reordering them in patterns that now favored and now challenged the decor. There had never been anything like it.

So the "intimate" revue learned that it was, after all, no less expensive to put on than any other show. Design mattered just as in the *Follies*: and design costs. Principals in a modern-dress musical comedy might easily get through the entire evening in only two or three changes. In revue, the principals wear a different costume for every number and sketch they appear in, making for quite a bill. The extremely appealing cast and the abundance of wonderful songs attract us to *The Band Wagon* today. But when it was new, it was the dazzle of its look that astonished the town.

Then, too, there was the show's heavy dance plot. Tilly Losch led three numbers entirely or largely devoted to dance. In "The Flag," she appeared alone in glittering gold from neck to train under a cap topped by glittering stalagmites, a bewitching sight. John Barker introduced the vocal of "Dancing in the Dark," then ceded the stage to Losch and the Rasch girls, performing on a mirrored floor swept by shifting lighting patterns. Last came the earliest Dream Ballet I can trace in the musical's history, "The Beggar Waltz": homeless vagrant Fred Astaire falls asleep outside the Vienna State Opera, whereupon Johnson's revolve gives us the interior,

---

* Johnson's is also an irritating name, because he blithely advanced his middle initial in his billing, then deleted it, then readvanced it, right through the decade. At Palgrave, we strive for accuracy in recording program citations, but this is too much. He shall be Albert Johnson for the rest of the book. The R. stood for Richard.

where Astaire imagines himself partnering Losch, the company's star ballerina. The revolve brings us back to reality. Astaire looks up as the gala Losch departs the opera house. She meets his glance and pauses. *Was* it a dream? Or did they really ... no. She simply tosses him a purse and leaves. Blackout.

It may seem strange that Losch and not Astaire was *The Band Wagon's* dancing star. But Fred had plenty to do in the songs and sketches, for *The Band Wagon* accomplished the deftest integration of ensemble yet seen in a star revue. Remember, too, that Astaire wasn't really a solo dancer at this time. He was not only half of a team with sister Adele: he had protectively been throwing the act to her all their lives. So most of his dance spots were actually their dance spots, though their recent shows *Funny Face* (1927) and *Smiles* (1930) had each singled him out for an important solo with the men's chorus.

The first Astaire duet, "Sweet Music," came right after the opening, "It Better Be Good," in which the audience watched the cast taking *its* place in theatre seats and planning to be hard to please. The first of the evening's stage revolves then took the public into a miniature revue made entirely of clichés, as if *The Band Wagon* wanted to brag a bit in the *Three's A Crowd* manner about how renovative it was going to prove. Indeed, the *New York Times* review was headed "Beginning a New Era."

"Sweet Music" is simply a charm song in which Fred introduces one of the first of his career-long trick moves, in this case dancing while playing the accordion. But the Astaires' second number, "Hoops," is one of *The Band Wagon's* most lovable episodes, and it put the revolve to singular application. The set, of a Parisian park, is like so many of the show's sets little more than a construction at stage center, to free the revolves for action. A low fence surrounds a huge slab of abstract greenery, while *enfants terribles* Louis (Fred) and Marie (Adele) roll their hoops past a balloon seller, a nurse with a baby carriage, a trysting couple, two nuns, a gendarme, and so on. The song itself sets up the dance: the kids get into mischief and note how many people are having sex, especially adulterously, and the dance, coordinated with the two revolves, allows the pair to stay in view even as they drive their hoops and harass the bystanders. The climax plays with not only the revolves but the public's familiarity with the Astaires, who developed (in *The Love Letter* [1921]) a trademark exit used once in each show, the runaround. With the revolve spinning them about the central slab, they guided their hoops in ever wider circles till they gained the stage left wings at the orchestral button. Blackout.

Astaire had one dancing solo, "New Sun in the Sky," and Helen Broderick's big moment was a takeoff on the pert soubrette, "Where Can He Be?," which she sang in the company of the male chorus while so intent on her posing and prettying that they all deserted her. John Barker—the one strong voice in the company—had a duet with Roberta Robinson, "High and Low," and the chorus enjoyed a "the stars have passed out in their dressing rooms" number in "Confession," in which the girls tell the boys of their almost sinfully pure lives. "I always go to bed at ten," is the start of one quatrain. And the fourth line tells us "But I go home at four."

The all-important next-to-closing spot was another number for the Astaires, "White Heat." Here the central piece of decor was what looked like a steamer's smokestack, and again the revolves invaded the choreography as the ensemble—like the Astaires in white tie and top hats, girls as well as boys—tore the place up. Choreographer Rasch is now recalled mainly as the schoolmarm of a bunch of haughty operetta ballerinas; don't get Agnes de Mille started on the subject of Albertina Rasch. But one aspect of the decade's new dance techniques required ballet people to try their hand at the hoofing arts—the mindset that would lead to "Slaughter on Tenth Avenue" five years after this.

As for *The Band Wagon*'s sketches, critics then and historians since call them the best batch yet, and of course even a just okay bit can play well in clever hands. Except for Losch, *The Band Wagon*'s stars were all comics, whatever else they did. The most praised of the sketches is "The Pride of the Claghornes," a spoof of southern ways—the unbelievably ancient and dilatory black house servant (Philip Loeb) to the tottering colonel (Frank Morgan) and wife (Helen Broderick), the mint juleps, the offstage chorus running through an atmospheric selection of spirituals, the high-spirited daughter, Breeze (Adele), her stupendously dim-witted fiancé (Fred), the dialect:

COLONEL: You found [Breeze] a-sittin' and a-cryin'. Where was she a-sittin'?
WIFE: In the a-sittin' room.

Breeze is a-cryin' because of her terrible secret, certain to destroy her engagement: Breeze is a virgin! The sketch ends as she is forced to leave the old plantation, her father cursing the younger generation and its lack of respect for the fine old ways of the south.

I personally prefer "The Great Warburton Mystery," with Morgan as the trusty English inspector in a murder case. Simply the first view of the stage as the lights come up is a goof: the corpse slumped in a chair of the library, the various suspects—of course in evening clothes—grouped on the other side of the stage, the butler, the two policemen. *The Band Wagon* completely avoided burlesque of a hit play or film; part of its originality lay in a wish to start all its fun from scratch. Still, "The Great Warburton Mystery" teased the public with, so to say, coin of literary-theatrical currency, because the audience's prior knowledge of murder mystery protocol gave the sketch its energy. Of course, the inspector gets a big buildup for his entrance. Of course, he will be coolly authoritative and cut right to business:

INSPECTOR: (looking not at the corpse but at the butler) Is this the dead man?
POLICEMAN: No, here, sir.

Nothing else in the sketch is quite as funny; solving the crime involves checking the size of everybody's bottom. Anyway, the butler did it.

After all that, the reader may be surprised to learn that *The Band Wagon*'s run, at the New Amsterdam, was a bit short of eight months—a fine stay for the time, but deflating for the first masterpiece in revue, even given the economy's chilling effect on theatregoing. Unfortunately for those who missed the show, it turned out to be the last joint appearance of the Astaires: Adele departed during the post-Broadway tour to marry into the English aristocracy and retire, causing the usual swamis to predict disaster for Fred. What had he been, they asked, but a brother? As we'll see, his first solo outing, *Gay Divorce* (1932), not only gave him a hit but created a new persona for him as a sardonically romantic bon vivant, all set for his RKOs with Ginger Rogers to music by Irving Berlin, Jerome Kern, and the Gershwins.

The Band Wagon itself passed into fond memory. When Columbia's Goddard Lieberson set about recording classic scores that had preceded the era of the cast album, *The Band Wagon* was the only revue score thus revived. The performance, featuring Mary Martin, sings yet on CD as

I write. And when MGM readied a Fred Astaire backstager for 1953 with old (and one new) Schwartz and Dietz numbers, it bore the working title of another *Band Wagon* number, "I Love Louisa," originally set on a carousel with the cast in lederhosen and dirndls. Yet the words "The Band Wagon" seemed so certain an imprimatur that in the end Metro had to buy them (from Fox, which owned the rights to the stage show) out of simple prestige.

Revue is the most ephemeral of the musical's genres. For this one to have outlasted so many other titles over the decades tells us how effectively it proclaimed the new form. The 1920s had been saturated with revue. The 1930s would see far fewer of them; but most of the great ones turn up in this time. This is just as well, for the book musical was making very little history.

2

CARRY ON, KEEP SMILING: MUSICAL COMEDY I

One interesting aspect of the 1930s is how thoroughly the old styles of musical show had been banished. There was a lot of overlapping between the primitive First Age, of the nineteenth century, and the Second Age, from 1900 to 1920: in the comics' "business," in the use of the beauty chorus, in genres of song, in set and costume design.

By 1930, however, the echo of old ways lay mainly in the last two musicals starring Fred Stone, *Ripples* (1930) and *Smiling Faces* (1932). Stone was a genuinely beloved figure, an acrobatic clown with a performing family (wife, two daughters, and one son-in-law) and a public of old-timers and their kids who liked their shows clean as an antibiotic. Indeed, when not fussing at the "obscenities" that Herbert Fields, Bert Lahr, and others were committing, critics never tired of reminding readers that an evening of Stone was so innocent that—this is the *Telegram*'s Douglas Gilbert on *Ripples*—"a child can take his parents to it."

That was the problem. Working up from the circus and vaudeville, Stone became famous as the Scarecrow (to the Tin Man of his partner, Dave Montgomery) in *The Wizard of Oz* (1903). With a libretto and some lyrics by Oz himself, L. Frank Baum, this show was a tremendous hit, albeit in the already fading First Age form of extravaganza: fairy tales using spectacle and vaudeville specialties. Montgomery and Stone's popularity was such that they reinvigorated the form, Stone doing so singlehanded after Montgomery's death, in 1917. By the 1920s, Stone's vehicles were Broadway hits (and huge touring attractions) because of the expert showmanship of his producer, Charles Dillingham. He made sure that Stone's audience could count on good music, a feature that extravaganza seldom enjoyed; Victor Herbert and Jerome Kern each composed two scores for Dillingham's Stone titles, and Ivan Caryll three.

Still, however well produced, these shows were written on an antique model, and time was nagging at Stone as sure as wife Ann Shoemaker does on his appearance as Katharine Hepburn's father in the RKO *Alice Adams* (1935). Stone's last twenties show, *Three Cheers* (1928), had done well, though in fact Will Rogers had had to take over before the opening when Stone suffered a plane crash. He survived, albeit with massive injuries, including two compound fractures of the left leg, fractures of the right thigh, jaw, and left wrist, and dislocation of the left ankle and right shoulder. ("Otherwise," Brooks Atkinson dryly noted, "Mr. Stone was not seriously injured.") Stone had all Broadway's support when he returned for *Ripples*, complete with the customary trick entrance, dropping out of the flies onto his back in a tulip bed as if kicked there by a mule; and Stone hoofed on his crutches, joined by daughters Dorothy and (in her debut) Paula, the girls on crutches, too. You see how loosely these shows were structured: they breathed with their performers.

Ripples got *The Band Wagon*'s booking, at the New Amsterdam. However, as a modern-day Rip Van Winkle with the expected dreamland adventure, Stone was hardly keeping up with *The New Yorkers* or even *Everybody's Welcome*. *Ripples* closed after 55 performances, a stunning defeat for a star who once could run any show for two years, counting New York and the tour.

Smiling Faces, which tried to get away with one of those legacy-with-a-catch plots, was no different. Big Hope Emerson cried, "As your fiancée, I have some rights!" And Stone replied, "I'll say you have," as he felt her right biceps. "It's big as [Jack] Dempsey's!" The show had toured the hinterland before daring New York, as if sensing that it would not be welcome. At 33 performances, it clearly wasn't; and Stone was over.

Nevertheless, noting Dillingham's profits through the 1920s, Florenz Ziegfeld must have been wondering why Florenz Ziegfeld wasn't producing an extravaganza, because its elements of star comic and spectacle were Ziegfeld elements as well. Ziegfeld's one entry in this form, *Simple Simon* (1930), was built around Ed Wynn by Guy Bolton (and Wynn), using a Rodgers and Hart score. The idea, presumably, was to renovate the corny old format with wisenheimer drollery, and it almost worked.

Typically for extravaganza, the show began in the modern era, at Coney Island, where Wynn, as one Simon Eyyes, runs a news shop. All the principals of the coming storybookland action turn up first in contemporary dress: the Cinderella heroine (Doree Leslie), her Prince Charming, a certain Tony Prince (Alan Edwards), cutups Jack and Jilly (Will Ahearn, Bobbe Arnst), the bad guy (Paul Stanton), and so on. Exposition accomplished, we move into *Babes in Toyland* territory, albeit in the company of the jiving "Don't Tell Your Folks," "Sweetenheart," and even "Ten Cents a Dance," though the last had nothing to do with the storyline. In fact, Wynn used it as a chance to show off another of his crazy inventions, a tricycle-*cum*-piano. Etting was perched on it, and she sang the wail of a taxi dancer while Wynn circled the stage. You never got that in a Fred Stone show.

Wynn was ideal for the infantile plot, however, for his persona was that of the childish zany zigzagging between a love of simple things and a zest for inventing those gadgets. *Simple Simon*'s included, besides the mobile piano, a mousetrap all locked up so the dear little creatures won't get hurt, and a cigarette lighter with match attachment, because lighters never work. Wynn's moment of contact with the natural world, on the line "Oh, *how* I love the woodth!" in a picnic scene, became a catchphrase of the day.

Unfortunately, *Simple Simon* arrived during the losing streak that bedeviled Ziegfeld's last four years on earth. After the excitement created by the opening of the Ziegfeld Theatre with *Rio Rita* and its second tenant, *Show Boat*, the location became what it had been before the theatre was built: foreign country. Both *Rio Rita* and *Show Boat* were event enough to draw crowds. But Fifty-fourth Street on Sixth Avenue discouraged walk-in business and was at least partly to blame for the successive failures of *Show Girl* (1929), *Bitter Sweet* (1929), this same *Simple Simon*, *Smiles* (1930), the last *Follies* put on by Ziegfeld himself (1931), and *Hot-Cha!* (1932).

They didn't know it at the time, but the helter-skelter star-comic vehicle was on its way out, though its stronger avatars produced hits for a generation more. They even produced, for *Fine and Dandy* (1930), probably the greatest set of notices ever accorded a show doomed to oblivion. *Brigadoon* was not more highly praised than this title, and it's odd to note just how vulnerable to memory a *Fine and Dandy* can be. Of its score, by

Kay Swift and her still pseudonymous husband, Paul James, everything vanished but for the title song, which served in television's early days for transition music and magic acts. Even *Fine and Dandy*'s star, one of the most celebrated jesters of the age, left behind a silent ovation: Joe Cook.

Cook of the Rube Goldberg machines, the digressive, improvised tirades, and the sophistry that outsmarts your logic was at his best in *Fine and Dandy*, as a factory employee caught in a shakeup in the firm's hierarchy while romancing the factory owner's daughter. Cook rises from nobody to manager (and almost destroys the business with spendthrift reforms). This should not be mistaken for a reflection of Depression labor relations. Cook tended to rise: in *Hold Your Horses* (1933), he started as a hansom-cab driver and ended as mayor of New York; and he loved to don fancy duds and colorful uniforms. Anyway, by *Fine and Dandy*'s finale Cook was not only no longer the factory boss but entirely unemployed.

He did get the girl (Alice Boulden), which was unusual for a star comic. But then, Cook's shows were not unlike conventional book musicals containing green zones for Cook shtick. Donald Ogden Stewart's *Fine and Dandy* book accommodated a scene plot much too busily narrative for the kind of joker who overwhelmed his shows—and Third Age jokers tended to do so. Act One moves from the factory machine room to a country club, first in the caddy house and then—to make room for a Joe Cook golfing sketch—in a sand trap. Then it's back to the factory for more plot: a story show in which the story almost matters.

So *Fine and Dandy*'s score is not entirely unintegrated. Cook was in only one number—that title song, a duet with Boulden. The rest of the tunestack was apportioned in customary early-thirties style—Eleanor Powell's dance numbers, "The Jig Hop" and "I'll Hit a New High"; siblings Boulden and Joe Wagstaff's cheer-ourselves-up duet, "Let's Go Eat Worms in the Garden"; Boulden's solos "Can This Be Love?" and the torchy "Nobody Breaks My Heart." James' lyrics veer from clever to cliché, and he dabbles in false rhymes. His wife showed promise, though for some reason she never wrote another book musical. Her melodies lack distinction overall, but she jiggles them distinctively, jollying "Worms" with such syncopation that its release just gets up and charlestons. "Can This Be Love?" is utterly conventional in its intentions, and yet Swift launches the refrain on the fourth tone of the scale in the tonic, catching exactly the edgy wonder that the dramatic situation needs. To be fair, her husband got into the zany Cook spirit in the title number, as Cook suggests famous duos for him and his girl to impersonate, from Napoleon and Josephine to Amos 'n' Andy.

These thirties comics can mystify us moderns. A highly convulsing moment of *Fine and Dandy* was Cook's sudden asking of the question, "Do you think birds should throw little boys at stones?" Is that funny? Or try Bobby Clark, pretending to be a doctor and training his stethoscope on a fat man in *Here Goes The Bride* (1931): "He has mice." *Here Goes the Bride* was an up-to-the-minute piece satirizing divorce. Like *The New Yorkers*, it was "by" Peter Arno, who co-wrote the book (with Roger Pryor), guided the set designer with sketches, and drew the logo: a bride complete with bouquet, furiously gazing on a spooning couple, the man similarly dressed to marry. Paul Frawley and Victoria Cummings played a pair headed for Reno, Clark played Frawley's valet, and Clark's partner, Paul McCullough, played Clark's valet. An unusually lively score, by composers John W. Green and Richard Myers and lyricist Edward Heyman, sought to bring the vocabulary of show music into the realm of slang and conversational realism with "One Second of Sex," "Well, You See—I, Oh—You Know," "My Sweetheart 'Tis of Thee," "Music in My Fingers (when I wake up 'til I go to bed)," or "Remarkable People We." Arno had got his financing from Paramount Pictures; the studio's publishing house rushed virtually the entire score into song sheets, and second-unit staff built short subjects around Ethel Merman, singing the two most likely hits, "Shake Well Before Using" and "Hello! My Lover, Good-Bye." But the critics liked only the crazy sets, and *Here Goes the Bride* died in a week.

Al Jolson is now recalled as a singer above all, especially as the star who made Hollywood's breakthrough into sound in *The Jazz Singer* (1927). The title itself emphasizes Jolson the vocalist, and the articulated portions of this part-talkie were almost exclusively musical. However, Jolson was by then a sixteen-year Broadway veteran, and a Jolson show typically had the structure of a star-comic vehicle. Jolson's management was the Messrs. Shubert, and Mr. J. J. was addicted to importing German-language operetta in Broadway remakes, so he put Jolson into one of them, *The Wonder Bar* (1931). The Viennese original, *Die Wunder-Bar*, had been staged environmentally at the Kammerspiele, in 1930, as if in a nightclub (not unlike Sam Mendes' *Cabaret* revival). The show went on to Munich, Budapest, and London; but Mr. J. J.'s co-producer, Morris Gest, commissioned a completely new version, using the storyline and some of the original Robert Katscher music but developing something special for Jolson's Broadway. Refurbishing the Nora Bayes—a rooftop venue over the Forty-fourth Street Theatre—Gest and Mr. J. J. welcomed the public into the very show itself, to serve as cabaret customers while Jolson emceed, ad libbed, hogged the stage, and sought to reinflame an audience grown tired of his talkies.

The Wonder Bar's plot involved that old wheeze the stolen jewels, and also an adulterous affair between jewel thief Rex O'Malley and lovely lady Wanda Lyon. Of course, this was just an excuse for a variety bill, as when Patsy Kelly spoofed the ballerina's dying swan as a dying flamingo; or when Jolson, without blackface makeup, sang a mammy song in French. "A mountebank in the heroic vein," Brooks Atkinson called him. The show did not draw, however, though it reached a satisfying completion at Warner Bros. with Jolson and an all-new cast turning the piece into a Busby Berkeley backstager as Wonder Bar (1934).

At least Joe Cook, Clark and McCullough, and Al Jolson were among the conjuring names of the day. Who was Ted Healy? A wan-faced nobody without trademark shtick, Healy must have been the least popular headliner around. Next to Healy, El Brendel was fit for Molière. Perhaps Healy was the only comic free to work when The Gang's All Here (1931) was put together. Russel Crouse's book, supporting a score by composer (and co-producer) Lewis Gensler and lyricists Owen Murphy and Robert A. Simon, used for background the Atlantic City boardwalk of pokerino parlors, joints, and dens. The story proper involved a Romeo and Juliet romance between the offspring of medicine-show con man Indian Ike Kelly (Healy) and a millionaire (originally Dallas Welford). Two major dancers of twenties musicals, Ruby Keeler Jolson and Zelma O'Neal (who had introduced "The Varsity Drag," in Good News!), and new thirties discovery Hal LeRoy, also a dancer, floated around the edges of the abundant plot, and the rest of the cast made up the hustlers and stooges of the Boardwalk: Dr. T. Slocum Swink, "Baby Face" Martin, Big Casino and Little Casino (a dwarf), Two on the Aisle, and so on. The show had atmosphere, if nothing else.

But it had nothing else. The Philadelphia and Newark tryouts saw frantic revisions as Oscar Hammerstein and Morrie Ryskind came aboard to fix the book. (Hammerstein took over the direction as well.) Ruby Keeler and Dallas Welford departed, replaced by Gina Malo and Tom Howard. "Too much show," said *Variety*. It's a curious comment. One could say as much of *Show Boat* or *Follies*. But almost all the critics wrote something of the like; George Jean Nathan thought *The Gang's All Here* had more there in it than *Strange Interlude* and *Back to Methuselah* put together. In *The New Yorker*, Dorothy Parker agreed, while sternly noting that "Above all, Zelma O'Neal should never wear sailor pants." Gone in 23 performances, *The Gang's All Here* took with it one of the liveliest production numbers of its day, the opening of the last scene, set in a nightclub. The number was "Speak Easy," modeled directly on Ravel's *Bolero* in the use of an ostinato under a crescendo of exotic melody. After Frank Swanee introduced the vocal, Tilly Losch's fifty-seven-person ensemble of singers and dancers set the Imperial Theatre blazing with hot rhythm. It remained a memory for the few who saw it; today, commentators speak only of the bemusingly titled "By Special Permission of the Copyright Owners I Love You," whose first line runs, "I asked your father, he said, 'O. K.' "

The worst aspect of Depression show biz was the chill put on theatregoing. This closed many a production that, in good times, might have sailed by on a star, a hit tune, or simply the name of Florenz Ziegfeld. His *Hot-Cha!* (1932) had all the Ziegfeld things—top talent in Bert Lahr (opposite the somewhat less top Lupe Velez), with June Knight and Buddy Rogers as the romantic leads and dancers Eleanor Powell, Veloz and Yolanda, and the De Marcos; a score by the now DeSylva-less Ray Henderson and Lew Brown; the usual any-old-book-will-do script, by Brown, Henderson, and Mark Hellinger; and the pictorial splendor of set designer Joseph Urban.

It was Urban's job to guide the action from New York's Golden Fleece Club (hit by a raid at the end of scene one) to the train station and the train en route to Mexico City and the big bullfight, and it was Lahr's job to take on the bull. Lahr had the tempestuous Velez to contend with as well. Even Tarzan couldn't tame her, and she once menaced Norma Shearer with a stiletto for wearing red to Carole Lombard's white party. Velez's *Hot-Cha!* establishing song, "Conchita," was a kind of primordial "I Cain't Say No," the shrugging lament of a girl made to be loved. "Do they ask me," she sang, to a spry Latin beat, "to be a sweet coquette?" The answer, of course, was no: they ask her to shake her castañet.

The whole thing was profoundly silly and coarse (the subtitle was *Laid in Mexico*), and it should have gone over. Ziegfeld had spanned eras, moving from Second Age styles into some of the most typical twenties musicals in *Kid Boots* (1923) and *Rosalie* (1928), not to mention the forward-looking *Show Boat*. Yet *Hot-Cha!* struggled for three months and change, closing in the red.

If Ziegfeld, Lahr, and company can't draw, what's going to run? Of course, there was that aforementioned problem that hard times struck just when the music was running at its emptiest. The songs have no profile; they're radio spots. *Hot-Cha!*'s lyrics offer scarcely a line—a word, even—of definition. The act-opening ensembles are so perfunctory that the authors didn't bother giving them titles; the program listed both as "Opening Chorus." Other than Velez's "Conchita," June MacCloy's homesick "Little Old New York," Lahr's comic spot with eight chorus girls, "I Make Up For That In Other Ways," and "The Procession of the Day of the Bull Fight," we could be in Greenwillow. The love and charm songs are sinfully contentless, as Knight and Rogers, in various combinations, suave their way through "You Can Make My Life a Bed of Roses," "Say (what I wanna hear you say)," "It's Great To Be Alive," and "There I Go Dreaming Again."

Some producers avoided the problem, if accidentally, by combining the variety and narrative formats, freeing the songwriters to create point numbers like "Hoops" to be performed as onstage spots. After all, there's more dramatic detail in "Hoops" than in the entire *Hot-Cha!* score. Earl Carroll had given the world nine revues when he veered off into *Murder at the Vanities* (1933), a whodunit set onstage and backstage from the finale of a Saturday matinee through the curtain calls of that evening's performance. There was a lot more onstage than off, allowing Carroll to run plenty of *Vanities* numbers—seven before the first substantial book scene. Typically, he made do with an unimportant cast (including Bela Lugosi) and a dull score. It took the Paramount adaptation a year later to glamorize the piece, with Kitty Carlisle, Carl Brisson, Jack Oakie, cop Victor McLaglen, and, finally, a big song hit, "Cocktails For Two."

Take a Chance (1932) ran on much the same idea without the murder case. But producers Laurence Schwab and B. G. DeSylva were smarter than Carroll, engaging a topline cast and a topline songwriting team,

DeSylva working with two composers simultaneously, Richard A. Whiting and Nacio Herb Brown (who complicates this already unwieldy assortment through having billed himself, just this once, as Herb Brown Nacio). The producers wrote their own book, with some help from Sid Silvers.

It's a mouthful, and *Take a Chance* has a loaded history. One of the very few musicals to close out of town in disaster, go into drydock for heavy revisions, and reopen, it was originally called *Humpty Dumpty*, which suggests its amorphous nature. It was a kind of revue, framing a play-within-a-play with the adventures of the rich family that has backed it. The onstage numbers illustrated events in American history, thus anticipating another disaster, *1600 Pennsylvania Avenue* (1976). Co-producer and co-author Schwab had been directing as well; he stepped aside in favor of Edgar MacGregor, a popular journeyman of the day. Bobby Connolly was brought in for new choreography. Protagonist Eddie Foy Jr. was replaced by Jack Haley, who had done so well in the leads of two Schwab shows, *Follow Thru* (1929) and *Free For All* (1931). DeSylva also wrote a new brace of songs, with Vincent Youmans. Finally, the show's title was changed, supposedly because DeSylva, arguing with the dubious Schwab, had urged him, "Let's take a chance!"

As it happens, Schwab and his usual partner, Frank Mandel, had taken a chance on Sigmund Romberg's *The New Moon*, closing it in Philadelphia in 1927 to rework it and try again. A hit. A classic, even. Persuaded, Schwab, with DeSylva, retained the concept but changed the details. *Take a Chance* still followed the to-and-fro of the family that capitalized a show, still called *Humpty Dumpty*. Out of town the family had been Jewish, led by dialect comic Lou Holtz; now the family was the ever-so Raleighs, led by blond hunk Jack Whiting. The scenes of American history were mostly cut, to emphasize the love plot between Whiting and *Humpty Dumpty*'s leading lady (and our *Hot-Cha!* heroine), June Knight.

The score was much strengthened by Youmans' additions, a total of five when *Take a Chance* finally reached New York. For Ethel Merman, Youmans and DeSylva wrote two raveups, "I Got Religion" and "Rise 'n' Shine." Whiting and Knight got "So Do I" and the melting "I Want To Be With You." For Knight alone, Youmans composed one of the earliest of the "sweet or hot?" numbers so popular in this decade and into the 1940s: sing classical (or old-fashioned American ballad) or toot jazz?

"Should I Be Sweet?" 's refrain keeps jumping from a soothing $\frac{4}{4}$ to a crazed $\frac{2}{4}$ and back.

The rest of *Take a Chance*'s score was good enough, with a risqué fox-trot in "Turn Out the Light" and a hit tune in "You're an Old Smoothie," for Merman and Haley. But the stand-out was one of the great showstoppers of all time, Merman's "Eadie Was a Lady." Sung within *Humpty Dumpty*'s action in New Orleans in the 1890s, it found Merman and the chorus saluting a long-gone daughter of joy who "had class with a capital K." The pounding beat in minor key, the bawdy saga, and Merman's drop-dead trumpet made the scene the talk of the town. *The New York Times* troubled to print the lyrics, and that fastidious crank George Jean Nathan declared it the greatest number the American musical had yet produced.

Whiting and Brown would return to Hollywood, where they had already launched successful careers with the earliest film musicals. But Youmans, who would compose (with lyricists Edward Eliscu and Gus Kahn) four perfect numbers for the first Fred Astaire–Ginger Rogers teaming, *Flying Down to Rio* (1933), became the first Third Age giant to retire. Stalked by illness and failure, and a difficult man to deal with, he would be seized by an idea—an imitation *Lady in the Dark* for Mary Martin, for instance—then somehow fail to pursue it. When Hollywood called, he relentlessly haggled deals into nothing, and even discouraged MGM from filming his bio. They got to Gus Kahn, but not to Vincent Youmans! His last attempt to return to Broadway, *Vincent Youmans' Ballet Revue* (1944), contained no Youmans music and collapsed on the road. Two years later, he was dead.

But the first of his successors had already appeared, in the person of Harold Arlen. Doctor Jazz's Broadway debut as sole composer of the evening (with lyricist Jack Yellen), *You Said It* (1931), bears not a hint of the Arlen of "I Had Myself a True Love" or "A Sleepin' Bee." Billed as "a musical comedy of young America," *You Said It* was a college show, centered on our old friend Lou Holtz as a campus con man. Mary Lawlor, the heroine of Tait College in *Good News!* four years earlier, was on hand as the more daredevil heroine of Keaton College, getting mixed up in bootlegging. Her love interest, Stanley Smith, had played opposite Lawlor in MGM's 1930 *Good News!* film, so perhaps producers Yellen and Holtz were hoping for repeat business by *Good News!*'s 557 audiences.

This might explain the almost insipid music with which Arlen introduced himself to the book musical after the *Nine-Fifteen Revue* (1930) and the eighth *Vanities* (1930), both with lyricist Ted Koehler. As well, both offered hot Arlen, including "Get Happy" for Ruth Etting in the first show and "Hittin' the Bottle" in the other. And the songs that Arlen and Koehler wrote for Cab Calloway's Cotton Club appearances include the outrageous "Triggeration" and "Kicking the Gong Around," hot to a fault.

So *You Said It*'s score passes for white, in such titles as "Learn To Croon (a sentimental tune)." Coincidentally recalling one of Youmans' *Take a Chance* numbers, "Sweet and Hot" does proclaim Arlen Harlemania, syncopated and centered on a "blue" note (i.e., the flatted third of the scale). Lyda Roberti, in a relatively minor role, so startled the audience with this number that it got an encore on opening night, and Roberti became a town topic. Not for the song, really, but because she was a highly evolved example of a thirties type, the platinum blond bombshell who is also a comic. Roberti's extra-heavy Polish accent added to the fun, and I'm looking forward to her second appearance in this chapter, some pages hence.

Arthur Schwartz and Howard Dietz aren't newcomers to us, but the team has yet to produce a story score together. (Each had already worked on at least one book musical with other partners, in New York and in London.) After their five Broadway revues, Schwartz and Dietz dared a full-scale narrative in *Revenge With Music* (1934), and while this is not a classic title it does bring us to some historical reckoning.

First of all, the show has one of the decade's finest scores, romantic ("You and the Night and the Music," "When You Love Only One") and playful ("Never Marry a Dancer," "That Fellow Manuelo," the serenely affectionate "Maria"), which suits a comic look at the nature of love in a place as Latin as Spain. The lyrics are very thirties in their lack of references specific to the plot and characters, except for, say, the mention of Navarre in the verse to "When You Love Only One." This is the nagging flaw of the decade; that's why I bring it up from time to time. Audiences of the 1940s and 1950s take "I got to Kansas City on a Friday" or "Mother's a Swede and Father's a Scot" for granted; such autobiographical precision is rare in the time I write of. Still, the music feels right for the story, even if "You and the Night and the Music" started (in waltz time, not in "Music" 's $\frac{4}{4}$) as "To-night," with lyrics by Desmond Carter, for an Anna Neagle movie called *The Queen's Affair*.

Revenge With Music's plot finds fiancés Maria (Libby Holman) and Carlos (Georges Metaxa) keeping Maria out of the arms of the grabby Gobernador (Charles Winninger). They are romance and he is no more than a commotion in their lives, a forgery of romance. When Carlos mistakenly believes that Maria has betrayed him, he speeds off to seduce the Gobernador's wife (Ilka Chase), in the revenge of the show's title. And, of course, Carlos is the real thing, no forgery, so he and the Gobernadora make a little night music.

Dietz wrote the book from Pedro de Alarcón's short nineteenth-century novel *The Three-Cornered Hat*, which similarly informed Hugo Wolf's opera *Der Corregidor* and Manuel de Falla's ballet bearing the novel's title. Dietz's script lies on the dull side, which is probably why *Revenge With Music* lasted only 158 performances. The opening is typical—an inn scene, as gypsies dance to guitar music and customers set the tone:

MAN: Here, Manuelo, more wine!

SECOND MAN: Fill up these glasses, Manuelo!

MANUELO: I can't be in all places at once.

and so on. In fact, Dietz never gets out of the rut of cliché, functional rather than interesting dialogue, and dumb jokes.

However, *Revenge With Music* is one of the first musical comedies written entirely around its plot and characters. A missing link between *Show Boat* and *Oklahoma!*, the work completely avoids the set-piece blackout sketch we find in star comic shows, the specialty dancers who simply turn up and go into it (*Revenge With Music*'s specialty dancers are Spaniards creating atmosphere: they have a right to turn up), the cutely unnecessary numbers. Like a twenties operetta, *Revenge With Music* pursues its narrative from opening to finale with an integrated score (albeit with those vague lyrics) and a book that for all its lack of vivacity never wanders from the driveline. The "musical play" is now in development.

Naturally, for more information on this genre, we turn to our brand-name composers and lyricists, for they always seem to be somehow or other connected to experiments in rationalizing the musical; and it is comic opera, which then became operetta, which in turn evolved into the musical play, that hosted these experiments. True, musical plays need solid scripts. But the first essential nonetheless is a wonderful score. The best parts of a musical occur during the music.

I say that even though a poor script can destroy the entire evening. Vincent Youmans, when not losing fortunes on his own productions, such as *Great Day!* (1929) and *Through the Years* (1932), worked for Florenz Ziegfeld on *Smiles* (1930). Historians love to point out what a sure thing *Smiles* sounded like in conception: Marilyn Miller and the Astaires (which is already almost unthinkable star power) heading another lavish Ziegfeld-Urban spectacle, Youmans to work with a fresh discovery in Harold Adamson (he had been graduated from Harvard that very year), and all filling out an idea dreamed up by Noël Coward.

Isn't something wrong already? What's so great about an idea? Isn't everything in the execution? Now let's hear the idea: Marilyn Miller plays the title role, a French wartime waif looked after by four soldiers—an Italian, a Frenchman, a Brit, and an American (Paul Gregory), the last of whom will vie with Astaire for her grown-up hand in the main action, after a prologue in 1918 France. The Astaires will be society snobs won over by the dauntless Smiles, a Salvation Army lass.

What an idea! How did they dare to write *Brigadoon* or *The Music Man* without an idea by Noël Coward to protect them? *Smiles* was a disaster. Worse: an out-of-date one, retrieving the kind of thing Miller and the Astaires were doing in the 1920s. One sympathizes especially with Youmans, who like Ziegfeld could do nothing right at this time but who unlike Ziegfeld had enjoyed only a decade's career to this point. (Ziegfeld had been on Broadway since the end of the First Age.) The *Smiles* problem was—as you suspected—the script, another flat tire of a book by Ziegfeld's inevitable William Anthony McGuire. Yet for some reason Ziegfeld kept whacking away at the score, crowding Adamson with veteran lyricists and badgering Youmans for hits. "Time On My Hands" is the surviving title, and anyone screening the Astaire–Rogers film *Top Hat* can enjoy the staging concept of Fred's big *Smiles* number, "Say, Young Man of Manhattan," in which (to Irving Berlin's "Top Hat, White Tie and Tails" in the film) he shoots down a line of chorus men with his cane.

If not Youmans, then surely Rodgers and Hart—who, as we will see, will rival Cole Porter as the guiding spirits of the thirties musical. Thus far, we have collected two of their three early thirties shows; let us now retrieve *Ever Green* (1930), lost to history because it was produced in London for English management and never came over. *Ever Green* was a big show, put on by the West End's foremost producer of musicals, Charles B. Cochran. Though partial to revue, Cochran took on book shows as well, especially foreign ones that had proved themselves elsewhere— Offenbach, Lehár, Christiné, and Broadway titles from Cohan and Kern to Porter. Cochran also commissioned new scores from visiting Americans, and so had produced a revue with a Rodgers and Hart score, *One Dam Thing After Another* (1927), whose cast included Jessie Matthews and Sonnie Hale. Apparently, not much passed between the two at the time. But, in the following year, while appearing together in Cochran's Noël Coward revue *This Year of Grace!* (1928), Matthews and Hale fell in love.

Unfortunately, each was already married, and the consequent divorces—especially Hale's, from the extremely popular musical star Evelyn Laye—made Matthews and Hale into tabloid monsters. Matthews was subjected to a public lashing, though it was in fact Hale who antici- pated Edward VIII's refusal to go on "without the help and support of the woman I love." This was just when Cochran decided to produce *Ever Green*, with starring roles for the controversial pair. She would play a young dancer who pretends to be her own sixty-year-old grandmother, he a fellow entertainer who breaks up their romance because he's too young for her.

"Odd," Matthews called it. Yes, one could call it odd. In her memoirs, Matthews tells how Cochran suddenly sought to avoid a scandal by pair- ing Hale not with Matthews but with Ada May. Something is wrong with that story, for May, an American who came over as the dancing soubrette in the London production of the DeSylva, Brown, and Henderson show *Follow Thru*, was a little-known performer who never got anywhere. Cochran had a personal as well as professional investment in May's appeal, and she was to work prominently for him, introducing Noël Coward's highly dramatic "Half-Caste Woman" in *Cochran's 1931 Revue*. But would he have set her before all London as *the* lead in a show he felt so strongly about that it remained his favorite ever after, the Cochran Masterpiece?

In any case, Jessie Matthews felt strongly about *Ever Green*, too, and Harriet Green became her most famous role (especially in its 1934 movie version, all but denuded of its plot and score). Though the show was a hit, there can't have been any wish to take it to New York, because its characters are all ultra-English and, worse, much of this backstager is about the *French* stage. The action has moved to France by the third scene, and but for an excursion to a Spanish fiesta to open Act Two it stays in France for the evening. Another problem is *Ever Green*'s curious format, a mosaic of revue numbers held together not by a revue's through-line but by a genuine (if extremely thin) musical-comedy narrative.

What made *Ever Green* successful in 1930 was the usual Cochran splendor—for, like Ziegfeld, he did spend the money—and some extra publicity surrounding the show's brand-new theatre, the Adelphi. Right down on the Strand, where the Gaiety, the Opera Comique, the old Strand near Somerset House, the Savoy, and earlier theatres on the Adelphi's site had seen the very creation of musical comedy, the new Adelphi seemed to glamorize the noisiest and dirtiest thoroughfare in the West End.

We are missing out on some excitement, clearly, and *Ever Green* remains one of Rodgers and Hart's least-known scores, as occult as *Betsy* (1926) or *Chee-Chee* (1928). Yet *Ever Green* includes some of this team's most interesting items. This is not, let it be said, a breakthrough piece. On the contrary, like *Pal Joey* (1940) it is made as much of performance spots as of situation numbers, and nothing in *Ever Green* fixes a character as well as "Bewitched" does. Still, the first number, "Harlemania," spoofs the lawless abandon of "jazz" with a musical sense of humor and an irresistibly dancey release; and "Dear! Dear!" sports a wonderful syncopated and chromatic hook in the accompaniment between each A and B section. In fact, the entire *Ever Green* score is "fiddled" for push beats and altered chords, as if making some summation of the twenties revolutions in pop music. The refrain of "In the Cool of the Evening (I must say, 'I've got to get hot')" sings scarcely a single note *on* the beat, the entire melody instead slithering over its $\frac{4}{4}$ as if trying to shake off the "cool" of the first line for the "hot" of the second.

The music of *Smiles* is charming, and *Ever Green* is effervescent—but we are looking for something genuinely distinctive in musical comedy, something to tower above the *Hot-Cha!*s and *You Said It*s. Perhaps the Gershwins will give us the unique, especially in 1933, a mere two years before *Porgy and Bess*. The show is *Pardon My English*. An Aarons-Freedley project initiated by Aarons alone but supervised largely by Freedley, this title might almost be an exhibition piece in what can go wrong in the Aarons-Freedley format.

Indeed, their partnership did not survive the show's tryout hell and Broadway failure. The idea, at least, was sound, for the star was Jack Buchanan, who had made a hit with audiences here in visiting English revues in the 1920s. Billed just under the title, in heavier type, was Jack Pearl, radio's "Dutch" comic who, as Baron Munchausen, perpetrated one of the era's most tiresome catchphrases: whenever a listener challenged the Baron's tall tales, he would reply, "Vass *you* dere, Sharlie?"

The Gershwins were by now at the very top of their game, so the two Aarons-Freedley essentials—star talent and star score—had been positioned. The book, by Herbert Fields, was the customary Aarons-Freedley foodle stew, made slightly novel in its setting, contemporary Dresden, Germany. Folded into the plot was a burlesque of Prohibition in that one must frequent German speakeasies to imbibe not liquor but the forbidden soft drink. And the plot itself did turn on a quaint hook: Buchanan played a man with a split personality, changing from his usual debonair English self into a tough-talking bootlegger (and back again) every time he's struck on the head. For the romance, he had girl friends to match his split self: the ingenue (Josephine Huston, the last in a series of girls in this part) when debonair, and *You Said It*'s Lyda Roberti, his moll when tough. Tying it together, Jack Pearl was Dresden's ditheringly ineffective chief of police and the ingenue's father.

Great; but now come the mistakes. Fields wrote an insanely verbose libretto, though he did include a series of Munchausen-shtick scenes for Pearl, wisely addressing his public's expectations. And the Gershwins, at least, cannot be faulted. George (or his music director or dance arranger) gets off a cute quotation of Weber's opera *Der Freischütz*, borrowing its famous Act One fanfare to introduce some discordant oom-pah in the number "Dancing in the Streets." A duet for the romantic leads, "Isn't It a Pity?," shows that Ira was one of the few writers promoting character-specific lyrics, with allusions to Hermann, Fritz, Hans, and even Schopenhauer. The song hung on over the years as a marginal standard, but the entire score is solid second-rate Gershwin, and that's saying a lot. Roberti was especially well served in the all-important second spot after the opening chorus. "The Lorelei," on Heinrich Heine's siren of the Rhine, offers one of Ira's juiciest lyrics, to a swinging melody that really opens up when the chorus sings harmony under the vocal. Kim Criswell liked it so much that she not only revived it but named the CD after it.

Nevertheless, from the start of the tryout, *Pardon My English* was in despair. John McGowan, who had co-written the *Girl Crazy* (1930) book for Aarons and Freedley, was called in as script doctor. But the patient was at once agitated and enfeebled. Only Jack Pearl's bits were landing, and when Jack Buchanan expressed a fervent wish to depart, management replaced him with the unknown George Givot, an odd way to treat a star part.

The team of Carl Randall and Barbara Newberry was spliced into the action, because they were not only engaging dancers but choreographers themselves.* However, numbers written for specific characters were reassigned to Randall and Newberry, including "The Lorelei," a perfect Lyda Roberti number (even if her tiny voice couldn't carry past the eighth row). The idea is to let the vamping Roberti pay tribute to a golden-age vamp of the higher culture, a superb Ira Gershwin joke. Giving it to the American Randall and Newberry divests it of content.

The notices were terrible, and it may be that business was further discouraged ten days after the New York opening, when the camarilla of plotters and idiots surrounding Germany's President Hindenburg persuaded the senile field marshal to appoint Adolf Hitler as chancellor. Front-page photos of the resulting parade of storm troopers can't have inspired a surge at *Pardon My English*'s box office.

They should have called David Ives in on the tryout instead of John McGowan, because Ives' concert version of *Pardon My English* at Encores!

* Historians are very cognizant of the now absolutely forgotten Randall because of an accident involving very remembered people. Have you ever wondered who Bill is, in *Show Boat*? True, "Bill" is just a song that Julie sings; there needn't be a Bill. But there *was* a Bill: and it was Carl Randall. He originated the role of Willoughby "Bill" Finch in Jerome Kern's *Oh, Lady! Lady!!* (1918) opposite Vivienne Segal (who was still on Broadway thirty-four years later, in the *Pal Joey* revival). Segal it was who would have introduced "Bill," but apparently the number fell into that—I say again—very vulnerable "first song after the opening chorus" slot, and was both too silly and too slow to go over. Besides, Segal's fondly sarcastic description didn't suit the charismatic Randall, especially the line "Whenever he dances, his partner takes chances." So "Bill" was dropped, eventually to make history in Oscar Hammerstein's slight revision of P. G. Wodehouse's lyric, for yet another memorable name, Helen Morgan.

in 2004 finally fixed the show. Following the old plot, Ives wrote a new script, making no attempt to observe thirties style if fifties shtick or modernist burlesque would better serve. Jack Pearl's lengthy radio-style harangues were dropped and his character worked more organically into the scenes. The business of the hero's two personalities was emphasized far more than in 1933—smartly, as the running gag of his getting banged on the head is the one thing that distinguishes the narrative.

Some of Ives' free-associative buzz-term wordplay has the flavor of lines the Marx Brothers might have blurted out to enliven their stage shows. At the end of *Pardon My English*'s storyline, when the hero is about to awaken in, finally, the personality he will have for life, the attending psychiatrist warns that, if he recognizes the ingenue, he'll remain the English bon vivant. If he recognizes the crazy Polish blonde, he'll remain the German tough guy. "And," Ives' doctor continued, "if he recognizes me, he'll be a waitress from Hamburg named Lulu."

One of the biggest laughs found a housemaid named Magda looking forward to marrying the customary Guy Bolton Silly Brit stereotype, in this case one Dickie Carter. "Then," she solemnly exulted, "I could be Magda Carter!" However, the audience was oddly slow to catch Ives' most bizarre joke, when bootlegger and moll mocked both his other self, "the limey," and the ingenue, "the filly." Wait a minute. Filly? Limey? Suddenly turning formal and standing shoulder to shoulder, the two broke into a familiar Christmas song as "The filly and the limey, when they are both full grown . . ."

Director Gary Griffin and choreographer Rob Ashford kept everything moving at top speed with utmost charm, and the cast was excellent. Brian d'Arcy James gave a James Cagney spin to the bootlegger, perfectly balancing the zaniness of it all with a sincere share in the love plot, one of the secrets of playing this brand of musical. His two romances were Jennifer Laura Thompson and the effervescent Emily Skinner. Given the crazy ploys of the Ives-Griffin worldview, one kept expecting Skinner to sidle up to one of the other women and "attach" herself, in an hommage to *Side Show*.

It's amazing how well *Pardon My English* played in 2004, considering its stunted history. In 1933, it was a musical-comedy disaster, so if the Gershwins cannot enlighten us in their own age, surely Jerome Kern will. Remember, he is now in his post–*Show Boat* era. He is liberated, eloquent, almighty. He composes only three shows for Broadway in this first half of the 1930s, however, and of them only *Roberta* (1933) is a genuine musical comedy. So *The Cat and the Fiddle* (1931) and *Music in the Air* (1932) will be along presently.

The sheer fame of the title *Roberta* suggests a smash. But it was rather the determination of producer Max Gordon that pushed the production through to success. The problem was a funless book about too little story, drawn by Otto Harbach from Alice Duer Miller's novel *Gowns by Roberta*.

"Extremely unimportant and slightly dead" was John Mason Brown's opinion in the *Evening Post*. The narrative did avoid the excessive and implausible twists with which twenties habits bedeviled thirties musical comedy, but the tale just clumped along while waiting for the American football hero (Ray Middleton) to jilt his manipulative fiancée (Helen Gray) and resist the flirtatious Slavic coquette (our favorite Pole, Lyda Roberti) to end up with the dress designer who is also an expatriate Russian princess (Tamara; not to be confused with Tamara Geva, Tamara Toumanova, Tamara Long, or Pinky Babajian). Nothing else happens all evening, except that Middleton's buddy Huckleberry Haines (Bob Hope) has a swing band and the Americans are in Paris, where Middleton's Aunt Minnie (First Age veteran Fay Templeton, just turning sixty-eight at the time) runs a chic dress salon under the name of Roberta. Templeton's one scene had to be staged around her sitting in a chair; when the lights came up, she was burning old love letters in the fireplace, and at the scene's end she died.

Harbach's book is not only tedious but horribly short on humor, despite the determination of Hope and Roberti to slay with shtick. There is one good laugh, when Hope offered to pep up Roberta's next fashion show with his band:

HUCK: My orchestra could put new life into your models.
AUNT MINNIE: That's what I'm afraid of.

Roberta's glory is, of course, the score. It's off-kilter, because of its seven major numbers three are rather grand (Templeton's solo accompanying the burning of the letters, "Yesterdays"; "Smoke Gets in Your Eyes"; the big duet "The Touch of Your Hand"), three are rooted in swing ("Let's

Begin"; "Something Had To Happen"; "I'll Be Hard To Handle"), and "You're Devastating" (a new lyric to a melody from *Blue Eyes*, "Do I Do Wrong") is the typical Kern ballad *hors série*. It is too straightforward, so to say, to suit operetta, yet it's big for musical comedy, so effusively lyrical when set next to *Flying High*'s "I'll Know Him" or *Everybody's Welcome*'s "As Time Goes By." Also off-kilter is the choice of singers for the ballads: Tamara sings that big duet with a minor figure, another Russian émigré, prince to her princess; and "You're Devastating" is first given to Hope as a vocal spot with his band.

Nevertheless, *Roberta*'s orchestration, by the inevitable Robert Russell Bennett, favors swing throughout the evening, putting the piano forward as if this were Gershwin. It's a sound that Kern disliked but felt necessary in so contemporary a work. Note that two of *Roberta*'s most famous numbers, "I Won't Dance" and "Lovely To Look At," were not in the show, but rather were added to its score for the 1935 film version. Today, they are so much a part of *Roberta: The Concept* that even Bill Tynes' New Amsterdam reading had to include them despite Bill's oath of fidelity to original texts.

Interestingly, the reviewers who so carped at the book failed to appreciate Kern's music. Historians, too, have rebuked Harbach's lyrics for a bit too much of the operetta "forsooth" and "chaffed" in the ballads. Yet Harbach's swing patter falls conversationally on the notes, and he—or someone—contrived a slick send-up of scat by combining Polish and swingtalk for Roberti's reprise of "I'll Be Hard To Handle."

Critics underpraised the *Roberta* talent generally. Producer Gordon and Kern had a terrible row in Philadelphia, the first leg of the tryout, for Kern was directing the show himself and Gordon fired him, to bring in Hassard Short. Short was the most creative director of the time and did not come cheap, and Gordon incurred more expense to ensure that the gowns for the fashion-show sequence drew an enthusiastic response from the public. Further, Gordon contributed to the dance history he had helped start (in *The Band Wagon*) by ordering up a ballet, "Blue Shadows," from choreographer José Limón.

In short, *Roberta* was an imposing production with an imposing score; and the critics failed to treat it as such. Worse, Brooks Atkinson called the kiddingly sexsational Roberti "coarse, shrill, and gauche." This is especially unhappy in view of her death, in 1938, at the age of twenty-eight.* Considering that George Murphy and Sydney Greenstreet were also in the cast, it's hard to know why the notices weren't more enthusiastic. Still, *Roberta* played 295 performances, making it the longest-running book show of the 1933–34 season.

As with Rodgers and Hart's *Ever Green*, we take interest in Kern's London show *Three Sisters* (1934), for this was a collaboration with Oscar Hammerstein, and anything by the authors of *Show Boat* bears on the history of the American musical. A Drury Lane spectacle, *Three Sisters* was meant to conform to the English style, though the English critics resentfully tore it apart. "How long is Drury Lane to be the asylum for American inanity?" asked James Agate in the *Sunday Times*, referring to the theatre's six-year occupation, from 1925 through 1930, of five American musicals in a row, four of them by Hammerstein; and of yet more Drury Lane Hammerstein in 1933, albeit in the continental *Ball at the Savoy.*

In a narrative that moved from 1914 to 1924, *Three Sisters* followed the fortunes of Tiny (American Charlotte Greenwood), Dorrie (Adèle Dixon), and Mary (Victoria Hopper) Barbour. Tiny is engaged to a policeman (Stanley Holloway). Dorrie captivates a lord (Richard Dolman). Mary marries an entertainer (Esmond Knight), who immediately deserts her, creating a heartbreaking second-act curtain. Act Three emphasizes wartime, and Dorrie is eventually reunited with her husband.

It's a bit skimpy for a big show. But then, with six principals to develop, Kern and Hammerstein created an unusual number of character songs. More unusually, for the first-act finale the authors had choreographer Ralph Reader design one of the inaugural Dream Ballets. It began with Greenwood's lullaby, "Somebody Wants To Go To Sleep," as she cuddled the dozing Hopper, who then entered her Dream to see how dearly her busker needed his liberty: because women cannot get along without him. Interestingly, both Hopper and Knight played themselves in the Dream— Knight in flowing white blouse, tights, and boots to mid-thigh, and Hopper in a pre-Raphaelite white gown—whereas back on Broadway it would be more typical to give actors dancing doubles in Dream Ballets.

---

* The curious can sample Roberti in a brace of thirties films, best of all the bizarre *Million Dollar Legs* (1932), perhaps the zaniest film ever made, and I'm not forgetting *Duck Soup*. Roberti plays the spy Mata Machree, the woman no man can resist. One must be prompt, though. As her butler explains, "Madame is only resisted from two to four."

Kern and Hammerstein honored English musical-comedy tradition with a production number for a soubrette supported by chorus girls in matching frocks and chorus men in tails. Here, it was Dixon's "Lonely Feet," later used in the *Sweet Adeline* film (1935). Performed in a sequence at the lord's estate with the manor house in the background and the playing area diminished by greenery and a practical bridge, the staging conformed to the deluxe charm that English audiences thought essential in their musical shows. Dixon's other number was the "I Won't Dance" that ended up in the *Roberta* film (with mostly new lyrics by Dorothy Fields). Hammerstein's original lyric is slim, trim, and naive, and of course it doesn't mention "The Continental" (because *Three Sisters'* narrative chronology precedes that song's inception, in 1934; the Fields rewrite, a year later, brings it in). Now a standard, "I Won't Dance" let off scarcely a ripple in *Three Sisters*, perhaps because of a delicate performance. It was meant to establish Dixon as the sweetheart of the sisters, to Greenwood's sarcastic realist and Hopper's romantic. Perhaps as reluctant as the critics to credit American writers for pulling off an English musical, the public resisted supporting the show, and it closed in two months. Ten of its songs have been recorded in one place or another, yet it remains the most obscure of Kern's thirties titles.

It is up to Irving Berlin, with librettist Moss Hart, to give us—finally—a musical comedy with content, *Face the Music* (1932). Produced by Berlin's business partner, Sam H. Harris, this work shares creative staff with Max Gordon's *The Band Wagon*—George S. Kaufman, Hassard Short, Albertina Rasch, Albert Johnson, costumière Kiviette, and Robert Russell Bennett. However, despite some writers' belief that *Face the Music* was a revue or something like one, it was a story piece—in fact, a satire, partly on police corruption, partly on the theatre, but mainly on the effect of the Depression on all aspects of American life. The first full-out scene (after a bit of this and that "in one") presented the Automat, where Boy (J. Harold Murray) and Girl (Katherine Carrington) lunch with the bankrupt American leadership class:

CARRINGTON: Guess who that is at the Swiss cheese and rye.
MURRAY: Coolidge?
CARRINGTON: Coolidge? He ate here *before* the Depression.

Making the point musically, they close the scene with "Let's Have Another Cup O' Coffee," another of those amiable paeans to the good times ahead, deliberately quoting the designated clichés ("silver lining," "April shower") to spoof the form.

The entire show is a spoof. Mary Boland, as the wife of a police sergeant (Hugh O'Connell) was a spoof woman, a haughty camp biddy who could bring a strangely exotic innocence to a line like "When I was fourteen years old, my father took me to one side and explained about the Shuberts."* Boland's meeting with unemployed thespians Murray and Carrington kicks the plot into motion, for Boland's husband the sergeant is eager to back a show and loaded with money in an age when only the crooks are rich. Boland invites the young couple to tea:

BOLAND: I begin to pour at four.
MURRAY: Right in front of everybody?

Why is a cop interested in moving into theatre production? And where did he get all that money? Those familiar with *Fiorello!* (1959) will recall the state investigation led by Judge Samuel Seabury into the corruption of New York Mayor James J. Walker's administration. Boland's husband needs to launder boodle, and thus is born *Rhinestones of 1932*, produced by bumbly Hal Reisman (Andrew Tombes). The critics bomb it, as the sergeant was hoping they would. But Tombes simply tarts the show up with nudity and smutty jests, and the show becomes a hit. This is great for Murray and Carrington but disaster for O'Connell. Just as Maurine Watkins suggested, in the play *Chicago* (1926), that justice, the news media, and show biz were interlocked, so does Moss Hart, as Reisman now plans to "produce" the inquiry into police corruption, as *Investigations of 1932*.

Hart's book is not consistently funny, but it's built on an arresting idea, not least because, to common knowledge, gangsters Waxey Gordon and Dutch Schulz had backed Ziegfeld's *Hot-Cha!*, among other items. At that, Berlin's score lacks narrative drive, preferring the generalized music

---

* Why risk a feud with big Broadway brokers? Before *Face the Music*'s opening, Hart detoxified the line as "about the facts of show business."

making of "Soft Lights and Sweet Music"; "I Say It's Spinach (and the hell with it)," from a *New Yorker* cartoon caption; and the delicately Latin "On a Roof in Manhattan." When the implicated police sergeant flees the city, Murray gets "Manhattan Madness," not so much a plot number as jazz-maddened abstraction of the speed and noise of the place.

Still, *Face the Music* would seem to be another of the missing links, for here is a show with a point of view, even if the score didn't support it in any real sense. *Face the Music* is also a backstager, a form that thrived on Broadway only in the 1930s, possibly in response to the ubiquitous Hollywood form. Few twenties shows roved behind the curtain. *Sally* (1920) climaxed with its heroine's *Follies* debut, but it wasn't about putting on the show. *Manhattan Mary* (1927) was; and *Show Boat* and *Sweet Adeline* (1929) deal partly with theatre folk and their work. However, in the 1930s a host of titles treats the real life of entertainment. Besides those mentioned in this chapter, there were most prominently *The Cat and the Fiddle*, *Music in the Air*, *On Your Toes*, *Babes in Arms*, *Very Warm For May*, and *DuBarry Was a Lady*. *Face the Music* actually included only one onstage scene, in Carrington's number "Dear Old Crinoline Days," in which Irving Berlin parodies not only the nostalgia number but the kind of nostalgia number that Irving Berlin himself liked to write.

Meanwhile, something rare occurred at Jolson's 59th Street Theatre in late 1929, a season of revivals drawn from the late First Age and Second Age: five by Victor Herbert; Reginald De Koven's *Robin Hood*; Gustav Luders' *The Prince of Pilsen*; and three titles from the Berlin-Vienna repertory. Revivals were not unheard of at the time, but they were usually no more than touring productions that dropped in for a week or two. What happened here was that the Shuberts had built a theatre too far uptown to attract trade. They had defied the theatre world by erecting the Winter Garden, at Broadway and Fiftieth Street, on the site of the old Horse Exchange in 1911, when most new auditoriums that counted as part of "Broadway" were being raised to the immediate north and south of Forty-second Street. The gamble paid off for the Winter Garden, because Broadway was in the grip of an almost reckless expansion that would fill the West Forties with new theatres for two more decades. But business did not comparably march north to the Jolson.

Eager to put the Jolson to use, the Shuberts set director Milton Aborn in charge of a low-budget reclamation of Herbert's *Sweethearts* for a two-week run. It did so well that more Herbert—Mlle. Modiste, with original heroine Fritzi Scheff—had to be extended and moved to the Casino Theatre to accommodate a lively reception; and the season was on. Aborn relied on stock decor but featured such singers as Ilse Marvenga (the original Kathy in The Student Prince) in Naughty Marietta, Tessa Kosta in The Fortune Teller, Greek Evans (another Student Prince alumnus, having created the prince's tutor) in Robin Hood, comic Al Shean (of Gallagher and Shean, and an uncle of the Marx Brothers) as the protagonist of The Prince of Pilsen, and Charles Purcell, hero of Maytime and Dearest Enemy, in The Chocolate Soldier.

Today, in the age of the revisal, we look back hoping for faithful renderings. But there was some meddling with texts even then. Robin Hood, the oldest of the series, lost some numbers and gained new ones composed by Louis Kroll, who conducted the Aborn revivals. Babes in Toyland was denuded of its elaborate (therefore expensive) prologue. The Prince of Pilsen got a wholly new script and an interpolation from the same authors' Woodland, "The Song of the Nightingale." All the same, here was an illustration of the continuity of the musical: one based entirely on its scores. Excepting the season's one work that is still widely performed today, The Merry Widow, these shows do not incorporate the survival-ready librettos that we expect from such modern classics as Gypsy or Fiddler on the Roof. But the parlor piano, 78s, and then radio kept all this music in the public ear. (Even such seemingly old-hat and therefore discardable titles as Robin Hood and The Prince of Pilsen were performed on the air into the 1940s.) Knowing the songs made the public want to hear them in context.

Perhaps this is why Florenz Ziegfeld decided to revive Show Boat in May of 1932, a mere three years and two weeks after the original production had closed. Replacing two of the leads with Dennis King and Paul Robeson, Ziegfeld otherwise reunited virtually the entire original cast in the original production and ran the show in that three-thousand-seat monster house that Earl Carroll had built, now renamed the Casino. (That old Casino that the Mlle. Modiste revival moved to had meanwhile been demolished.)

The second coming of Show Boat lasted 181 performances, remarkable for a work that had recently played for seventeen months, and I think this tells us how important the new sound of the Golden Age had become.

Kern, Berlin, Rodgers and Hart, the Gershwins, Cole Porter, Vincent Youmans, and DeSylva, Brown, and Henderson set forth music too captivating to be allowed to float away in passing. However, the lyrics were going to have to match the quality of melody, and this would not come easily to a Depression business desperate to mint go-everywhere commercial hits.

3

We're Off to Feathermore: *Nymph Errant, Anything Goes,* and *Jubilee*

In one way, Cole Porter is the outstanding author of thirties scores. Only Rodgers and Hart rival him in prominence, because the other great Third Age names did much less work in the 1930s than in the 1920s; and such newcomers as Harold Arlen, E. Y. Harburg, and Kurt Weill would not really have impact till the 1940s.

As for this rival pair, Rodgers and Hart claim nine Broadway titles in the 1930s, seven of which ran at least half a year—an excellent showing for the Depression, even after New Deal economic policies assured a steady rise in theatregoing cash flow from about 1936 on. Remember, too, that the Rodgers and Hart shows of the decade's latter half, from *Jumbo* (1935) to *Too Many Girls* (1939), produced by far the bulk of the team's standards and cabaret treasures heard today. This is a period all but stuffed with Rodgers and Hart—so much so that three of their scores—*On Your Toes, Babes in Arms,* and *The Boys From Syracuse*—are virtually standards as wholes. Doesn't this make Rodgers and Hart the champion authors of the thirties score?

But Porter is exponential. Of his eight thirties Broadway titles, no more than four lasted half a year or more, and only *Anything Goes* (1934) can be called a standard score, at that in its two revival versions with Porter interpolations. However, those Rodgers and Hart scores are very much alike in the way they delineate character and in overall musical construction, whereas the three Porter scores that mark his theatre work in the early middle of the decade vary greatly in what they choose to depict and especially in musical construction. Above all, Porter raises very pertinently the question of how artistic one is free to be in a popular art. As we'll see, others were untroubled. The serene confidence of George Gershwin's genius—sorry, but no other word is correct here—led him without interior conflict to *Porgy and Bess* (1935), even if it seemed a long shot to many, doomed, one might say, to the succès d'estime.

Porter had no use for art that invited admiration but not commercial achievement. The very notion seemed an oxymoron to him, which is partly why the typical Porter standard is ready to wear while some Rodgers and Hart standards might be more effective if one knew something of their context. For example, why is the lady a tramp? Does she sleep around? No: she's a vagabond, dropping into and then out of the *Babes in Arms* narrative because she is too independent to put down roots.

Of course, by the time of *Kiss Me, Kate* (1948), Porter had succumbed to the Rodgers and Hammerstein revolution, and his songs then tend to the contextual. But early Porter reminds us that, while Rodgers and Hart were trying to break in by writing shows, Porter never had to break in, because he was well off and social. Such people blithely captivate parties at the piano, word gets around, and history says *now*.

Porter actually made commercial recordings, piping away in an amiably off-center voice, the twang of a soigné banshee. If the sound of the man was unlikely, so was his material: dreams of a love so intense it devours; an acerbic view of marriage disguised as wry social satire; and junkets into a world of sensual wastrels, some imagined (the late—in fact, lynched—Miss Otis, the hostess of death Mrs. Lowsborough-Goodby, the ugly Americans Mr. and Mrs. Fitch) but most quite real and cited by name. When less noteworthy people turn up in Porter's art, they are mere categories, such as "the janitor's wife" who enjoys a more satisfying love life than a Porter heroine.

His colleagues maintained an innocent streak in their jesting and respected an incorruptible majesty of romance, but Porter always pushed the taboos, and his view of romance was ultimately a tragic one. Rodgers and Hart write the breathless "My Heart Stood Still"; Porter writes "Love For Sale." True, Hart has his cynical side, but meanwhile his partner Rodgers is soaring—as in "Falling in Love With Love"—thus to compromise Hart's regret with rapture.

Porter writes not only lyrics but *music* of regret, because love is not consecrated but appetitive, a torture inflicted on mankind by "the gods," who can unleash passions that shatter the world. Again and again, Porter refers to the ecstasy and horror of love at its hottest—its amazing power to affirm the ego but also its destructive impulses. "I Hate You, Darling" is a characteristic Porter observation and "Get Out of Town" a typical Porter plea, because his love is outlaw. It's homosexual, and Porter, despite a life that stylishly respected the cautions, never pretends that it isn't.

Of course, Porter romances are strictly Boy Meets Girl, or at least Judge Meets Lilo. But Porter's lyrics insistently tug at the sophisticate's euphemisms. As early as in *Hitchy-Koo 1919*, in "My Cozy Little Corner in the Ritz," Porter gets a double meaning out of the word "queens." Later, "lavender" and even "gay" turn up. True, Lorenz Hart was as playful as Porter. The aficionado will have collected, in *By Jupiter* (1942), an Amazon warrior's comment that "a sailor has a boy in every port." And both Hart and Porter worked extensively with Herbert Fields, who pioneered the ribald musical-comedy libretto. Yet Porter resists a tenderness that conquers Hart. Hart believes in love, even the other people's kind: Wait Till You See Her! When Porter indulges, however, he is at best "going in for" it: What Is This Thing Called Love?

Perhaps Porter's homosexuality empowered his satire, for it placed him at an observant remove from his favorite subject, the rituals of courtship and marriage. Porter delves into the humiliations and blisses of romance far more variously than anyone else in the Third Age, and he even writes from the woman's point of view. The number of Porter's "woman" songs is astonishing: "The Laziest Gal in Town," "Find Me a Primitive Man," "The Queen of Terre Haute," "My Heart Belongs To Daddy," "Most Gentlemen Don't Like Love," "Give Him the Oo-La-La," "All I've Got To Get Now Is My Man," "Make a Date With a Great Psychoanalyst," "A Lady Needs a Rest," "Why Marry Them?," "I'm in Love With a Soldier Boy," "I Hate Men," "A Woman's Career," "No Lover," "What Do You Think About Men?," "Never Give Anything Away," "Every Man Is a Stupid Man," "Without Love (what is a woman?)." These are not simply songs for women characters, like *America's Sweetheart*'s lightly carnal "I Want a Man," or songs taking the long view of woman's contribution to civilization, like *The Girl Friend*'s "The Damsel Who Done All the Dirt," to call on Rodgers and Hart again. Porter's lyrics for women reach more deeply into their experiences, now toying with them and now rebelling against them. Alone of his sort, Porter is a gender equalizer.

On the other hand, the celebrated Porter, the Porter of the mass market, is perceived as the dispenser of lift and release, for instance with his list song, adducing comparisons especially from the great names of the great world, spotlighting everyone from Aphrodite to the Countess di Frasso. Lorenz Hart mentioned only the genuinely famous, whom any American might place; Oscar Hammerstein's characters didn't name-drop; and Ira Gershwin's idea of a celebrity was the Lorelei. It was Porter alone who carpet-bombed pop music with the names of the archons and clones of city culture, and doing it inspired him to devise theatre music unlike that of Hart, Hammerstein, and Gershwin. Porter's song is preposterous, earthy, and aware, not just a list song but a song that one of the listed might sing at something like 3 A.M. on the ninetieth floor.

In anecdote, Porter seems the dilettante, taking his work on jaunts to Giza or Singapore as other men commute and, overhearing a chance phrase, impishly crying, "Title!" and immediately planning a song around it. The unknown Porter is a craftsman. Launching a Porter medley during a show at the Waldorf-Astoria in 1957, Lena Horne referred to "the always surprising Cole Porter tunes." Right. A Porter verse, for instance, is often unusually elaborate, more "built" even than the chorus. The first lines of the verse to "I've Got You On My Mind," from *Gay Divorce* (1932), ingeniously anticipate the refrain—note for note, but in a different rhythm. In the same way, a Porter coda—literally the "tail" of a song—can be very expansive, pushing beyond pop's traditional AABA format.

More than anyone but Jerome Kern, Porter constructed songs around musical ideas not meant to be fitted to lyrics. "Blow, Gabriel, Blow" takes off on the toot of a horn—"Do you hear that playin'?" the first line *replies*—and "You're the Top" similarly starts not with words but with a hook, the rhythmic mechanism that structures the melody and plays on through the number, shaping its statement and response. "Swing That Swing," from *Jubilee* (1935), is almost wholly musical, a song made of jazzy blares for the brass that punctuate lyrics spoken rather than sung.

Porter's most characteristic musical tic is his insistent use of minor keys. A favorite example is "I Love Paris," doleful in c minor until it wells into C Major for the exuberant close. Still, as Porter observes in "Ev'ry Time We Say Goodbye," "how strange the change from major to minor": for he doesn't use the emotional release inherent in reaching the major as much as he uses the ambivalence of switching back and forth between major and minor. Porter's art is wholly ambivalent, in fact. It needs yet fears love, adores yet ridicules society, happens to like New York yet loves Paris. A typical Porter melody is so uncertain that it travels between the two basic rhythmic beats, $\frac{4}{4}$ and $\frac{3}{4}$, as in "I Get a Kick Out Of You," which glides from quarter and half notes to triplets and back virtually from measure to measure. Thus the tune seems to float, unattached, above the accompaniment.*

It isn't only syncopations and the beat-beat-beat of the tomtom in Porter. It's rhythm itself: unexpected jazzy explosions in the middle of a ballad; such propulsive energy that songs seem to be racing themselves to the finish; a flood of Latin dances. This is nervous music, Ritz-Carlton ragtime. Only George Gershwin is as celebrated for his beat. But Gershwin has drive; Porter has *pulse*. He is seductive, sinuous. What made "Night and Day" one of the biggest international song hits of its era was its sex appeal—the sensual effect of the urgently repeated notes in the verse and the title phrase, of the descending chromatic lines spanning nearly an octave, of the flashy breakout on "oh, such a hungry yearning," of all this ambivalent wondering with a solid beat pumping through it. No, it isn't sex appeal. It's sex.

So the London show *Nymph Errant* (1933), a major Charles B. Cochran event starring Gertrude Lawrence, was perfect Porter: the picaresque of an English finishing-school graduate who tours much of the European world and finds Temptation in every inch of it. There is no plot per se: Evangeline Edwards bids goodbye to her chemistry teacher and four schoolmates—one each from England, Germany, France, and the U.S.—and proceeds to have adventures in as many different places as possible, including a railway carriage, a French seaside resort, Paris, Venice, Athens, Smyrna, a Turkish harem, the desert, and, back in Paris, on the stage of a cabaret. For a binding element, each of the heroine's former schoolmates turns up at some point. Still, in effect, only Lawrence's Evangeline enjoys any continuity, so apart from her numbers the music

---

* We don't necessarily hear this, because singers tend to deliver versions of a song rather than the song itself. Even Ethel Merman, who introduced "I Get a Kick Out Of You" with Cole right there at the piano coaching her, slurred the distinction between the twos and threes, not to mention singing, throughout her career, a wrong note in the verse of "You're the Top" (on "I always have found *it* best"). The only performance of "Kick" that is sung correctly in terms of its note values is that of Kim Criswell on John McGlinn's restoration recording of *Anything Goes* on EMI.

must consist of one-offs for various specialty performers. It's a score made of party turns, like those of Porter himself.

Based on a naughty novel by James Laver, *Nymph Errant* had a book by Romney Brent, a performer (one of the original cast of the *Garrick Gaieties*) with writing ambitions. Brent directed the show as well, and Agnes de Mille won her first credit as choreographer on the production. The American revolution in bringing ballet into the musical had not yet influenced the West End, however, so there was no extended dance sequence of the kind we noted in, say, *The Band Wagon. Nymph Errant* was meant to be indistinguishable from the local product, a genuinely English show, and Porter even created two comic quartets of the kind favored by Noël Coward especially, often sung in one to cover a scene change and utilizing singers who didn't have actual character roles but couldn't be called simply "ensemble," either. One thinks of *Bitter Sweet's* "Green Carnation" or *Operette's* "The Stately Homes of England." *Nymph Errant's* quartets were "Neauville-sur-Mer," for atmosphere at the start of the resort scene, and "Ruins," a tourists' lament; there was a comic sextet as well, a servants' tarantella in Venice, "They're Always Entertaining."

Otherwise, the *Nymph Errant* score is pure Porter in content if somewhat Anglo in presentation—a modern take on historical figures in "Georgia Sand," or a wry look at society sensuality in "The Cocotte." Marie Cahill's cut solo from *The New Yorkers* surfaced here; originally called "But He Never Says He Loves Me," it was now "The Physician." It explores a somewhat gay notion: the good doctor is utterly entranced by his patient, but only physically, not emotionally. She wants to be rescued; he wants to trick. Another modern "history" turned up, in "Solomon," written for another *New Yorkers* alumna, Elisabeth Welch, and set in a Bibleland Paris-Harlem in which the eunuch is named Rastus Brown and the king's thousand unfaithful wives ride "diamond-studded" Hispanos to Ciro's.

The number became Welch's theme song; she was still singing it sixty years later, at the Porter centennial gala, in Carnegie Hall. Unfortunately, all these go-everywhere novelty solos reveal how unintegrated the thirties musical was even when it was striving for integration. It's better when the songs simply stop the narrative, when characters with no true role to play in Evangeline's voyage just step forward to delight us. But when the script tries to ramp up to a number, one hears the whine of vexed machinery, as when the Paris cabaret impresario implores Evangeline to appear in his revue:

ANDRÉ: Mademoiselle, in one season I can make you a star.

. . . . . .

EVANGELINE: No! I couldn't, really!

ANDRÉ: But why not? You are so *complètement délicieuse*. Oh, I am mad for you. Please!

The orchestra strikes up, and Evangeline replies with the verse to "It's Bad For Me," beginning "Your words go through and through me." But there's something contrived about the procedure, especially as the number is Evangeline's solo and André now has to sit still and listen to what more realistically would have been a continuation of their mutual dialogue.

Worse yet is the set-up for "The Physician"—which, we may recall, was originally written for the character of the *New Yorkers'* Park Avenue grand dame with plenty of leisure for dalliance with doctors. Reassigning it to Evangeline—an innocent schoolgirl in excellent health—stretches credibility, as she addresses an officer of that Turkish harem:

EVANGELINE: I'm fed up, Ali. I might as well be back with Aunt Ermyntrude. I can't stand it, I tell you.

Ali sympathizes, and photographs reveal how much smart showmanship could cover up these *bêtises de livret,* with the vastly fat Ali a kook in eyeglasses, darning a sock with a gigantic shako-like turban on his head, and Gertrude Lawrence a lovely scream in her seraglio robes and accessories. Still, what motivation does Ali have to ask if this new girl has ever been in love (which he immediately does)? And when Lawrence answers in the affirmative with "In school, two years ago, I had measles," and the boys in the pit once more warn us that another party turn is before us, aren't we right to feel that Evangeline *is* appearing in cabaret, after all? This isn't how book shows are supposed to work. Worse, this coarse segue is completely out of synch with Porter's delicate use of musical themes sounded by the orchestra during dialogue scenes to keep the show's throughlines in the ear.

So the evolution of the book show was still in its struggling stage. Indeed, Romney Brent must have become convinced that *Nymph Errant* was terminally primitive for all Cochran's extravagance, for he wrote a second musical on Laver's novel in 1946, this time with composers George Posford and Harry Jacobson and lyricist Eric Maschwitz. *Nymph Errant* had known sluggish near-success at the Adelphi in 154 performances; the new version, entitled *Evangeline*, occupied the Cambridge for a single month. Frances Day played the lead.

Not till 1982 was *Nymph Errant* seen in the U.S., at Equity Library Theatre, with Kathleen Mahony-Bennett as Evangeline and Bob Riley as Jo, Aunt Ermyntrude's gardener, who concludes the storyless story by offering the heroine the Ultimate—no, the First—Temptation: an apple. Seven years later, London got a second taste of the show in a benefit concert of the entire score, including cut numbers. Each of the solos was assigned to a different star, who would parade out to an ovation-inducing fanfare that only emphasized the work's disjunct nature. Still, it was interesting to hear Maureen McGovern playing coloratura scat games with "It's Bad For Me," Alexis Smith putting the finishing touch on "The Cocotte," Andrea McArdle getting a show-stopper out of "Georgia Sand," and Kaye Ballard trying to top McArdle with the number that replaced "Georgia Sand" during the original run, "Cazanova." Lisa Kirk took "The Physician," Marie Santell got "How Could We Be Wrong?," and Elisabeth Welch reintroduced her "Solomon."

Perhaps learning from *Nymph Errant* what not to do any more, Porter returned to the plotted show and the story score when back on Broadway for his next item, *Anything Goes* (1934), the second-longest-running book show of the decade.* *Anything Goes* was a Vinton Freedley project, Alex Aarons having moved to California. So the star songwriter was making the numbers on star performers (William Gaxton, Victor Moore, Ethel Merman, and, under the title, Bettina Hall) on a farcical plot line set somewhere in particular, for site-specific fun.

---

* A few revues broke the 1,000-performance mark. No thirties book musical even came close to 500, though eleven titles of the 1920s surpassed that figure. The champ of thirties narrative works is *Of Thee I Sing*, at 441 performances. *Anything Goes* reached 420, followed by *DuBarry Was a Lady* at 408 and *The Cat and the Fiddle* at 395. No other title comes close. Hard times.

That setting, framed by a first scene in New York and a finale in England, was an ocean liner. Now comes the factoid that haunts *Anything Goes* to the present day: its action told of a wacky shipwreck, and the show was about to start rehearsals when the *Morro Castle* suffered an explosion off the New Jersey coast and sank with a loss of 134 lives. *Anything Goes'* book, by Guy Bolton and P. G. Wodehouse, would obviously have to be denuded of its shipwreck; but the authors lived in Europe (in different countries, besides) and were unavailable for last-minute revisions. Freedley begged a rewrite of his director, Howard Lindsay, but Lindsay couldn't write a new script by himself and wouldn't collaborate with anyone but the unknown Russel Crouse. Freedley finds Crouse. Crouse says yes. This launches the twenty-eight-year career of Lindsay and Crouse; and meanwhile *Anything Goes* is saved.

This tale has taken in three generations of theatre historians, including, to his shame, your reporter. Now for the truth. It happens that musicals of this time were often written "off" a matrix scenario, and Guy Bolton's for *Anything Goes* survives. It would appear that Bolton was to outline the action and Wodehouse separately to flesh it out, while Porter would decide where the précis called for music and slip a number into that slot.

These treatments were not synopses but detailed scene-by-scene break-downs complete with suggested lines of dialogue and "business" (the old term for "shtick"). Bolton wrote the scenario so early that "Ethel Merman" and "Gaxton" don't have character names. These may seem a likely romantic pair—the fifty-eight-year-old Victor Moore was long past his Boy Meets Girl—but this trio was really on hand for comic roles. Moore was a gangster, a joke in itself because of his self-effacing presentation. Gaxton stows away on the cruise and is thus forced into and out of disguise, and Merman loves him in vain, as he is in pursuit of Bettina Hall.

It sounds potential, but the erratic Bolton was at his dimmest here, contriving an action without a plot. For the entire show, it seems, characters come in and go out and do it again: but virtually nothing happens, especially not a shipwreck. What actually troubled everyone in regard to the *Morro Castle* tragedy was a subplot involving a mad bomber terrorizing the ship.

Lindsay and Crouse didn't simply remove the bomb throughline. They wrote a new script. A few elements of Bolton and Wodehouse remain— a missionary and his two backsliding Chinese converts, Gaxton's disguises and attempts to steal Hall from an English lord, and Moore's character generally. Lindsay and Crouse eased very happily into Victor Moore territory, as he shilly-shallies about without ever quite getting what's said to him yet always veering off into comments that are somehow contiguous and irrelevant at once:

LADY: Have you ever lived in California?

MOORE: Well, I served a few years in San Quentin.

LADY: San Quentin? Is that anywhere near Santa Clara?

MOORE: Well, Clara wasn't there when I was. Whatever became of Clara?

While reimagining *Anything Goes*, Lindsay and Crouse tightened it. Bolton in particular wrote librettos as *romans-fleuves*, simply coursing along wherever his imagination took him. Lindsay and Crouse tried to limit their materials the better to exploit them. To Bolton, the two Chinese Christians were bric-à-brac; Lindsay and Crouse bring them into the action. This creates one of their best jokes, on the appearance of a certain Plum Blossom (Merman in disguise), seduced and abandoned. Her deceiver is accused of "taking Plum Blossom to rice fields" and bringing back "Plum Tart."

So *Anything Goes* is more than a great score. Thirties musical comedies were dizzy pieces; *Anything Goes* is dizzy but centered. Not to beat poor Guy Bolton over the head with his scenario: but how could he have included a spoof of a revivalist meeting and not realized that Merman was born to play that shady idol the revivalist preacher? Bolton's Merman is just a broad—it was Lindsay and Crouse who made her the combination of Texas Guinan and Aimee Semple McPherson named Reno Sweeney that defines this show's sarcastic vitality. Indeed, the most significant part of *Anything Goes* that is entirely missing from Bolton's conception is the goof on American celebrity as beyond criticism and the law. Lindsay and Crouse saw it clearly, as did Porter, of course: Merman the Evangelist and Moore the Criminal are American show-biz stars, joined by Gaxton the Stowaway when he is mistaken for Public Enemy Number One.

Even without the nonexistent shipwreck, the *Anything Goes* legend still sounds nutty. Why was Lindsay that determined to work with Russel Crouse, so tangential to The Street that Freedley couldn't locate him through standard professional channels and finally just happened to see him looking out a window on West Fifty-second Street? Yes, Freedley's office was in the Alvin Theatre, which he had once owned, and Crouse worked for the Theatre Guild, whose office was in *their* theatre, the Guild, just across the street. It's still nutty. Further, Crouse's curriculum vitae consisted of co-writing the book to two failures. One of them, *The Gang's All Here*—the show with the Atlantic City characters—has appeared in these pages as having one of the most excoriated librettos of the decade.

In any case, let us consider how suitable *Anything Goes* was as a "Cole Porter show." *Nymph Errant* liberated Porter's elitist side. *Anything Goes* democratized him, letting him revel in the swing of American language and content and the dead-on pow! of the American singing style. There's no hit tune like an American hit tune. English musicals of that day didn't have hit tunes: they had vocal gems.

Best of all, *Anything Goes* had Ethel Merman singing four of the five major numbers, hit insurance. Reno Sweeney was only the third story role that Merman had played, but already the five authors knew what they were working around: a tough broad with no pretensions and no tolerance of the pretentious. Onstage, she had a sense of humor and could take her lumps like a sport; offstage, she was spectacularly foul-mouthed and took umbrage easily. No wonder she suffered a lifelong failure to amaze Hollywood. The movies liked dangerous women, rough women, and even a few independent women. Merman was a phallic woman, castratingly blunt. When Alan Jay Lerner asked Julie Andrews if he could add a new solo for her in the two performances preceding *Camelot's* opening night, Andrews replied, "Of course, darling, but do try to get it to me the night before." When Irving Berlin tried to change a lyric in *Call Me Madam* at a comparable late moment, Merman looked right into the face of the man who Jerome Kern himself said *was* American music, the man who, one show earlier, had given Merman the hit of her life in *Annie Get Your Gun*. And in words so nakedly aggressive that I try to quote them at least once in every book I write, she slammed out, "Call me Miss Birdseye of 1950. This show is *frozen!*"

The four leading numbers that Merman sang in *Anything Goes* sound utterly unlike almost everything in *Nymph Errant*. Clearly, Porter was selecting and developing elements of his talent, but, also, he was celebrating the American sound of American art: "I Get a Kick Out Of You," "You're the Top," "Anything Goes," and "Blow, Gabriel, Blow" are freshets of sass after the jaded *complainte* of the cocotte or the dainty syncopations of "Experiment," a kind of operetta version of a rhythm number. Interestingly, all four of Merman's major *Anything Goes* songs, however portable, are locked into the *Anything Goes* narrative. The serenely regretful "Kick" warns us that Merman loves Gaxton in vain; he wants the soprano. So Merman and Gaxton can be pals, cuing in "You're the Top." The title song explains the show's premise: the new pop culture entirely lacks moral discrimination. And "Blow" fixes Merman as that singing evangelist, profanely combining the two least harmonious forces, jazz and religion.

Merman had a fifth number, "Buddie, Beware," designed simply to give her a solo before the traveler curtain in the second half of Act Two and, as mentioned, replaced very early in the run by a "Kick" reprise. The other important number in *Anything Goes* was Gaxton's duet with Bettina Hall, "All Through the Night." This replaced "Easy To Love," which apparently gave Gaxton trouble. It does have a slightly larger vocal range than "Night," but, more pertinently, it dwells significantly at the bottom of that range, exactly where Gaxton's just-barely voice lacked tone. Then, too, "Night" is easier to sing because it's unusually rhythmic for a ballad, almost a march, with plenty of orchestral backup, while "Easy To Love" makes demands on the singer's ability to sustain a legato with very little accompaniment from the pit band. Ironically, "Easy To Love" was later used in Porter's score for the Eleanor Powell film *Born To Dance* (1936), where it is sung, very affectingly, by someone with even less voice than Gaxton, James Stewart. But then, Stewart was singing into a microphone, not having to fill the Alvin Theatre eight times a week.

Interestingly, *Anything Goes* anticipates Porter's only other universally popular score, *Kiss Me, Kate*, in that more or less every number is of major weight or at least very tuneful. Some of *Nymph Errant* doesn't deserve to be heard more than once—the drearily wan "Cocotte," perhaps, and certainly "Back To Nature With You" and "Plumbing." But *Anything Goes* is first-rate throughout, including even the number written to cover the first scene change, from the (real-life) Weylin Caprice Bar to the afterdeck of the ship, "Bon Voyage"; even the second-act opening,

"Public Enemy Number One," laid out as a madrigal celebrating the presence of a genuine celebrity on board, a wanted criminal.

Typical of *Anything Goes*' richness is Bettina Hall's one star outing, the show's eleven o'clock number, "The Gypsy in Me." Utterly unmotivated, it allowed the dignified heroine to play saucy lady with flamenco turn, and but for the five overwhelming hit tunes might have caught on as a semi-standard. Similarly overlooked for decades was the "Sailors' Chanty," generally called "There'll Always Be a Lady Fair," a quartet also used in one as a scene-changer. Easily the most unknown of the original *Anything Goes* titles is "Where Are the Men?," a swirling waltz whose only purpose was to give choreographer Robert Alton something to do with the middle of the first act.

The songs cited in the four paragraphs above comprise the entire *Anything Goes* score, save Victor Moore's one number, "Be Like the Bluebird." Ten songs with the two smallish choral pieces comprise a lean tunestack, but after so many musical comedies with generic scores, Porter's precision dazzled. The chromatic descent of the melody in "All Through the Night," the breathless pileup of jaggedly syncopated phrases in the title song—the musical depiction of a world crazed by fad—or even the image of "the moon over Mae West's shoulder" in "You're the Top" all typify why Porter is the least obsolete of all his coevals today. Even Rodgers and Hart—whom theatre buffs may prefer for the sheer range of their shows—cannot challenge Porter's survival. It was Porter who received the ultimate tribute in a rock anthology album, *red hot + blue*, in which present-day singers reimagine his art in their personal styles. There are even two rap cuts.

One reason why Porter is so much with us is because *Anything Goes* is. Although the 1930s produced many famous titles, they tend to be works we seldom see, such as *Of Thee I Sing* or, even rarer, *The Cat and the Fiddle*; or compositions in forms other than operetta or musical comedy, such as *Porgy and Bess* or *The Cradle Will Rock*; or Rodgers and Hart shows that return despite dummkopf books because the music is so good.

Anything Goes is the essential thirties musical; it never really closed. It shows the customary flaws of the era: mechanical love plot, songs performed in one that come out of nowhere. And Paramount's two filmings did not promote it. The first, in 1936, credited its screenplay to three of the original authors (Wodehouse is stiffed), and it generally follows the storyline. Merman's in shot, playing to Bing Crosby, in Gaxton's character. Charles Ruggles and Ida Lupino are acceptable substitutes for Moore and Hall. But "All Through the Night" and "Blow, Gabriel, Blow" are gone, and that is simply absurd. Paramount's second *Anything Goes*, again with Crosby, roamed even further from the source.

Of course, a hit this big goes to London—but in what form? The history of the transatlantic production of musicals falls into three periods. In the first, from the late 1800s to 1920 or so, the original work serves as a matrix for a new piece. From 1920 to exactly April 29, 1947, there is much less rewriting and even the occasional souvenir of the original, as when Bobby Connolly's choreography is seen in both New York (1928) and London (1929) *New Moons*; or when *Bitter Sweet* (1929) comes to Broadway (1929) in a facsimile of the original staging, albeit with a new cast.

I feel that we can map the start of the third (and present) period of the Broadway and West End show bank to the precise day because that is when *Oklahoma!* opened at Drury Lane. It was performed in its original production in every particular and with Americans in roles they had performed on Broadway or in the national company. Since then, this replica approach has been preferred almost as a rule.

Anything Goes thus benefitted from the second period's reasonable sense of fidelity, as Charles B. Cochran produced a fresh yet respectful version, in 1935, commissioning P. G. Wodehouse to spiff up the verbal content for local enjoyment. Broadway's most constant romantic lead, Jack Whiting, played Billy to the Reno nouvelle of Jeanne Aubert, a French star who, you may have noticed, had appeared on Broadway. Whiting's romance led him to Adèle Dixon, whom we met in Kern and Hammerstein's *Three Sisters*. The London *Anything Goes* played the Palace, in the center of West End coming and going, but it was a no more than moderate success.

Is there something exclusively American about this celebration of swindling and masquerading? In any case, for the first major revision, at off-Broadway's Orpheum Theatre, in 1962, Guy Bolton himself refitted the book, and a solid helping of the 1934 score was amplified by six other Porter numbers. The additions included "It's De-Lovely" (from *Red, Hot and Blue!* [1936]) and "Friendship" (from *DuBarry Was a Lady* [1939]), which appear to have been sneaking into the show in various regional and stock productions during the 1940s and 1950s. Thus, Bolton's work lay mainly in situating the new songs in the action and rearranging the

story to take place entirely aboard ship, thus accommodating the
Orpheum's limited scenic facilities.

The run of 239 performances in a theatre seating no more than 299
suggests a very modest "maybe" success. But the cast, headed by Hal
Linden, Eileen Rodgers, Mickey Deems, and Barbara Lang, was unusually
high-powered for off-Broadway. If for that alone—and getting its own
recording—this *Anything Goes* attracted some attention, and its version
became the only one offered for production. Once again, the show sailed
to London, as the first musical produced by Cameron Mackintosh, in
1969. With James Kenney, the crooning rather than belting Marian
Montgomery as Reno, Michael Segal, and Valerie Verdon, it may have
lacked charisma control, for it closed almost immediately.

Anything Goes a bomb? And note that, here once more, the score was
diddled, with "I Get a Kick Out of You" not heard before the eleven o'clock
spot—remember, Porter *started* his music with this title in 1934—and
"Let's Do It" shoved in as another interpolation. Still, we notice that each
revision attempts to rationalize the book's relationship with the songs—for
instance, to find more music for the heroine while dropping her unsuitable
"Gypsy in Me"; to bring the typical Bolton-Wodehouse Silly Brit character into the score in a duet with Reno, "Let's Misbehave"; to establish the
minor character of Bonnie with numbers (such as "Heaven Hop" and
"Let's Step Out") so that she serves a purpose other than simply being the
character accidentally left over from the long-vanished "Where Are the
Men?" In other words, the typical lumpy thirties musical comedy was
being integrated as few thirties musical comedies had been in their time.
Oddly, credit for the book did not specify "revised by Guy Bolton," as at
the Orpheum; only Lindsay and Crouse were mentioned at all.

The culmination of *Anything Goes* revisions came with the 1987
Lincoln Center production, one of the modern era's most persuasive
reworkings of an old piece. I need to emphasize this praise, for all too often
the rewriting of shows treats the original coarsely, even recklessly, so vio-
lating its form, content, and spirit that the result is wholly ersatz. Who was
it that conducted the reclamation of this sixty-three-year-old relic so faithfully that it was true to itself while directly addressing the public of today:
director Jerry Zaks, choreographer Michael Smuin, music director Edward
Strauss, orchestrator Michael Gibson, dance arranger Tom Fay? Or was
it simply the new book writers, Timothy Crouse (Russel's son) and

John Weidman? For besides sorting out character interaction in a way that soothes the disconnects of the 1934 script, the revision does something all but unheard of today, bringing back as much of the original score as possible—considerably more than the 1962 edition, by the way.

This really is *Anything Goes*, not just a Cole Porter sing-off using portions of the *Anything Goes* narrative. "The Gypsy in Me" and "Buddie, Beware" were reinstated after decades of obscurity, and "Easy To Love" joined them, finally taking its place in the show it was written for. Few knew that "There's No Cure Like Travel," the first half of the chorus that covers the set change from the opening bar scene to the ship, was being heard for the first time, having been dropped from the show in 1934 in favor of the other half of the number, "Bon Voyage." Presumably, the music was regarded as a throwaway and was cut to half to take advantage of a speedy change of decor. But the two melodies play off one another amusingly and make a splendid effect when sung in counterpoint.

The treatment of Elisha Whitney and Lord Evelyn Oakley also demonstrates how carefully *Anything Goes* was rebuilt. In 1934, these were non-singing comic roles. But important characters cannot play entirely outside the music today; modern audiences expect more reasonably proportioned scores. So Whitney got an interpolation from Porter's Yale days, "I Want To Row on the Crew," and Lord Evelyn got "Gypsy," which suits his giddy jesting far more than it did the heroine that Bettina Hall had played.

"Friendship" and "It's De-Lovely" were probably retained because they have been part of *Anything Goes* for so long; and they are useful in, respectively, giving Victor Moore's character a second number and firming up the love plot. A third interpolation, "Goodbye, Little Dream, Goodbye,"*

* Though a Porter number of the mid-1930s and thus sound *Anything Goes* material, "Goodbye" is technically not from a Porter show. Written for Frances Langford to sing in the film *Born To Dance* (1936), it was dropped and went right into *Red, Hot and Blue!*, for Ethel Merman. It's hard to imagine a better mating of singer and song—can't you imagine that voice going grand at the start of the release ("For the stars have fled from the heavens")? Apparently, however, Porter then wrote "Down in the Depths (on the ninetieth floor)" for the same slot as Merman's first solo, and while "Goodbye" is lovely, "Down in the Depths" boasts one of Porter's snazziest lyrics. (This is the one with "the janitor's wife.") The music, too, is distinctive, with a strong pulse that suggests an urban din heard from the top of a tower. Michael Leeds' *Red, Hot and Blue!* revision for Goodspeed Opera House in 2000 managed to place both of these torch songs, but in 1936 "Goodbye" was dropped, finally to serve as a musical bonbon for Yvonne Printemps in a London play called *Oh Mistress Mine* that same year. (This has no connection to Terence Rattigan's 1944 Lunt-Fontanne vehicle *Love in Idleness*, which the Lunts played on Broadway two years later as *O Mistress Mine*.)

was a rarity worthy of revival—and it gave the sweetheart her only solo, at that one defining her true feelings for the hero. Most unexpected was the use of Porter's own rendition of the title song with which to launch the overture; and Porter's return at show's end was thrilling: in a photograph lowered from the flies to smile down on the instrumentalists, who were playing the show from the poop deck overlooking the main stage. Porter might well smile. Aside from the extra numbers, all but one of the songs heard when *Anything Goes* opened in New York, on November 21, 1934, were performed in full at Lincoln Center.

And yet the most telling moment of revision was the addition of some dialogue and the reassignment of a single line of a song during the "Easy To Love" scene. The hero serenades the sweetheart with it. But the moment has bite because she is trapped in an engagement to a man she does not love—Lord Evelyn. After the hero's two choruses, she is apparently as determined as ever to marry the Brit:

HOPE: If you don't let me alone, I'll make a scene.
BILLY: (with the quiet confidence of the Boy who knows that, according
     to the musical-comedy rulebook, he *must* Get Girl) You love me,
     Hope. You're going to marry me.

Hope Harcourt and Billy Crocker. It is Hope who sings the number's final line, giving the romance an intimacy and power it completely lacked in 1934.

Patti LuPone, Howard McGillin, and Bill McCutcheon headed the Lincoln Center cast, though the below-the-title Kathleen Mahony-Bennett (ELT's errant nymph, you may recall) was playing a Hope so amplified in script and score that hers, too, might be thought a star role. With Anthony Heald's Lord Evelyn and Rex Everhart's Whitney, with Linda Hart as a now souped-up Bonnie, renamed Erma (she got "Buddie, Beware," sung not as a solo but with adoring sailors), and with Anne Francine as Hope's grand-dame mother (yet another Porter character named Evangeline, by the way), the new *Anything Goes* was well cast. Patti Lu surprised many with her vivacious comic style; and as hers are the score's best known numbers, her famously imprecise diction wasn't a problem. McGillin, a matinee idol who can really sing, reminds us how far the casting of the Boy in the love plot has come since the 1930s.

If there are no Bert Lahrs or Ethel Mermans today—and there aren't—at least there are no William Gaxtons, either.

As London was enjoying the fidelity of the third era in its hosting of American productions, the West End gave almost exactly the same show seen at Lincoln Center, in 1989. Howard McGillin came over to join comic Bernard Cribbins and a top-billed Elaine Paige. There was one very odd emendation of the New York staging when, for no discernible reason, a mussed-up, shirtless sailor came barrelling from stage right to left, trailed by a leering male passenger.

The Lincoln Center version is surely to remain Final *Anything Goes*; it's too wonderfully constructed to dispute, even in small ways. Trevor Nunn used it, albeit with some fiddling here and there, at England's National Theatre, in 2002.* Sally Ann Triplett (the original Sue in *Carrie*), John Barrowman (who had replaced McGillin in the Elaine Paige production), and Martin Marquez were the principals, with ingenue Mary Stockley and veteran Denis Quilley, in the last job of his life, as Elisha Whitney.

The Nunn version was a huge hit, transferring prominently to the West End, but we should note as well a Paper Mill Playhouse staging, in 2000, with Chita Rivera. Here the fiddling consisted mainly of enhancing the choreographic structure, with, for a novelty, a dancing Billy (George Dvorsky) and Hope (Stacey Logan). They turned "It's De-Lovely" into a rhumba of a Dream Ballet for five couples, and the entire cast got stepping in the title number, even Mrs. Harcourt (Eleanor Glockner).

Chita of course had her exhibition spots, most especially an arresting solo amid the hoopla of "Blow, Gabriel, Blow." She made an unusually elegant Reno, going diva in twelve different costume changes; her sailor uniform for "Anything Goes" was a knockout, with a blue shirtwaist over the nautical whites, surmounted by a pink tie. Interestingly, Chita put a spin on "I Get a Kick Out Of You" by singing it not as a wistful torch song but as a platonic jest, thus freeing herself to spend the plot working around the Billy-Hope romance rather than having to resent it. Here was

---

* Nunn at first intended to revive an English classic, *The Boy Friend*. However, at his meeting with its author, Sandy Wilson, Nunn revealed that he had alterations in mind and Wilson refused to countenance any. It was a brave stand to take, as his career was long over and a National Theatre *Boy Friend* would have made quite some hurrah. But Wilson is right: *The Boy Friend* is already perfect.

a chance, then, to watch a great performer make provocative choices, freshening a character in danger of becoming trite.

One might say that of *Anything Goes* itself. It is so readily performable that it may be too often around nowadays; but then it is irresistibly full of personality. The songs are not particularly plot-driven. But Porter did write a certain continuity into Reno's numbers; and a worldview permeates the show's lyrics in general. One hears no throughline in *Nymph Errant*'s score, while Porter's satiric vision—his America, so to say—bonds *Anything Goes*' songs, even if the show's very title suggests another of those emptily vivid musical-comedy buzz terms like *Helter Skelter* (1899), *Merry Mary* (1911), *Pom-Pom* (1916), *Pitter Patter* (1920), or *Heads Up!* (1929), a Rodgers and Hart show. *Anything Goes*: the glamour of celebrity has overwhelmed everyone's moral judgment.

So Porter could write his elitist party pieces or something more popular, always within his craftsman's compass. But there was a third option. What if Porter, newly self-assured after the huge appeal of the *Anything Goes* score, chanced an evening *filled* with music—character songs far more precisely turned than ever before in a Porter show and a great deal of plot numbers as well?

In fact: what if Porter abandoned the Aarons-Freedley construct, with which he had been associated with various producers since his first definitive success, *Fifty Million Frenchmen* (1929), and instead wrote a wholly novel work with real characters in it? That is, not a display piece for Gertrude Lawrence's indescribable charm nor an exploitation of the bantering flimflammer, whining human doodad, and belting broad that Gaxton, Moore, and Merman will themselves "create" for you, but rather a work conceived around a story, the music cut to fit that story, and the cast then assembled to enact the tale.

This piece concerned four British-like royals—King, Queen, Prince, and Princess—who run off to have adventures, each coupling with an *à clef* figure. The King joins up with partygiver Elsa Maxwell, the Queen with Johnny "Tarzan" Weissmuller, the Prince with an American song-and-dance star (this character has no apparent real-life source), and the Princess with Noël Coward, though of course the show's characters bear fictional names.

Jubilee (1935) is famous as the show that Porter wrote with Moss Hart while sailing around the world on the S.S. *Franconia* during the first five months of 1935. But note that they were physically together during the period of composition, not separated by a "treatment" from which writers could work apart from each other. This explains why *Jubilee* is unusually well integrated for a thirties musical comedy. It does have its allotment of mere atmosphere or scene-opening pieces, true. Still, not counting reprises the show contains twenty-two numbers both large and small, most of them delineating character and some partly built on conversations, giving *Jubilee* the flavor of a bawdy operetta.

It is not a celebrated score, and Hart's book rather lacks humor. Teased and prodded by Porter and cruise sycophant Monty Woolley, Hart did try a few daring touches here and there. No sooner have the Prince and his American, Karen O'Kane, met and danced (=loved) than Hart brings the lights up on the two of them in bed with the Prince in search of a cigarette. And here's the Queen trying to get a policeman to direct her to the latest film of jungle hero Mowgli:

> OFFICER: *Mowgli!*
> QUEEN: Yes!
> OFFICER: Oh, I adore him!
> QUEEN: What?
> OFFICER: He's divine, isn't he? That *body*!
> QUEEN: Well, there's going to be a hell of a shake-up in the Police Department, I can tell you that.

When the Queen enters the movie theatre, the original production went into mixed-media mode, showing a portion of *Mowgli and the White Goddess*; and the Mowgli, one Charles Rausmiller, made his personal appearance after the showing dressed only in his loincloth. We expect that today, but this was an inflammatory baiting of the social cautions in 1935.

Hart was good at specifying character, a quality that we have seen failing in thirties librettos not made on stars. Karen O'Kane is one of those vivacious charmers with a pet tic, crediting Dorothy Parker with various colloquialisms, and Porter works this into the verse of "Just One Of Those Things," revealing how collaboratively the two authors collected their inspirations. The Noël Coward figure, called

Eric Dare,* comes through best in his music, where Porter can refer to the style of song Coward wrote. This is especially true of the droopy waltz "When Love Comes Your Way." In fact, it was first written for Gertrude Lawrence to sing in *Nymph Errant*; even so, it might well have been a doting spoof of "I'll See You Again" or "Lover Of My Dreams," a part of Coward as basic as the better-known patter songs—and, as we'll see, the sample of the latter that Porter created for Eric Dare in *Jubilee* is one of his masterpieces.

Perhaps the most vivid of the *à clef* characters is Eva Standing, the Elsa Maxwell copy, if only because Maxwell was so faithfully duplicated. Eric Dare is modified Coward, really more like a Coward creation than like Coward himself; and Charles Rausmiller is simply an "Aw, shucks" farmboy–movie star. Eva Standing, however, really *is* Elsa Maxwell, in all her dialed-to-the-topmost-setting connectedness: everyone's "an angel" and "my most intimate friend." You name a celebrity and Maxwell-Standing "discovered" him. Everything's beautiful. Everyone's happy. Here's Eva making a rare exception:

EVA: Everyone *adores* doing things for me. . . . Grace Moore wanted to sing for me tomorrow night, but I wouldn't let her. I've *turned* on singers!

A FRIEND: Grace Moore?

EVA: My most intimate friend! I discovered her, you know—took her *right* to Gatti-Casazza! Dear Gatti—he's the sweet of the world. Too marvelous. I adore him.

Jubilee is about celebrity, in fact—about being one or meeting one. *Anything Goes* warned of America's amoral fascination with fame, but in this show fame has become the first virtue, a morality itself. This makes it in a way the ultimate Cole Porter show, for several reasons. The obvious one comprises the celeb sightings that crowd the lyrics in this work especially. Among the relentless plugs are those who are still famous today,

---

* This must be one of the most canny sobriquets ever given to an *à clef* figure. There is something of the literary, the precious, the timeless, the self-regarding, the adorable, and the demanding in the sound of it: and that was Coward. Also, Eric was the name of Coward's only sibling. More important, Coward was artistically a very *daring* figure, one who baited the cautions almost as a rule.

such as Greta Garbo, Cecil B. De Mille, Bing Crosby, Henry Ford, "Fritzy Kreisler," H. G. Wells, Paul Revere, Romeo and Juliet, Abelard and Héloïse, Cain and Abel, and even Porter's own regretful Miss Otis. There are also those no longer famous but known to aficionados of certain kinds, such as Will Hays, Father Coughlin, and Clifton Webb's mother. Most amusing to us today are the citations of those whose fame is now extinct but who were known to every member of *Jubilee*'s original public, such as O. O. McIntyre, Lucius Beebe, Walter Hampden, and Dizzy Dean (who also gets a look-in during "Conga!" in *Wonderful Town*). In her own wonderful category resides the early-nineteenth-century French beauty and *saloniste* Mme. Récamier.

More relevant to Porter's style is the gigantic *Jubilee* score itself, arguably the most interesting of all Porter's oeuvre. The best? I shall be careful here, for those who love Porter nominate *Kiss Me, Kate* (1948) first of all, and the well-versed amateur will know of *Out Of This World* (1950), nearly comparable for its wealth of melody and verbal mischief. *Jubilee* might be Porter's exhibition piece, a parade of: Porter genres, genres unknown to Porter outfitted in the Porter manner, and one-offs that Porter never tried again.

One oddity is that *Jubilee*'s two standards did not take off when the show was new. "Begin the Beguine" and "Just One of Those Things" had to be rediscovered, "Beguine" on Artie Shaw's best-selling 78 released after *Jubilee* had played the last of its 169 performances.* But then, with so much music to absorb in one evening, the public could not keep up with Porter's rate of invention, especially as so much of the action unfolds in the lyrics. Thirties audiences were not used to tracking a musical's scenario through its songs. As we've seen again and again, the script told the story and the score intermittently celebrated. In *Jubilee*, script *and* score told the story.

---

* Paradoxically, this classic swing instrumental, one of the outstanding documents of pop-music history, was the B side of the disc. The release title was *Rose-Marie*'s "Indian Love Call," almost unrecognizable in Shaw's avid sendup, with the band men shouting out punctuational noises and Tony Pastor contributing a vocal chorus that wins the prize for Least Amount of Rudolf Friml Actually Sung on a Friml Recording. "Begin the Beguine" is played straight. There is no vocal, just the sounding of the hook—a smoothly throbbing swing version of the accompaniment Porter himself wrote—and then Shaw's clarinet over the band. It was commonly said in the industry that "the intro sold the record." No: it was Porter, and Shaw's technically spectacular rising glissando at the climax.

For instance, what was one to make of Mowgli's establishing number, "When Me, Mowgli, Love," a jest on hare-brained heroes and Hollywood jungle-movie lore? The verse starts off on an almost modal melody over little more than a pounding in the bass on a single note, and the accompaniment of the refrain's A sections—a syncopated teetering between E Flat and D Flat Major chords—suggests the turgid stirring of an elephant herd. The number's vocal compass is extreme, sitting low for much of the refrain yet straining high in the release; all told, it needs a singer with absolute freedom from a deep B^b to a high G, an octave and a sixth. It's an extraordinary way to bring Mowgli into the score, with fantastical lyrics that picture those elephants looking on through binoculars as Mowgli enjoys an all-nighter. In Porter's output, there are other numbers as naughty or as clever, yet nothing even remotely as fanciful in both musical scene-painting and verbal wit. It's almost too brilliant, the kind of thing best absorbed and savored on repeated hearings, not something one easily collects on the spot.

Jubilee does have its Porter-as-usual pieces, such as the rhythm number— the beguine, of course—in an art deco nightclub set. Karen O'Kane sings the vocal as part of her club act, the Prince then Boy Meets Girls her, and the two take to the floor to empty it of all the other couples, in tribute to the pair's dancing expertise but more precisely of their romantic chemistry. Note that *Jubilee*'s choreographer, Albertina Rasch, did not stage this number. It demanded a combination of ballroom narcissism and contempo finesse that Madame Rasch may have lacked, so director Hassard Short called in the busiest exhibition dancer of the day, Tony De Marco.

"Begin the Beguine" itself is so luxuriously delineated that it's akin to the slow movement of a pop symphony, the entire thing generated from the launching figure of the fifth, sixth, and major-seventh intervals of the scale over an undulating accompaniment. This is the hook that so beautifully served Artie Shaw when he swung the beguine, a haunting effect that Porter needs in order to establish the dance as a musical madeleine, the very playing of which "brings back a night of tropical splendor." The melody is sleek, innuendo set to maracas—until the climax, an importunate statement on high that dies away to slivers of the main strain, reaching up and falling back to nothing. The song is not about beginning a beguine but about its fragility, its end. The lyrics say so in frankly defeatist terms, but it is the musical construction that "explains" the song.

Along with the rhythm number is of course the list song, for the Prince and Karen, "A Picture Of Me Without You." This starts with a smoky, after-hours jazz prelude of seven sung lines of conversation before reaching the song itself, a truly innovative touch. The number is innocent enough in its cascade of similes—but this is the aforementioned view of the couple in bed together after a bout of whoopee. It gives the duet a devilish spin unavailable to "You're the Top."

Jubilee gives us also a genre very much a part of Porter's professional worldview, the ballad with an easy-as-pie melody over grade-school harmony. Porter's first hit, "Old Fashioned Garden," from *Hitchy-Koo 1919*, must have taught Porter the wisdom of cajoling lazy ears every now and then. Porter tended to write these numbers for Hollywood. Some readers may think of "Hey, Babe, Hey" or "True Love," but the outstanding example is "Don't Fence Me In," Porter's most successful title of all. *Jubilee* has one such, too: "Me and Marie," a waltz presented as the hit tune of the King and Queen's youth, and deliberately nostalgic in its diatonic chording.

Jubilee's twenty-two numbers contain so many delightful bits that one has to admire Porter for never ham-and-egging his way through a scene-change or lights-up piece the way, for instance, DeSylva, Brown, and Henderson did. (Think of *Good News!*'s "On the Campus" and "Today's the Day," both available for moderns' inspection on the 1996 Wichita cast CD.) "What a Nice Municipal Park" has too much verve for what is in effect an excuse for a dance, and the sextet "Gay Little Wives" sings out in the curious metre of $\frac{3}{2}$ and thinks nothing of jumping from A Flat Major to the extremely distant key of E Major without warning. "Polished, urbane, and adult playwrighting in the musical field," Porter observed at this time, "is strictly a creative luxury." Yet in *Jubilee*, Porter indulged himself, setting the scene establishing Eric Dare entirely in song, as the acolytes eagerly await his arrival in a comic lament, swinging at length into a smashing waltz when Eric appears and they greet each other. Then, without an intro worthy of the name, Eric jumps into the aforementioned patter song, "The Kling-Kling Bird on the Divi-Divi Tree."

This was the first song written on that *Franconia* cruise. The party put up at Jamaica, where, so legend tells, Porter hears something strange in the air and asks what it is.

"Kling-kling."

"What?"

"Kling-kling, sir. Kling-kling *bird*."

Porter wants it pointed out.

"There."

"Where?"

"*There*. Divi-divi tree where, sir."

"The kling-kling bird on the divi-divi tree," Porter amusedly repeats. Then, smiling: "Title!"

Or something like that. "The Kling-Kling Bird" is Eric's recounting of his romantic adventures on his own world cruise, and it is ultimate Porter in its grandiose structure (an extremely lengthy rondo), its powerful and diverse rhythmic energies, its playfully bawdy content, and its casual juxtaposition of the old-fashioned and the ultra-contemporary. Call it Gilbert and Sullivan in heat. Everywhere that Eric travels, the kling-kling appears, to warn him away from sex—with women. The double meanings count among Porter's most outrageous, as with Eric's diversion with a Pacific Islander, who suggests he "visit her volcano," or with Eric's relationship with a cannibal woman who invites him to "come inside and make poi."

With Mary Boland heading the cast as the Queen, the King was Melville Cooper, and the younger royals were Charles Walters and Margaret Adams. Opposite them were, respectively, Mark Plant, May Boley (who actually resembled Elsa Maxwell), June Knight, and Derek Williams. Fifteen-year-old Montgomery Clift played their majesties' younger son. It was a good cast. But don't the four celebrity figures need outsized performances—the kind one gets from stars or, at least, highly specialized entertainers? And then wouldn't the four royals all but vanish unless they, too, get the star treatment? Brooks Atkinson didn't worry about it: he gave *Jubilee* possibly the greatest notice ever presented to a musical that failed to turn classic. "A rapturous masquerade," Atkinson wrote. "A visual masterpiece." "A light-stepping parade of splendor." "A tapestry of show-shop delights." Indeed, Atkinson couldn't find a flaw, and except for two critics who merely liked or accepted the show, all the daily reviewers gave it a rave.

Yet *Jubilee* proved vulnerable when Mary Boland made an early return to Hollywood, replaced by Laura Hope Crews, *Gone With the Wind*'s future Aunt Pittypat. Instantly, the show died. As if having learned a painful lesson, Porter wrote only in his most basic vein till *Kiss Me, Kate*, eleven shows later—and even *Kate* does not rival *Jubilee* for sheer vivacity of invention.

There was no *Jubilee* movie. Aided by the eventual popularity of "Begin the Beguine" and "Just One of Those Things," the title hung on in some powerful yet unclear way. Too much of the score works only in the narrative context, but at least Bobby Short included a third *Jubilee* number on his Porter retrospective, the Princess' "Why Shouldn't I?" Built on the fearful hunger that Porter detects in romance, this song is virtually a consultation with the gods in charge of reckless acts. It suits the Princess well enough, but it is really a motto song for Porter himself. On the line "Miss Peggy Joyce says it's good," Short's tone shapes all the power and fame and fury of the rich and popular and loveless gay that Porter was into a single image: a frenzy caught, for one moment, standing perfectly still in a mask.

What else, listeners may have wondered, lies in this tantalizingly unknowable score? Two years later, Columbia issued Porter's own renditions of nine other *Jubilee* numbers, recorded for use by the cast in rehearsals. More recently, the groups devoted to musical-theatre archeology have made reviving *Jubilee* a priority. Both Bill Tynes' New Amsterdam Theatre Company and Ian Marshall Fischer's London-based Lost Musicals lavished their finest efforts on the work, though proper casting remains a challenge. The New York performance came off well in Rebecca Luker's Princess, Davis Gaines' Mowgli, Alyson Reed's Karen, and Carole Shelley's Eva Standing; others were weak or incorrect. In London, Denis Quilley and Vivienne Martin led a more balanced but less showy lineup.

By far, the most notable cast was that of a 1998 benefit for the Gay Men's Health Crisis at Carnegie Hall, with royals Bea Arthur, Michael Jeter, Damian Woetzel, and Alice Ripley, and new-found friends Bob Paris, Tyne Daly, Sandy Duncan, and Stephen Spinella. Herbert Ross staged it, and—most unusually for the concert format—everyone was off book. Like the two previous concerts, this one aggrandized the already heaping score by reinserting a major number for the Queen, backed by Mowgli and the boys, all in swimming attire. Dropped in Boston, "There's Nothing Like Swimming" does not elucidate plot or character in any necessary way. But it is one of the gayest concoctions of its time, not only in the toothsome visuals but in Porter's gleeful use of the term "Neptune's daughter." This most exclusive of parish kennings denotes the gay man who chases sailors, and the phrase's true meaning stayed so arcane even as the term entered general use that MGM naively made it the title of an Esther Williams film in 1949.

The century's outstanding quirky WASP, Cole Porter took the thirties musical in a marriage realer than his legal one, to socialite Linda Lee. He more than anyone helped the musical adjust to its ineffable yet all the same substantial gay identity. Lorenz Hart had to work through his partner, Richard Rodgers; Porter's partner was Ethel Merman. Simply casting Tarzan in a musical is an absolutely unencoded gay act, and writing that musical on a cruise aboard the *Franconia* seems to challenge the American musical's historical emergence out of a subculture made by the children of penniless immigrants. And note that Porter took Moss Hart—one of that subculture's great success stories—along with him. Throughout his career, but especially in the 1930s and most of all in *Jubilee*, Cole Porter was the Unique Person in the Broadway authors' club, the only one who didn't resemble the others.

4

HARLEM ON MY MIND: THE BLACK SHOWS AND *PORGY AND BESS*

The black musical and the mainstream black musical star were inventions of the 1920s. A black show called *Clorindy, or the Origin of the Cakewalk* famously played Broadway as early as 1898 (albeit as a roof-garden one-act), and Bert Williams appeared in eight of Ziegfeld's *Follies* during the 1910s, a unique record for repeat work in that most visible of revues.

Still, not till the flash success of *Shuffle Along* (1921), the first black musical on Broadway since *Mr. Lode of Koal* (1909),* was a genuine cycle of black shows set into operation. The 1920s saw over a dozen such productions, and the high energy level of the dancing made the best of them must-sees not only for the public but for professionals looking for innovations to absorb. New stars appeared: the dainty dynamo Florence Mills (tragically cut down in her youth before the 1920s ended), Bill Robinson, and Ethel Waters.

There was no development whatsoever in the 1930s, because the black formats were still undergoing establishment when Depression economics discouraged their public. The narrative shows were the most vulnerable; typically, the outstanding producer of the twenties black revue, white Lew Leslie, remained the entrepreneur of note in this arena, sticking with

---

* Both *Mr. Lode of Koal*, at the old Majestic, and *Shuffle Along*, at the 63rd Street Music Hall, played that area around Columbus Circle that can't truly be called "Broadway" but wasn't exactly anything else. The houses were of Broadway proportions, and now and again prominent thespians worked in the neighborhood. Keep in mind, too, that only one block east of the Majestic (which became a TV studio), *Kiss Me, Kate* played its entire two-and-a-half-year run, at the New Century on Seventh Avenue and Fifty-eighth Street.

Robinson and Waters and never venturing out of the revue structure into a story show.

Lew Leslie's Blackbirds of 1930, the third of seven Leslie *Blackbirds* titles (counting London as well as New York), assigned the score to Eubie Blake and Andy Razaf, where Leslie's *Blackbirds of 1928* had sung in the white blackness of Jimmy McHugh and Dorothy Fields. Ethel Waters, the dancing duo of Buck and Bubbles, Mantan Moreland, Broadway Jones, Flournoy Miller, and other stalwarts of the scene headed the 1930 cast. The evening's burlesques singled out not only the prison melodrama *The Last Mile* and *All Quiet on the Western Front* but even *The Green Pastures*—tricky to do, as *The Green Pastures* is nearly burlesque in the first place. "Memories of You" and "You're Lucky To Me" were the popular numbers, with a New Dance Sensation in "Lindy Hop," unusual in this genre in being addressed especially to senior citizens. "Watch the way that *they* go," the lyrics advise us: because the new step "cures them of lumbago." Waters offered the double-entendre ghetto number, "My Handy Man Ain't Handy No More," and a miniature minstrel show held the eleven o'clock spot, with Waters as interlocutor and Moreland as Mr. Bones.

In short, it was typical, and too much so. The sheer novelty of black music theatre had worn off; critics and public demanded something more substantial. *Blackbirds of 1930* closed in a bit less than two months, but Leslie snapped back the next year with *Rhapsody in Black*—and this one was different. Billed as "a symphony of blue notes and black rhythms," the work stripped the African-American revue to certain basics: solo and choral song with a smattering of dance, the whole performed by a dozen or so principals and the Cecil Mack Choir against the simplest possible unit set of playing area backed by dark drapes. There were no comic sketches, and most of the dancing was assigned to Valaida (Snow), who offered the "Harlem Rhumbola" and "Dance of the Chocolate Soldier," a militaire tapped out on a set of oversized drums. The latter's music was "March of the Toys" from Victor Herbert's *Babes in Toyland* (1903), a curious selection for a show entitled *Rhapsody in Black*. Ethel Waters again led the lineup, in such numbers as "What's Keeping My Prince Charming?" and "You Can't Stop Me From Loving You" (both with Blue McAllister). The Cecil Macks sang spirituals, a vocal arrangement of the *Rhapsody in Blue*, and—speaking of curiosities—a Hebrew folk song, "Eli, Eli."

It's often uncomfortable to read critics' comments on the black shows, however innocently meant. *The Evening Post's* John Mason Brown thought *Rhapsody in Black* had "precious little of that white-teethed, broad-grinned and insinuating gagety [*sic*; "gaiety"?] which heretofore has been the redeeming feature of many a brown-skinned revue." Translating from the high middle racist, I think he means that the show wasn't black enough: not fun.

But it may be that Leslie was trying something else for a change, a black show without black cliché—minstrel-show jokes, whirlwind dance routines, "handy man" blues smut. And isn't the infusion of alternate ethnicities in Victor Herbert, Gershwin jazz, and Jewish song something beyond mere curiosity, perhaps a comment on how Broadway categorizes its art? Could Leslie have been promulgating multicultural progressivism before its day? But the critics found the evening pompous. "Academic" was Arthur Pollock's opinion, and Richard Lockridge wrote, "Not even Miss Waters is a revue." The low-budget mounting was able to squeak out 80 performances, a deflating run for a work possibly meant to create a sense of dignity and even cultural philanthropy in the matter of ethnic music. Undaunted, Leslie went on to *Blackbirds* shows in 1933, 1934, 1936 (the latter two in London), and 1939 before ending the series.

Composer and lyricist (and even straight playwright) Donald Heywood was ambitious enough to travel to Africa for study, in order to authenticate his style. But Heywood never had a *Blackbirds of 1928*. His first score, for a revue called *Africana* (1927), was heard through 72 performances and gave la Waters her Broadway debut. She was much noticed by the critics, as was Mae Barnes (much later the maid of the "Happy Habit" in *By the Beautiful Sea*) in Heywood's *Hot Rhythm* (1930), another revue. This show, for which the usually ambitious Heywood wrote only lyrics (to Porter Grainger's music), was very like cabaret without tables, as emcee Will Morrissey was down in the aisles chatting up the clientele. Heywood wrote both music and words for at least part of *Blackberries of 1932*, but it was gone in three weeks.

Then Heywood made his history, in a second *Africana*, in 1934. For once, a Heywood show was no revue but a grandiose Congo operetta, and Heywood had written almost all of the book, music, and lyrics. He told of a Europeanized African prince who returns home in times of social turbulence: *Kwamina* (1961) without the mixed-race romance. Trouble began when opening night got off to such a late start that the public had started clapping in rhythm. And then came The Incident.

Digesting this event from contradictory reports, we gather that, early in Act One, a man in either evening clothes or a camel's hair coat strode down the aisle during a musical number and physically attacked the conductor, Philip Ellis (not author Heywood doing a first-night-only podium gig, as we sometimes hear). Some say the intruder had an iron bar, others that he pulled a chair out of the orchestra pit. Ellis defended himself with another chair while the orchestra and performers went right on playing and singing. The sole woman critic, Wilella Waldorf, admitted in print that she had wanted to head for the hills. Noting that her colleagues held place, however, she, too, decided to maintain on-site critical detachment.

Meanwhile, folks in the front rows, who had assumed the fracas was part of the show, realized that nothing as completely terrible as *Africana* could have rehearsed anything this interesting. They jumped up and subdued the assailant, who identified himself in night court as one Almany Daouda Camaro. He had apparently served in the French Foreign Legion with Heywood, and claimed that the two of them had planned the *Africana* scenario. Camaro had simply been protesting his lack of credit and profit participation. A lenient judge gave Camaro a suspended sentence, and *Africana* closed after 3 performances. Indeed, while calling *Africana* "arty Harlemania," *Variety* reported that "half the house" deserted during intermission.

Heywood had no luck. Two years after this second *Africana*, he suffered another disastrous premiere with *Black Rhythm*, a backstager that he not only wrote in its entirety but co-directed. The cast included Avon Long, Jeni LeGon, the Wen Talbott Choir, and the Savoy Lindy Hoppers, a typical lineup. But of course there was nothing typical about a Donald Heywood opening night. This time, two stink bombs were set off in the theatre—three if we count *Black Rhythm* itself. The show closed within a week, and after he wrote one last straight play, *How Come, Lawd?* (1937), Heywood's byline was retired.

It is often said of the black book musicals of the era that they relied on narrative simply as an anchor for skits and specialties. That could be said as well of the white shows. It was not so readily apparent, because the 1920s hosted many white operettas, musical plays, or musical comedies under the musical-play influence, and these did not make room for vaudeville spots. However, as there were few black operettas or musical plays, there was no purely integrated black format to counter the typical slapdash organization of the ghetto shows.

So *Hummin' Sam* (1933) proved just another example of a black book show with a specious libretto and a program filled with variety acts. Its booking already says a good deal: the New Yorker Theatre, originally the Gallo Opera House and a place so jinxed that virtually nothing that dared its stage lasted longer than two weeks till the *Cabaret* revival moved in at the millennium. *Hummin' Sam* lasted one night. It was based on Charles T. Dazey's extremely popular melodrama *In Old Kentucky* (1893), by 1933 unavailably antique. To be sure, *Hummin' Sam* used only the outline of the plot, about a jockey who wins the Big Race and, thereby, True Love. The white dramatis personae obviously went black and the setting was updated, but *Hummin' Sam* preserved the play's typically turn-of-the-century stunt of using live horses on treadmills during the derby sequence to climax the second act (of three) with genuine excitement.

It's an odd project, mating one of America's oldest forms with one of its newest: not unlike seeing words like "reefer" and "triggeration" on the title cards of a D. W. Griffith silent. Even odder was *Hummin' Sam*'s twist on a twist. *In Old Kentucky*'s jockey is a young woman, a piquant novelty for 1893. *Hummin' Sam* transgendered the jockey into a young man, but cast the role with Gertrude "Baby" Cox, playing in drag. Dazey's play made much of the jockey's battle with her fiancé's snobby family; *Hummin' Sam* substituted villainous gamblers visiting from up north.

It sounds just nutty enough to have been strangely enjoyable, but the credits fall to nobodies and a director isn't named at all. The cast, too, had neither stars nor the reliable support that came up with the twenties titles, such as comics Tim Moore or "Pigmeat" Markham. Who were Madeline Belt (as Cox's light of love), Edith Wilson, Speedy Smith, the Two Chesterfields, comics Jones and Allen, or the Three Sepia Songbirds? And doesn't the tunestack suggest another generalized winging—"How the First Song Was Born," "Aintcha Glad You Got Music," "Dancing, and I Mean Dancing?"

Even the black star shows were having trouble staying open. *Brown Buddies* (1930) had Bill Robinson, rivaled by only Ethel Waters in headliner power, along with favorites Ada Brown and Adelaide Hall (much later in the Lena Horne show *Jamaica*) and also Maurice Ellis (the original Genesis in *Seventeen*, also much later). A book show so liberated that it had the same problem as white musical comedy, a dumb script, *Brown Buddies* followed a group of comrades before, during, and after the Great War. It got a nifty piece of publicity when, during the Pittsburgh tryout, Robinson attempted to foil a robbery and got shot by a cop; he had to play the New York premiere with his arm in a sling. And 113 performances is not a bad run—the longest of any black musical comedy in the entire decade.

At that, *Porgy and Bess* (1935), a black opera, ran only two weeks longer—though it reopened in a successful revival and has been running ever since, one way or another. Probably the single most unusual work ever to be called a "musical," *Porgy and Bess* owes its existence to a number of factors operating simultaneously in the 1920s. One was the folk-play movement. Another was the Theatre Guild. A third factor introduces the Great Man theme, in which history is changed by an individual able to mate his ambitions with the power to execute them: a Napoléon. And a fourth factor is *Show Boat*.

Interestingly, Kern and Hammerstein themselves had to abandon plans to make their own *Porgy and Bess* so that Gershwin could realize his. This takes in also the shadow of Al Jolson, who had it in mind to play Porgy as a culmination of Jolsonian blackface—of, even, America's native musical form, the minstrel show, whence the notion of whites playing blacks partly derives.

All of this must be understood in the context of race relations, particularly in their impact on twenties Broadway. The atmosphere was sympathetic among theatre people and the enlightened public, aggressively resistant among legal authorities. Luckily, their power to control the content of theatre was, one might say, vitally moribund: in a last-gasp series of show trials that hampered O'Neill, jailed Mae West for a week, and was all but over by 1930.

Meanwhile, the folk play had sprung into being. Primarily associated with black shows put on by whites with black casts, the folk play utilized language and mores to dramatize a subculture so thoroughly that this revelation of a way of life was as central to a play's being as its plot, characters, and theme. The entertainment was a lesson. Without the accessibility of the folk play, it would have been impossible for DuBose Heyward to turn his 1925 novel *Porgy* into a drama (in collaboration with his wife, Dorothy). And without the Theatre Guild, *Porgy* would not likely have been produceable, because it's a relatively big show both in scene plot and cast—sixty individuals in the Guild's original production, in 1927. Paul Green's *In Abraham's Bosom* (1926), arguably the most powerful of all the black folk plays, could get no better booking than the Provincetown Playhouse in the Village, and while it did move to Broadway, even a batch of rave notices couldn't support it, and it closed: only to reopen back downtown after it won the Pulitzer Prize.

But the Theatre Guild played to a subscription audience, and was thus free to put on anything its board fancied. Even so, *Porgy*'s huge cast did end up performing in somewhat budget-pinched decor, while David Belasco's production of Edward Sheldon and Charles MacArthur's *Lulu Belle* (1926) enjoyed a sensation because of the customary Belasco verisimilitude, including the spectacular representation of a busy Harlem intersection complete with working automobile. *Lulu Belle*, a spoken *Carmen* about a prostitute destroyed by the eroticism that she arouses, was Big Broadway. Typically, Lenore Ulric, who specialized in Exotic Ladies, played Lulu Belle in blackface.

There could be no such masquerade in the folk play. Sincere and almost humble in its outlook, the folk play found its correspondence in the musical in *Show Boat*, produced the same year as the Heywards' play. True, one of *Show Boat*'s principals played in blackface, but then *Show Boat* has many internal contradictions, the main one being that it is a musical comedy with an operetta's ballads and a serious drama's subject matter. Its success must have heartened Gershwin, but it did not inspire him, for he had already tried to arrange to compose an opera based on the novel *Porgy* in mid-1926, around the time that Edna Ferber's novel *Show Boat* was published. Moreover, Gershwin (with B. G. DeSylva) had experimented in black opera in *Blue Monday Blues*, a self-contained one-acter included in *George White's Scandals of 1922*. White dropped it directly after the opening, and in truth it's a naive little piece; the very music seems to be in blackface.

In all, it took Gershwin nine years to turn *Porgy* into an opera, from the day the idea first struck him to *Porgy and Bess'* opening night at the Alvin Theatre, on October 10, 1935. Had the age not been intrigued by black theatre and the ever expanding power of American popular art—whether in *Rhapsody in Blue*, "Ol' Man River," or the eros that Fred

Astaire could unveil in "Night and Day"—*Porgy and Bess* would have been unthinkable. All the same, the fulfillment of this strange dream belongs not to the age but to Gershwin alone. He had important assistants in his librettists, Heyward and brother Ira; and in the Theatre Guild, which made worried noises about cost projections* but never doubted that *Porgy and Bess* must be staged, and only by the Theatre Guild; and in Kay Swift, Joseph Schillinger, and others in the Gershwin camp who helped in various ways, Swift in copying out the individual singers' music and Schillinger possibly in aiding Gershwin to some unknown degree in his mastery of orchestration. Nevertheless, I say again that *Porgy and Bess* is one man's achievement, and the unique position it occupies in the evolution of American art reflects the unique position Gershwin himself holds in a classical Tin Pan Alley where a concertante piece for piano and orchestra is tuned "in blue" and the orchestra is a jazz band.

This may be why, when *Porgy and Bess* was new, folks got exercised over whether to call it a musical play or an opera. Does it matter? As all the characters except the whites (in short roles) tend to sing virtually every line, it is an opera. But there are those who hear deference in the word "opera." They fret over the implication that this word denotes a work of authority and craftsmanship, whereas Gershwin—they usually do not dare say—was a primitive and his subject matter vulgar.

This viewpoint also relates to what was happening in the culture at the time, for two generations of composers had been actively seeking a way into the at first unknowable concept of American Opera, and all had conspicuously failed. Actually, the official "first" American opera, William Henry Fry's *Leonora*, after Edward Bulwer-Lytton's play *The Lady of Lyons*, appeared in 1845. But not till the early twentieth century were composers intent on engendering a native form of opera. Giulio

---

* *Porgy and Bess'* final budget was $70,000 at a time when a sizable musical cost upwards of $100,000. The opera's modest investment was possible only because the costuming—which normally accounts for a large part of a musical's capitalization—was quotidian by the very nature of the setting in Catfish Row. Another huge cast and an orchestra twice the standard size meant heavy running costs, but the Guild had that subscription audience to depend on, and it had had long experience in keeping spending tight. At times, its survival depended on it. Eight years after *Porgy and Bess*, the Guild tried another musical work, and though by 1943 a sizable musical could reach or even break $200,000, *Oklahoma!* came in at just $5,000 more than the original *Porgy and Bess*. And *Oklahoma!* wore costumes.

Gatti-Casazza, manager of the Metropolitan Opera from 1908 to 1935—the very year that *Porgy and Bess* was produced—tirelessly encouraged the creation of American Opera, ending up with a *Cyrano de Bergerac* (1913) that proved as unnecessary as the various musicals based on Rostand; or a *Cleopatra's Night* (1920), so tedious even with an orgy that it had to be paired with a Caruso-Scotti *Pagliacci* to get anyone to attend. The Met did have a success with three works built around the titanic singing actor Lawrence Tibbett in the 1920s and 1930s, especially Howard Hanson's *Merry Mount*, an extremely melodic and dramatic piece that also includes an orgy. But note that neither the Hanson nor the rest of the trio, Deems Taylor's *The King's Henchman* and *Peter Ibbetson*, survived the end of Gatti's regime.

Of course, no one knew in those days of Frederick Delius' *Koanga* (1897), performed but twice and only abroad despite American subject matter, or of Scott Joplin's *Treemonisha* (1911), undiscovered till the 1970s. What everyone knew was Virgil Thomson's *4 Saints in 3 Acts*, seen in Hartford, Connecticut and then on Broadway, in 1934. The orchestra and chorus were under the same leadership as those of *Porgy and Bess* the year after, Alexander Smallens and Eva Jessye. Oddly, the German-English Delius, the ragtime king Joplin, Thomson, and Gershwin all wrote, for black singers, works that otherwise have nothing in common. Thomson's piece could be said to be *Porgy and Bess'* opposite, as a plotless work without the slightest hint of jazz or folk culture. What *4 Saints* is, really, is chic, with its opaque Gertrude Stein libretto and scenic design made—literally—of cellophane. Thomson's was a miniature talent, rather like that of an old spinster chording out her hymns on the harmonium. But he was prominent in the American musical establishment, and one has the feeling that his confederates deeply resented the furore that *Porgy and Bess* created.

In fact, the commercial failure of that first Guild production, followed by the reaffirming 1942 revival at the Majestic (one of Broadway's biggest houses, for 286 performances, followed by an eighteen-month tour and a New York return at the even larger City Center for a further 64 performances) and the spectacularly successful international tour in the 1950s all go to suggest a victorious comeback after initial disaster. This is a favorite American parable, but it does not apply to *Porgy and Bess*. The excitement that this work aroused as "George Gershwin's opera" made it one of the biggest events of the decade. The tryout, a single week in Boston, was launched by the most applauded first night that anyone could remember, and grim little Virgil Thomson could not have been glad to hear it.

One odd note that we should sound here, in the light of how proud the Houston Grand Opera and the Met were, much later, to be performing *Porgy* complete or with very little cutting, is that Boston heard a nearly uncut *Porgy* at that first performance. The opening number, "Jasbo Brown Blues," had been omitted early on in production, to avoid incurring a surcharge for building an inset in the Catfish Row scenery. Apparently, all the rest of the vast score was performed at the Boston premiere. As the singers were working without microphones or matinée alternates, some music had to go—the "Buzzard Song," the prayer sextet during the hurricane, "Good Mornin', Sistuh!," some of the final scene. One further imagines that tucks were made all along the way.

At that, the original cast performed with less intensity than has become standard in this work, as their recordings attest. In the title roles, Todd Duncan and Anne Wiggins Brown were singers more than singing actors, he a teacher at Howard University and she a Juilliard student. The Serena, Ruby Elzy, and the Crown, Warren Coleman, had comparable backgrounds. In any case, there were so few opportunities for black opera singers then—the color bar in white companies would not effectively be broken till the next decade—that black singers were as a rule recitalists. Like Marian Anderson, who was fifty-three before she became the Met's first black singer, the African-American in the field of classical music sang Handel, Schubert, and spiritual. Their opera would consist of arias extracted to sing, concert-style, at the piano, not in the theatre.

It would seem that Gershwin and his director, Rouben Mamoulian, liked hearing *Porgy and Bess* more sung than emoted. Later Porgys would bring out the character's awkward heroism; Duncan simply brought out his warmth and strength. Later Besses would game with the hot-lady identity that she never quite loses in her romance with Porgy; Brown would not have disgraced her family with such truck. But Mamoulian had directed the play *Porgy* in the first place, and he knew what he wanted from the story. Then, too, he was more the theatre wizard than the psychologist. Mamoulian's staging lay as much in his individualizing of ensemble members (or, conversely, using them en masse for stage pictures during the wake and hurricane episodes) as in the principals' depth of personality.

There was as well the subversive figure of Sporting Life, in sharp contrast to the leads for his Harlemite devilry. It seems amazing that Cab Calloway didn't create the role, for Sporting Life's music is unmistakably modeled on Calloway's Cotton Club art, right down to the sarcastically unctuous tenorino inflections and the call-and-response scat section with the chorus singers in "It Ain't Necessarily So." We've met the team of Buck and Bubbles already; John W. Bubbles originated Sporting Life, and, rather than break up the act, Ford Buck came along as Mingo, a smaller role in something like the same vein.

As *Porgy*'s admirers returned from Boston with glad report, New York's cultural élite prepared for another of those art-world controversies *à la parisienne*, in which anyone with intellectual pretensions must take a side for or against. The nation's only prestigious classical-record label, the Victor Red Seal discs of Caruso, Toscanini, and Stokowski, had already finalized plans to give *Porgy and Bess* the first American-made show album to be recorded during a show's original run—in fact, four days after the opening.* Taking note of the genre confusion that the work produced, all the city's dailies sent both their music and theatre critics to cover the premiere, as had already occurred in Boston. Thus, in all, there can be no question that, whatever stand one ultimately took, the Matter of Gershwin's Opera was significant indeed.

"George Gershwin's personal holiday," Brooks Atkinson called it. "Something glorious." And note his very comprehending remark that the play *Porgy* "lacked the glow of personal feeling." It doesn't, in fact: but Atkinson had noticed how much Gershwin had added to the Heywards' text with numbers such as "My Man's Gone Now," "What You Want Wid Bess," or "Oh Lawd, I'm On My Way." Broadway's countless adaptations of straight plays into musical works count a few in which only the authors heard the score latent in the original—*Carousel*, for instance. What a hapless bunch of characters *Liliom* treats! And there are plays that, for certain reasons, could not have been revived in their original form and had to be transformed to survive—into *Mame*, for instance. Why attempt

* This was not an original cast recording. Our old friend Lawrence Tibbett and his fellow Met contractee Helen Jepson sang all the solo lines, leaving Duncan, Brown, and a few others of the original and 1942 revival casts to make *Porgy* albums for Decca, in 1940 and 1942.

Auntie Mame without Rosalind Russell when she left her portrayal on screen?

But *Porgy* called for music to complete its journey, just as the era called for a black story, Gershwin, and jazz to pin progressives' yearnings upon the map of American culture. It is not merely that *Porgy and Bess* had to happen. It is that it had to happen with George Gershwin, Rouben Mamoulian, the Theatre Guild, and even Todd Duncan, Anne Brown, and John W. Bubbles *happening* it.

"The style is at one moment of opera and another of operetta or sheer Broadway entertainment," wrote Atkinson's *Times* colleague Olin Downes, of the music desk. Oh, really? Let's have a look at the first scene of Act Two, to watch how Gershwin controls his generical elements and why Downes doesn't get it. Gershwin filled the score with leitmotifs, and, as the act begins, we hear one of them over pounding brass chords alternating g minor with a pile-on of G Major over D Flat Major; the leitmotif is adapted from Mingo's interjection into "A Woman Is a Sometime Thing." Now the curtain rises, and a bit of rushing music in the strings leads to Jake's Rowing Song, "It Take a Long Pull To Get There." Jake, who earlier sang "Sometime Thing," has that typical *Porgy and Bess* role, a minor principal helping to personalize the setting with character detail. What other opera—or musical, for that matter—so particularizes so many characters necessary to not the plot but the experience as a whole? *Boris Godunof* comes to mind, perhaps *Die Zauberflöte* (*The Magic Flute*). The fanatic will know Hans Werner Henze's *Der König Hirsch* (*The Stag King*). But one of *Porgy and Bess'* unique qualities is that, by its end, one has actually paid a visit to a real place—not to history or fantasy but a venue in American culture.

So the Rowing Song isn't just a decoration, but more insight into the life of Catfish Row. Jake's vocal line is very basic, with a slight twist in a use of the sixth tone of the scale; but the harmony is sophisticated, with major sevenths and, at one point, what appears to be the unknown chord of $B_6^{\frac{9}{7}}$. After the song, a fugato section on the Jake-Mingo motif accompanies a short bit of plot material in rhythmic declaration and recit, which blends into the "tuning violin" intro to the Banjo Song (thus in the score, and marked *Moderato con gioja*), Porgy's "I Got Plenty O' Nuttin'."

It's surely too late in the history of this indispensable American song to analyze it musically; let's simply admire its ebullient simplicity.

Of course, it serves a vital purpose in dramatizing the effect that Bess has had on Porgy. The lonely man with nothing to lose now lives in Grace. The authors do not even need to bring Bess onstage: everything is in the music's grin, even in the irresistibly gentle swing of the ensemble's humming under Porgy's solo in the second chorus.

A tonic G Major chord "buttons" the number and invites the act's first genuine break for applause. Such punctuational lacunae may have prompted complaints of the work's tendency to feel like a book musical even while operatizing. That is: aren't the leitmotifs and fugato sections from one work, and "I Got Plenty O' Nuttin' " from another? In fact, "Nuttin' " sounds "easy"—better, fundamental—not because Gershwin forgot himself and deserted the Philharmonic for Tin Pan Alley but because he wants to exploit the folklike amiability of the tune to develop his protagonist. Porgy's first-act solo, "They Pass By Singin'," is completely different, more "classical" yet also drawing on a folkish sound at its climax. This reveals a complex personality in somewhat unstable music, a philosopher of sorrow: "When Gawd make cripple, He mean him to be lonely." So "Nuttin's' " simplicity is character advancement: Porgy has been clarified by love.

Indeed, the notion that *Porgy and Bess'* set pieces are pitched in a style different from the interstitial material is to blame Gershwin for being the man chosen by destiny to bring jazz and Broadway together in the 1920s. Would critics of 1935 have been so ungrateful for this music if Gershwin had simply appeared out of nowhere? From Broadway he came, they cried: so Broadway he must be.

Yet what Broadway does one hear in the solo that follows "Nuttin'," Maria's "I Hates Yo' Struttin' Style," a barbaric *Allegro giocoso* in pure *Sprechstimme*, the syllables pitched rather than sung? What Make Believe Ballroom is ready for the "Buzzard Song," with its emphatic triplets and that biting harmony that, in any case, we hear throughout the opera? And has anyone noticed that "Bess, You Is My Woman Now," for all its lyricism, is really a discussion about whether or not Bess should leave Porgy alone and go off to the picnic on Kittiwah Island? Porgy's line about Bess having to "laugh an' sing an' dance for two" and Bess' refusal to go anywhere " 'less you shares de fun" are references to that picnic. And of course this makes the duet the center of the tragedy, for he prevails, she goes to Kittiwah, and there occurs the event—Crown's reappropriation of

Bess—that will lead to the destruction of the romance. For extra irony, after the Catfish Row folk have poured into the courtyard for "Oh, I Can't Sit Down!" and marched off to the boat, Gershwin ends Act Two, scene one in the last truly carefree moment in Porgy's life, with a reprise of the main strain of "I Got Plenty O' Nuttin'." This is tragic paradox. The play Porgy made it plain tragedy: the bad-luck buzzard, instead of being scared off (as in the opera), lands on Porgy's house. As he explains, "Once de buzzard fold he wing an' light ober yo' do,' yo' know all yo' happiness done dead."

In fact, it's remarkable how closely the opera follows the play, which is filled with lines later made immortal in music: "Give 'um to me. I'll fix 'um fo' yo'." "Porgy change since dat 'oman go to lib' wid he." "Yo' could whistle fo' me and' dere I was again a-lickin' yo' han'." More than any other play put through musical adaptation, the Heywards' Porgy was completely swallowed up by Gershwin's. But then, Porgy and Bess has been in turn all but overwhelmed by politics. Some black intellectuals thought it promoted lurid stereotypes, with its crap game and murders and "happy dust" (cocaine); and some black musicians resented this incursion into black material by a white composer. This seems rather bizarre considering that the Porgy story, from the start, was the work of a white novelist. In any case, black performers were glad of the job security, for Porgy revivals tended to favor veterans of previous productions. The original Crown and Jake, Warren Coleman and Edward Matthews, not only played again in the 1942 revival but sang their parts on the first full-length recording, in 1951.

The racial politics of the work were bigger than black and white, as when the Danish Royal Opera staged the first European Porgy and Bess in 1943, under German occupation. Although the Nazis eventually forced the company to drop the work from its repertory, mounting in the first place an opera by a Jewish composer in Nazi-held Europe was extremely courageous. Cultural politics continued to direct the gaze toward aspects of Porgy beyond its words and music. The 1952 revival toured not only North America and Europe but Egypt, Israel, South America, and Soviet Russia at the height of the Cold War; and this partly under State Department sponsorship.

The originality of Porgy and Bess is doubtless why it attracted so much attention in 1935, and why some needed extra exposure in order to absorb it. Duke Ellington despised "Gershwin's lampblack Negroisms" in 1935, but in 1952 saluted "the superbest, singing the gonest, acting the craziest, Gershwin the greatest." Formerly a novelty, an outrage, and a mad masterpiece, the opera patiently allowed everyone to become its best friend, as the score lent itself not only to strictly authentic recordings of every last note but also to extramural "interpretation." Ella Fitzgerald and Louis Armstrong, Cleo Laine and Ray Charles, Lena Horne and Harry Belafonte, and Diahann Carroll and André Previn have all teamed up thus, each in his singular way. Carroll takes the score down to lower keys in an unhackneyed selection that includes "There's Somebody Knockin' at de Do' " and "Oh, I Can't Sit Down!" Carroll's "It Ain't Necessarily So" is almost white, shorn of its Cotton Club call-and-response, and her "My Man's Gone Now" is turned into a pensive cabaret number, pure music rather than music theatre (though it is the most dramatic piece in the score). Only "I Got Plenty O' Nuttin' " fails in this approach, for while Previn's busy Dixieland piano is delightful, this title is too power-fully made of character information to dress in business casual.

Yet how many other thirties shows, or shows of any era, give the artist of a later generation so many different ways to bond with their music? For all its debt to movements of its day, Porgy and Bess ended up as ecumenical and timeless. And this despite Virgil Thomson's description of it—for one was allowed to speak one's mind in public at that time—as "a piquant but highly unsavory stirring up together of Israel, Africa, and the Gaelic Isles." One hears as if watching a dirty little mummy open his poison ring.

5

LEAVE IT TO KATARINA: OPERETTA BEGINS ITS FORTY-YEAR DEATH SCENE

Sigmund Romberg and Rudolf Friml were doing no better in the rest of the decade than in *Nina Rosa* and *Luana* in 1930. Indeed, Friml tried only once more, in *Music Hath Charms* (1934), before abandoning Broadway for a thirty-eight-year retirement stippled with oddjobbing in Hollywood. *Music Hath Charms* didn't last a month—but what did Friml expect, when Mr. J. J. Shubert gives him another of those plots with a flashback in which modern-day characters appear as their own ancestors or romantic counterparts, filled with numbers called "My Palace of Dreams," "Sweet Fool," "Love," "Cavaliers," "My Heart Is Yours?" What is this, Operetta 101? Taking roles played by Maria Jeritza and Allan Jones on an extended pre-Broadway tour, the newly cast Natalie Hall and Robert Halliday played a Venetian marchese and her blueblooded American swain in the present and, in 1770, a fishermaid and a duke. Critics generally loved the dancing, laid out by Alex Yakovleff around lead ballerino Paul Haakon; and Richard Lockridge, who hated operetta, loved this one, which is strange, considering how generic it was.

Romberg was doing slightly better, presumably because he partnered more wisely than Friml. *Music Hath Charm*'s libretto was the work of Rowland Leigh and the show's director, George Rosener, and the lyrics were by Leigh and the producer's son, John Shubert. Romberg spent the 1930s with Oscar Hammerstein for *East Wind* (1931), Irving Caesar for *Melody* (1933), Hammerstein again for *May Wine* (1935), and Otto Harbach for *Forbidden Melody* (1936). Actually, these were the lyricists only; Hammerstein collaborated with Frank Mandel on *East Wind*'s book,

Melody's book was by Edward Childs Carpenter, Mandel alone wrote *May Wine*'s book, and Harbach wrote all the words of *Forbidden Melody*. These are for the most part experts who built operetta big in the 1920s—*Rose-Marie*, *The Desert Song*, and *The New Moon*, not to mention *Show Boat*. More important, unlike Friml, Romberg was willing to evolve along with operetta, if someone but point the way. However, if Sigmund Romberg didn't know where operetta was going, who would?

East Wind, at any rate, marked a last attempt at a twenties Big Sing spectacle, with an all-specialist team of Laurence Schwab and Frank Mandel producing, Hammerstein directing, Bobby Connolly choreographing, Donald Oenslager and Charles LeMaire designing, and Hans Spialek orchestrating. Lockridge didn't like this one, complaining of the overloaded plot, "a melodramatic story of love, marriage, betrayal, partings, white elephants, mysterious Indo-Chinese secret societies, handsome army officers, sinister half-caste dancers, cabaret singers, murder, suicide, and tea plantations." Lockridge has omitted the main action, set in Saigon, in which French heroine Charlotte Lansing loves French army captain J. Harold Murray. Alas, Lansing is married to Murray's brother (William Williams), a dissipated wretch—an opium addict, in fact. Luckily, the sinister half-caste dancer Lockridge mentioned (slinky, inscrutable Ahi) murders the brother and herself in Act Two, leaving the way clear for the two leads' Paris reunion.

Note that Hammerstein was in something of a *Show Boat* mood, once again experimenting with adult subject matter, and letting Lansing become an alcoholic and sing a torch song, "I'd Be a Fool," rather as the alcoholic Julie sings "Bill." *East Wind* looked quite handsome, and the score, though completely devoid of the *Desert Song*–*New Moon* sort of Romberg hit tune, is agreeable. The best number, a sinuously dramatic title song for Murray and the ensemble with lots of extra choral lines and blocks of vocal harmony, is the very sound of twenties operetta. The show might have gone over with good notices, but everyone save columnist Ed Sullivan found the book insanely dreary. *East Wind* was consigned to the limbo of an occasional week at the St. Louis Muni, the giant outdoor summer theatre that never met an operetta it didn't like.

Having learned a lesson, Romberg now tried to normalize operetta in partnership with that archon of musical comedy George White. So *Melody* starts romantically but eventually gets kind of scrappy. Another of those three-generation plots begins when Evelyn Herbert cheats on her wedding night to rendezvous with composer Everett Marshall, whom she really loves. He dies in The War. (This being *Melody*'s operetta section, one needn't ask which war; in operetta, there's always A War.) Act Two concerns the next generation, with Herbert now playing her own daughter, and Act Three treats Herbert's granddaughter (toujours la Herbert), who triumphs in cabaret and enjoys the happy ending with a distant relation of the dead composer (not Marshall: Walter Woolf). Somehow, comics Hal Skelly and Jeanne Aubert managed to defy time, playing the same characters over the decades, though Gilbert W. Gabriel of the *American* accused them of "some rather weedy larking about." Still, they did lay down a thread of musical-comedy atmosphere early on, to prepare for the third act, not only modern-dress but almost indistinguishable in tone from such George White shows as *Manhattan Mary* and *Flying High*. Romberg really could write musical comedy if he had to, but *Melody*'s outstanding number was the Big Baritone Military Boom Boom With Male Chorus Restant, "Give Me a Roll on a Drum (or, if you *choose*, *a* rum tum-a-tum by Monsieur *Sousa*)." *Melody* lasted 79 performances.

Not only is Romberg not down yet, but *May Wine* is one of those history-makers that somehow never got famous but must have impressed the theatre people who saw it. The following *Forbidden Melody* was rather adult in subject matter, with its adultery among European diplomats, but *May Wine* is nearly transgressive. It follows the marriage of a milquetoast psychiatrist (Walter Slezak) and a hot Liebchen (Nancy McCord) taking him for his money. She loves a caddish baron (Walter Woolf again, now surnamed King and not to be confused with Tamara), and the obliging Slezak is so in McCord's grip that he allows Woolf to come along on the honeymoon.

It suggests an early Lubitsch talkie, perhaps a Nabokov novel. And it starts with a book scene in which Slezak confesses to the cops: he has murdered McCord. *And* there was no singing ensemble, just a lot of principals. *And* there was no dancing, except from the team of (later choreographer) Jack Cole and Alice Dudley. *And* the score was broken into musical scenes rather than songs. *And* the action cascaded along on a revolving stage. By the way, Slezak hasn't killed McCord. He shot a dummy.

Doesn't this sound fascinating? At 213 performances in the roomy St. James, *May Wine* did pretty well considering that once again Romberg failed to knock out a hit tune. Hammerstein went contempo—Vera Van's soubrette-steals-the-show spot, "Somebody Ought To Be Told (that I've arrived)," begins "I am young and plastic, I'm enthusiastic," and Romberg matched the words with haunting minor chords and an insolent "wrong" note on the last two syllables. Nevertheless, this spoken play with interspersed vocal sequences lacked the public melody number one that earns one's page in chronicle. Six years later, *Lady in the Dark*—another musical treating psychiatry—would get the glory in this innovative genre.

It is notable, even so, that at a time when Rudolf Friml gave up the business as unfriendly, Romberg was pursuing original ideas, especially because he had the reputation of—just every now and then—borrowing tunes from classical composers. In a favorite Broadway story, a guest at a party, enjoying a background piano rendition of the Barcarolle from Offenbach's *Les Contes d'Hoffmann*, asks fellow guest Romberg if he wrote that music.

"Not yet," Romberg replies.

If operetta's masters are retiring or being forced to re-equip, what happens to operetta's stars? Nothing: there weren't any, as we've said. But then, who was clerking the store? Howard Marsh and Norma Terris, *Show Boat's* romantic leads, led the company of *The Well of Romance* (1930), which featured Lina Abarbanell, the heroine of *Madame Sherry* (1910), in her last Broadway appearance in a musical. That did not distinguish this one-week flop, though it is the only operetta with a libretto by Preston Sturges.

In Abarbanell's youth, operetta had stars—such as the lady herself, famous for one role only, and that was not untypical. However, in the 1920s, Marilyn Miller is Sally, Sunny, Rosalie; and, in the next generation, Ethel Merman fields a gallery of Great Roles. Of course, Miller and Merman didn't work in operetta. Nor did Grace Moore, really: her appearance in the title role of *The DuBarry* (1932) was a one-off. Moore had graced Broadway four times in the early 1920s, but she was one of the twentieth century's great musical personalities, and destiny called her to opera, in Paris and at the Met, and in crossover films in Hollywood. As Moore's three 78 sides of the *DuBarry* score attest, she was the kind of singer rarely heard on The Street, with an intense *espressivo* that jazzed opera and ennobled pop.

Oddly, *The DuBarry* was fifty years old when Moore had her sensation in it. Composed by Karl Millöcker, it failed to establish itself on its 1872

Berlin premiere as *Gräfin Dubarry*. Then, again in Berlin, in 1931, with a rewritten libretto and an updated score, it took out a new lease of life with another spectacular singer who spanned the worlds of opera and the popular stage, Gitta Alpar. The similarly gifted Anny Ahlers played the French courtesan in London in 1932.*

Perhaps the casting of two such gala divas isolated *The DuBarry*'s title role as one beyond the range of the typical operetta lead when the piece came to New York. The production was especially lavish, with sets and costumes by Vincente Minnelli and a cost of $150,000. Moore amazed the critics, yet the show lasted only 87 performances, a strange waste of the unique Moore, who never appeared on Broadway again.

If a larger-than-even-opera star can't boost operetta, who can? Three skilled sopranos couldn't make a hit out of *Die Fledermaus* in 1933, but then this classic of European operetta—more or less *the* classic—did not truly draw on Broadway till the fourth try, as *Rosalinda* (1942). The first, as *The Merry Countess*, ran 135 performances in 1912, a good but unworthy showing. The second (alluded to in the present book's introduction for its use of a revolving stage), called *A Wonderful Night* (1929), played only 125 performances despite a superb production. This third try, as *Champagne, Sec*, lasted 113 performances with the imposing lineup of Peggy Wood, Helen Ford, and Kitty Carlisle.

Put into English by the Theatre Guild's Lawrence Langner (pseudonymously, as Alan Child) and lyricist Robert A. Simon, and first tried out at Langner's pet pocket theatre, the Westport Country Playhouse, this *Fledermaus* was apparently the most faithful of the Broadway versions, literally the work that Johann Strauss had written, rendered into English. It was even to have been the only Broadway *Fledermaus* actually called *Die Fledermaus*, but mysterious legal rumblings in Europe scotched the plan. Wood was Mrs. Eisenstein and Ford the scampy maid Adele, with George Meader as Mr. Eisenstein and, as the drunk jailer in Act Three, veteran comic John E. Hazzard, who dated back to the days of "Yama-Yama girl" Bessie McCoy and the first Kern-Bolton-Wodehouse Princess show, *Very Good Eddie* (1915). Kitty Carlisle had just turned nineteen and was

---

* About a year after the premiere, Ahlers died after a fall from the balcony of her residence. The official report was suicide, but those close to Ahlers strongly disagreed. It has been suggested that the pressure of stardom told on her, that medication misled her, even that she was sleepwalking.

making her Broadway debut in the relatively small role of Prince Orlofsky, a mezzo trouser part ideal for exploiting Carlisle's demonstration *chalumeau* low notes. With the first act broken into two scenes to bring this somewhat erotic comedy into the Eisensteins' boudoir and the decade's favorite arty dancer, Paul Haakon, leading the corps in the second-act divertissement, the show sounds enticing: authentic Strauss and sound Broadway salesmanship. But the economy held everything back in 1933: only one musical ran a year and only two others broke the 200-performance mark.

Ironically, the most expensively capitalized of all the decade's operettas was the most successful, *The Great Waltz* (1934). Counting a return engagement, it totaled 347 performances—at a theatre seating 3,822. This was the former RKO Roxy Theatre in Rockefeller Center, a movie palace renamed the Center Theatre after losing a lawsuit brought by another Roxy Theatre. Going legit for *The Great Waltz*, the Center gave producer Max Gordon a technical marvel of a place unmatched since the reign of the Hippodrome in the early 1900s.

The show itself claims a tangled history, being a new version of a new version. *Walzer aus Wien* (1930) used the music of Strauss Sr. and Jr. to tell of their rivalry, of Jr.'s on-and-off romance with Resi, the pastry baker's daughter, and of how the worldly Countess Olga arranges to have Sr. detained under force so that Jr. can conduct his own music before all Vienna at Dommayer's Restaurant.

So far, so good. A year later, *Waltzes From Vienna* played London with both libretto and music rearranged. Super-productions were the rage of London that year, and our own (if English-born) Hassard Short went over to contrive a suitably sizable exhibit. Still, not till Short took the piece (in yet another revision, with a book by Moss Hart) to New York could he turn the newly-named *Great Waltz* into the greatest show on earth. For that scene in which Jr. amazes Dommayer's, a garden set was changed into a ballroom with the addition of ten colossal columns, the lowering of eight gigantic chandeliers, and the raising of the orchestra out of its pit onto the stage to move to the rear as the playing area was overrun with hussars in shakos, rhapsodically swirling couples, and Jr. himself, to lead the orchestra of fifty-three in "On the Beautiful Blue Danube."

Guy Robertson played Jr., with opera singer Marion Claire as Resi and Marie Burke (London's *Show Boat* Julie) repeating her London Olga.

Dennis Noble, also from the London cast, rivalled Jr. for Resi's hand. Alexandra Danilova led the Albertina Rasch ballet corps, a real coup— but the star of the event was Hassard Short, billed twice on the program's title page. "Production conceived and directed by" stood above the title with Short's name in larger type than anyone else's, and, at the bottom of the page, one read "Lighting, staging, scenic and mechanical effects created by."

"More Moss than heart" was a joke going the rounds at the premiere and, in such a big auditorium, some primitive form of sound amplification was used, three decades before it became acculturated along The Street. Still, a cast of almost two hundred, a production cost of $246,000, and the sheer delight of the music attracted playgoers despite mostly bored and carping notices. Best of all, as far as the Rockefellers were concerned, the huge auditorium's payback potential made this sort of monster musical profitable.

Especially if it be a modern German-language piece that had enjoyed a successful English-language transition in London. So the next Center Theatre offering was White Horse Inn (1936), producer Erik Charell's spectacular Berlin musicalization of a quiet little comedy of 1897, Im Weissen Rössl (which is pretty much what the English title means). Critical report estimated the company at three hundred and, indeed, the cost at $300,000, the second-largest in the musical's history (after Jumbo) and a sum that would not become common for another twenty-five years. But then, White Horse Inn plumed itself on special effects—rain, animals, a tourist bus, a steamboat, an imported Alpine yodeler named Madame Reverelly, even a dance performed on a pogo stick. On one unusual note, the Ernst Stern scenery used in the Berlin premiere (1930) was seen again in London (1931), in Paris (1932), and now in New York, with producer Charell consistently in charge.

The adaptor of the libretto, David Freedman, did not tamper with the original piffle about an innkeeper (Kitty Carlisle) who loves an attorney (Robert Halliday) while being pursued by her headwaiter, Leopold (William Gaxton). Leopold's attempts to ruin the lawyer's vacation get him fired, but the lawyer prefers a businessman's daughter (Carol Stone), and, after some advice from Kaiser Franz Josef (Arnold Korff), headwaiter gets innkeeper. Note that Leopold is a part for a droll, not that con man pseudo-hunk that Gaxton claimed as his Fach. Jimmy Savo had been the intended Leopold, but he couldn't handle the songs. Charell fired him, and Gaxton was free.

One interesting thing about *Im Weissen Rössl's* score is its very contemporary sound. Of well-known German so-called operettas, only Pál Ábrahám's *Die Blume von Hawaii* (1931) sounds even more like musical comedy. But then, it's hard to know whom to credit for *White Horse Inn's* ready-for-Broadway pizzazz, for while Ralph Benatzky is the nominal composer, the original Berlin score is a hash of contributions and the American text even more so, with lyricist Irving Caesar spotting now Vivian Ellis and now Jara Benes.

The original is admittedly very loosely organized, to accommodate almost any sort of interpolation, and as the score gives Leopold an establishing song but nothing to innkeeper Josepha until she's suddenly duetting fondly with the lawyer, Charell had Benes and Caesar run up something dashing for Carlisle. Renamed Katarina (Josepha lacked tang), Carlisle would make a star entrance, assume control of all 3,822 seats of the house, and sing the typical musical-comedy hymn to *débrouillardise*, anticipating comparable numbers—such as "I Can Cook, Too," "Doin What Comes Natur'lly," "The Hostess With the Mostes' On the Ball," "A Little Brains, A Little Talent," and "Come To Me"—in "Leave It To Katarina."

The 223-performance run was good enough for the Rockefellers to take a more active interest in what was shaping up as an annual event, and the following year they commissioned something American to take Center stage for once—in fact, something set in Williamsburg, Virginia, for the Rockefellers had recently underwritten the colonial town's restoration. With Laurence Stallings and Owen Davis writing the book and a score by Arthur Schwartz and Stallings (with co-lyricist Albert Stillman), *Virginia* (1937) told how a troupe of actors from London's Drury Lane visited America in 1775. The romance involves a stalwart colonel of the Virginia Rangers (Ronald Graham) and one of the actresses (Anne Booth), and the plot itself centers on a vital secret dispatch for General Washington. As a Redcoat officer (Dennis Hoey) tries to intercept it, it keeps getting passed from one character to another, including *Porgy and Bess'* Buck and Bubbles, for *Virginia* included a strong dose of race relations along with the increasingly de rigueur quota of ballet.

It's worth remarking that, after the Broadway and then continental showmanship of Hassard Short and Erik Charell on the first two Center spectacles, the Rockefellers made do with Radio City Music Hall staff for *Virginia*, in director Leon Leonidoff and choreographer Florence Ragge. This may explain why *Virginia* did not enjoy its predecessors' success. The very size of the show precluded a tryout tour, so *Virginia* played in over-long dress-rehearsal proportions on opening night, which started at 8:20 and was still gluing along after midnight. Twenty-five minutes of cuts had been instituted by the second performance, but the critics all thought the show a gorgeous bore, and it ran only two months.

Is it Arthur Schwartz's most secret score? True, there's as well the extremely unheard *Park Avenue* (1946). But somehow Schwartz working with Ira Gershwin on a satire on divorce doesn't quite disappear as fully as he (or anyone) does into a Center Theatre behemoth musical lorded over by the grandiose Stallings and featuring as *its* Big Wonder Moment a perspective of the colonial army on the march (on treadmills), framed by flags and rockets and cleverly laid out to look like not just hundreds but thousands. For a decade or so, opera sopranos doing crossover on radio would select *Virginia*'s big ballad, "An Old Flame Never Dies." Now all is silence; and something tells me the people at Encores! would give a season of *The Black Crook*, *It Happens on Ice*, and *Dance of the Vampires* before they'd get to *Virginia*.

From the most elaborate operettas, we turn to the skimpiest: the Messrs. Shubert and their endless attempts to have another *Blossom Time*. Actually, that's the Shubert legend. Some of their tours and that Milton Aborn operetta project were indeed planned on Uncle Scrooge budgets. But the Messrs.* were often willing to spend the money, and few operettas are as trim as *Blossom Time*. If you go into the operetta business, you *have* to spend the money.

Still, Mr. J. J. did retain his habit of buying the rights to German-language successes and "adapting" them for Broadway, as happened with *Blossom Time*. The adaptation could be so overwhelming that the origi-nal's charm would be as drowned as Ys; rather a number of Shubert German operettas died on the tryout road after Dr. J. J.'s leeching treat-ment. *Three Little Girls* (1930), *Meet My Sister* (1930), and *Marching By* (1932) made it in, the first two to semi-success and the third dying in

---

* Almost all Shubert productions were billed as being presented by the two surviving (of three) brothers. In fact, Lee Shubert put on the straight plays, leaving the musicals to Mr. J. J.

12 performances, possibly because of a heavy case of adaptationitis. All three enjoyed the assistance of either Natalie Hall or her sister Bettina, making a quaint little series.

Both Halls were in *Three Little Girls*. Its original, *Drei Arme Kleine Mädels* (1927)—*Three Poor Little Girls*—was composer Walter Kollo's attempt to duplicate his 1913 success *Wie Einst im Mai* (which was also a Shubert success, as *Maytime* [1917]). But this was yet another of those three-generation love stories, by now the musical's most exhausted cliché, and the English lyrics for *Three Little Girls* were by Harry B. Smith, so venerable that he dated well back into the First Age. Smith ended his career, at seventy-two, with *Marching By*, which Natalie Hall had played during the tryout only, ceding her role to Desirée Tabor for New York. To the despair of a purist or two, Jean Gilbert's *Hotel Stadt Lemberg* (1929) was at times hard to detect in *Marching By*, especially when the cast was tooting through such Harry Revel and Mack Gordon interpolations as "I've Gotta Keep My Eye on You (I've gotta kinda spy on you)."

On the other hand, two Shubert versions of German-language originals came to Broadway in 1937 in substantially faithful renderings. True, adaptor Edward Eliscu added a prologue to Franz Lehár's *Friederike*, showing contemporary American tourists in Weimar and designed to explain the historical context of the piece. It recalls a real-life incident, in which the young Johann Wolfgang von Goethe must renounce romance when he is summoned to the court at Weimar. Perhaps it was feared that some Broadwayites wouldn't know who Goethe was.

Hassard Short was the director, reminding us that, when he wanted to, Mr. J. J. Shubert hired the best. Short was then enjoying a tremendous reign in revue (*The Band Wagon*), musical comedy (saving *Roberta* out of town), and operetta (*The Great Waltz*), and while the incomparable *Jubilee* didn't draw bigtime, it nonetheless got the reviews of the decade. Further, Goethe was Dennis King, probably the best singing actor operetta had produced.

Respelled *Frederika*, Lehár's piece excited neither critics nor public. Brooks Atkinson thought the show made "a virtue of avoiding originality." It had been considered very daring in Berlin in 1928, because putting Goethe on stage was akin to blasphemy. Then, too, Lehár had abandoned his big romantic twenties style (as heard in *Frasquita*; the first

version of *The Land of Smiles*, *The Yellow Jacket*; *Paganini*; *The Tsarevitch*)
for an intimate musical play. Atkinson remained unimpressed for all that:
"The operetta formula has been refilled so many times that nothing more
than competence can be expected from anyone in the business." No wonder operettas weren't running: some people attended them anticipating
platitude. Of course, it is true that Atkinson was another critic frankly
unsympathetic to the modes and content of operetta: but his lack of
sympathy reflects that of the public.*

There was no platitude in *Frederika*, but there was plenty in *Three
Waltzes* (1937), the last work to get away with a three-generation
romance. The show did boast an amusing stunt in that, respecting the
time frame, composer Oskar Straus used music by Johann Strauss Sr. for
Act One (set in 1865), by Strauss Jr. for Act Two (set in 1900), and
invented his own music for Act Three, set in the present. As usual, the
two leads played ill-fated lovers separated by caste, then his son and her
daughter, then the third generation, for whom class distinction melts
away as they pledge their love on a movie set.

Clearly, *Three Waltzes* was not going to adorn an age that felt neutral
about Romberg, Friml, and even Lehár. Yes, the Strausses had known
great réclame in *The Great Waltz*. But wasn't that a success of showmanship? As it happens, *Drei Walzer* never made much of an impression in
Germanophone lands, though for some reason it has captivated the
French, its three-role female lead creating important personal triumphs
for Yvonne Printemps (who also filmed it), Germaine Roger, Suzy Delair,
and Mathé Altery. Our own Marie-Charlotte-Franzi was the indispensable Kitty Carlisle, opposite the Count Rudolph–Count Otto–Count Max
of Michael Bartlett.† The other lead is that of the heroine's confidant, a
comic role given to Glenn Anders, who aged ferociously for the third act

---

* Atkinson troubled to report a conversation he overheard between a couple in the row
in front of him just before the performance of *Frederika* began. I quote it (in script form)
because it seems quite the most banal yet mysteriously opaque anecdote of the 1930s:

MELANCHOLY LADY : I don't think I'm going to like this.
HER ESCORT: Why not? You liked *Tobacco Road*, didn't you?

† Now all you *Follies* buffs know what Roscoe was up to when not bringing on the
Weismann girls. Two of the critics could not resist commenting on how well Bartlett filled
out his tunic; serious students may want to dip into the file for further revelation.

especially. The run was 122 performances at the Majestic Theatre, once again in a production by Hassard Short.

Yvonne Printemps was the heroine also of Noël Coward's *Conversation Piece* when the original London production came over in 1934 with most of its West End cast. The work is rather like *Frederika* in its deconstruction of operetta's ostentatious aspects. In both, the chorus was used sparingly, the scenery was attractive but not heavy, and there was some dancing but nothing that Albertina Rasch could sink her teeth into. Both stories are set exotically, less in place than time, *Frederika* at Sesenheim and Strasbourg in Alsace in the 1770s and *Conversation Piece* in Brighton in 1811. One story is even true: Goethe really did love and part from Friederike Brion in his youth, though the action is still a bit implausible. *Conversation Piece* is fiction, and completely implausible: an older man takes up with a young girl in pursuit of a pet project of his. Along the way, she enchants a young man of means and position and at length seems to be ready to mate with him. But she makes a surprise return to the older man for the final curtain, demonstrating her devotion by quoting a line of private significance to them both.

That's right: it's *My Fair Lady*. Or, more properly, Shaw's *Pygmalion* with a coda, though it's doubtful that Coward noticed the similarity. His story differs from Shaw's in that the two leads are adventurers, the older man hoping to couple his protégée with a lord for the financial advantage. So the two are not entirely sympathetic; and Coward further distanced the show from us with artificial conventions, such as the somewhat irrelevant trio or quartet sung before the curtain during a set change, as we recall from *Nymph Errant*. *Conversation Piece* is rich with them—"Regency Rakes," "There's Always Something Fishy About the French," "Mothers and Wives," "There Was Once a Little Village." Coward also included a spoken prologue, delivered by three women each carrying an ivory stick topped by a little mask, promising a "polite but faintly raffish play." Note, too, that the show's title is a pun, for there was far less music than usual for an operetta, loading the evening with chat.

It's not an easy show to play. Coward, directing the London production, had to join the cast, replacing our *Nymph Errant* librettist, Romney Brent, as the older man; Brent begged to continue visiting rehearsals "and watch you find out what a bloody awful part it is." Nonsense, thought Coward. His blurb was ready: "The lyrics are good and the music excellent."

Yvonne Printemps' spectacular singing and eat-the-house charisma made the show a hit, though as she spoke no English she had to learn her role phonetically; her dialogue must have kept the public guessing. In New York, Printemps' *petit ami* Pierre Fresnay, who had spelled Coward in London, took over the role entirely. To no avail: a modest West End success became an outright Broadway failure, albeit in the oversized Forty-fourth Street Theatre, suitable for pageants only.

What *Frederika* and *Conversation Piece* have in common above all is the central operetta thing: song that is *molto espressivo*. Every note of Printemps' role is utterly beyond musical comedy, not least "I'll Follow My Secret Heart." It starts as an anxious conversation in which she sings and speaks and the older man only speaks, then bursts into a soaring waltz for her alone. Indeed, the two leading men in the story never sing a note, as if emphasizing operetta as a ladies' art. But no: for *Frederika*, despite its title, is entirely made on Goethe. Lehár had at his disposal tenor Richard Tauber, one of Germany's best singers of any kind of music from folk to opera.

One wonders, though, if it was wise to cast the baritone Dennis King in a tenor role. The key melody in *Frederika*'s ample underscoring turns on a kind of trill between the fifth and sixth of the scale in G Major, which eventually creates the melody of the *Tauberlied*—the big solo around which Lehár evenings navigated. Part of the sound of Lehár is the sound of Tauber: a high tenor gaming with falsetto cadenzas favoring high B flat. King was a looker, a resourceful actor, and a fine singer. But he *was* a baritone, and this calls for a lowering of keys and a lessening of brilliance in the sound. After all, the character is Goethe, full of youth, love, and poetry. As with *Show Boat*'s Gaylord Ravenal (which, remember, King also played, in the 1932 revival), a baritone doesn't really work. The score is organized around a lightly passionate sound, lilt with tension.

Have you noticed how many entries in this largely unimpressive catalogue were imported from Europe? *The Great Waltz, Champagne, Sec, White Horse Inn, Three Waltzes, The Dubarry, Three Little Girls, Meet My Sister, Marching By*, of course *Frederika* and *Conversation Piece* just above, three visits from the D'Oyly Carte company (in 1934, 1936, and 1939) with their absolutely *echt* Gilbert and Sullivan, and even something called *Gypsy Blonde* (1934), which turned out to be Michael Balfe's opera of 1843, *The Bohemian Girl*, with an updated libretto . . . all this supplied a bit more than half of thirties operetta production in toto, even without counting the Gilbert and Sullivan titles individually.

Clearly, no one had any great ambition to take up where Romberg had faltered and Friml given up—or almost no one. It's not certain exactly how Frederick Loewe saw himself fitting in on Broadway at this time, but to Broadway he came, in 1938, with *Great Lady*, to lyrics by Earle Crooker and book by Crooker and Lowell Brentano. However, *Great Lady* does not remotely suggest the kind of show or the style of music that Loewe became famous for. No fewer than three veteran divas led the cast: Norma Terris in the title role as American adventuress Eliza Bowen, with Helen Ford and Irene Bordoni; and romantic entanglements Shepperd Strudwick and Tullio Carminati. The work began with what was becoming the nearly de rigueur book scene, set in the offices of *Live* magazine in 1939. From there the action went into flashback, moving from 1793 to 1852 and from Providence, Rhode Island to Paris and New York.

Great Lady, which lasted only 20 performances after the excruciated critics could offer not a single reason to see it, had a notable corps de ballet if nothing else: Alicia Alonso, Nora Kaye, Jerome Robbins, Paul Godkin, and premier danseur (as they invariably put it) André Eglevsky. We hear little, however, of Alan Jay Lerner's Frederick Loewe in the music, as if Loewe was actually trying to sound generic. But then, the shows in which he prospered all had character and atmosphere— *Brigadoon*'s cathedral of spooks, *Paint Your Wagon*'s lawless gold rush, *My Fair Lady*'s Anglo class war, *Camelot*'s political mythopoeia, *Gigi*'s belle époque. Looking at *Great Lady*'s tunestack, we find lyricist Crooker striking operetta's tritest poses instead of polling his people on their needs and attitudes: "Though Tongues May Wag," "In the Carefree Realm of Fancy," "There Had To Be the Waltz," "Keep Your Hand On Your Heart." Crooker was Loewe's partner for five years of obscurity, till Alan Jay Lerner wrote the book to another Loewe-Crooker show, *Life of the Party* (1942), a victim of tryout implosion. By 1943, Crooker was gone and the new team debuted on Broadway with one of the most unknown of the post-*Oklahoma!* shows written by major talents, *What's Up*.

Let us sharpen our focus on thirties operetta in two of the better examples, both from 1932. Vincent Youmans' *Through the Years* stood among the least successful operettas of the time and Jerome Kern's *Music in the Air* among the most successful. Ironically, of the two only *Through the Years* claims a full-out recording, the sole Youmans score besides *No, No, Nanette* so treated.

Compare and contrast. *Through the Years* is an adaptation of a popular tearjerker, *Smilin' Through* (1919), credited to one Allan Langdon Martin. This turned out to be the writing name of the play's leading lady, Jane Cowl, and her collaborator, Jane Murfin. It's a fantasy, another of those generational things. In the play's first act, we learn that a young couple cannot marry because her uncle hates the young man's family. Act Two is a flashback: the uncle was to marry the girl's mother, but the boy's father, who loved the bride, burst in on the wedding and, aiming for the groom, shot the bride dead. Act Three brings redemption and forgiveness. The couple gain consent as the uncle is spirited off by the ghost of his beloved.

Music in the Air is an original, and wholly realistic. In contemporary Bavaria, boy and girl visit Munich, get involved in local show biz, quarrel, get hurt, and go home to patch it up and plan the wedding.

Of course, the last thing to take into account in an operetta is the plot. Still, it is noteworthy that Youmans and Kern use their respective stories as a key to the kind of music they will compose, Youmans to Edward Heyman's lyrics and Kern to Oscar Hammerstein's. For *Through the Years* is obviously sentimental and *Music in the Air* something of a romp. Thus, Youmans must graduate his signature musical-comedy sound to accommodate an emotional outpouring. Kern is busier: he has to make certain that the burlesque of show-biz egos and operetta convention doesn't overshadow the central romance. Then, too, Youmans must deal with the opening up of a play counting but a handful of characters. Where to place the dancey second couple? The chorus? And Kern must characterize the rustic opening and closing scenes of village life, with its birdcalls, choral society, and church bells, as well as the fast city lifestyle, with its zoo, its eccentrics, its erotic subtext, as when the operetta diva tells the village girl, "Maids' parts are always the last to be written in a play, my dear. They depend largely on whom the author meets during rehearsals."

One unique touch in the *Music in the Air* score is Kern's subdivision of each scene into a separate musical entity. The first he termed Leit Motif because the cry of a linnet inspires the village music master to compose "I've Told Every Little Star," and the tune runs through the scene. The village boy has written the words to the melody, so Scene Two, described as Etude, presents a performance of the song with an elaborate choral introduction that Kern himself arranged out of the *Adagio* of Beethoven's Third Piano Sonata.

The following scene, called Pastoral, follows the boy and girl's trip to Munich to try to get the song published. Other scenes are designated as Nocturne, Caprice, Humoresque, and so on; finally, back in the village, comes Rondo, because the scene consists almost entirely of "We Belong Together" played over and over under dialogue or sung by different characters until the postman arrives with printed copies of "I've Told Every Little Star." Village Boy gets Village Girl, those church bells peal out, and the curtain falls.

Another of this show's individual qualities is the way music runs through the action even when no one is singing or dancing. Following an experiment first tried in *The Cat and the Fiddle* (1931), which Kern wrote with Otto Harbach, *Music in the Air* is flooded with underscoring and odd little musical bits. Vocal passages sometimes lapse into dialogue than lunge back into song; or dialogue may be timed to be spoken to a melody "sung" only by the orchestra. There's so much music in the air, in fact, that it bullies the book, intimidates and overwhelms it. There isn't even much choreographic intrusion: *Music in the Air* was one of the few thirties musicals to limit its dance plot, to little more than two children's Ländler to launch a schoolroom scene and a showgirl's bubble dance later on.

There were only three major composers at this time whose style naturally accommodated both musical comedy and operetta and who could draw on both voices through nice shading in any given work. One of these was Sigmund Romberg: but the other two were Youmans and Kern. It's a handy gift when creating operetta *après la lettre*. Kern wrote "Who" but also "You Are Love." Youmans wrote (as co-composer with Herbert Stothart) *Wildflower* (1923), the operetta disguised as a musical comedy because operetta was temporarily out of favor.

So *Through the Years* has a rather elegant tone; even the fun numbers are highly musical. Of course, Youmans' librettist, Brian Hooker, made room for that second couple and chorus; the juvenile and ingenue help relieve the tragedy. Yes, the show ends happily for the youngsters. Still, at the show's center broods the uncle, whose life effectively ended forty years in the past, at the murder, and who lives only for his dead sweetheart's ghostly visitations.

Such numbers as the jaunty "Kinda Like You," for the two cutups, lend the spirit of DeSylva, Brown, and Henderson to the event, on a clever musical hook that Youmans often favored, repeating a four-note melodic cell while changing the accent with each statement. On the other hand, the breathlessly expectant "How Happy Is the Bride" inspires something special in Youmans, suiting operetta more than musical comedy yet with a flavor all its own. Also, note that while the setting is Ireland, Youmans made space for a single bit of pastiche, "Kathleen Mine." *Through the Years* is set in Ireland simply because *Smilin' Through* was; it is *Music in the Air* only whose setting creates the sound.

To be fair, Kern did not compose much German pastiche per se. There is that seasoning of Beethoven, that Ländler, and a certain folkish quality in the non-vocal melodies that constantly flit in and out of the score. It is really Hammerstein who lays down the cultural atmosphere, in such numbers as "In Egern on the Tegern See"* and "There's a Hill Beyond a Hill," which accompanies the young couple's trip to Munich as a choral escort by the village walking club, the sort of people who may yodel at any moment.

The experiences that the couple undergo are why *Music in the Air* was subtitled "a musical adventure." It is not a glad one, for both boy and girl are badly used by the operetta diva and her impresario boy friend; worse, the girl goes on in the diva's place and has a disaster, in a wicked turn-about of show-biz myth. Even so, the older couple are spoofs of theatre-world egotism, and the two kids, though not spoofs of anything, are comic roles in part. And note that, now that the operetta era is all but over, writers—or at least Hammerstein, *Music in the Air*'s librettist as well as lyricist—have finally learned to spread the humor throughout the action instead of entrusting it to one or two specialists, as almost invariably in the 1920s.

The second most integrated musical to that point in history (after *The Cat and the Fiddle*), *Music in the Air* in fact spread every one of its elemental

* Hammerstein indulged himself in an interior rhyme in this number, balancing "along the shore" with "one light more." It must have driven him crazy when, after one confused singer inverted the second phrase to "one more light," many others imitated the error. When the show was still running, Victor issued a two-sided medley picture disc (showing scenes from the production), and, already, house soprano Marjorie Horton was getting the line wrong.

characteristics throughout the action. The music even took part in sight gags, as when, in the zoo sequence, the dropping of sugar lumps into coffee was timed to plinks from the orchestra, three on offbeats as a waiter did the dropping, then a fourth as the impresario grabbed one more lump, on the last tonic chord.

One might even say that the integration extended to the orchestrator's desk, for Robert Russell Bennett chose a pit to serve the work pictorially, less an instrumentation than a palette. A haunting sound style suffused the Pastoral, with muted strings, bells, and marimba. Further, xylophone, celesta, and harp "mimed" the sound of water dripping from an exhausted old mill wheel.

There was one flaw in the musical program, the shameless plugging of "I've Told Every Little Star." But it does fall easily on the ear, with a verse that returns as the chorus' release. Best of all is the ingenuous lyric, a typically Hammersteinian construction of the most ordinary words and the simplest images. Through the use of repetition-with-development—from telling "ev'ry little star" to "ripples in a brook"; and starting with "I" but ending with "you"—Hammerstein makes poetry, as he loved to, out of the most everyday expressions.

Coincidentally, *Through the Years* played Oscar's uncle Arthur's theatre, the Hammerstein: it had passed out of the family by then and was renamed the Manhattan. The tryout was stormy, for Youmans was again his own producer, and while he generously sprang for a forty-five-piece orchestra, he was a great firer, and three of the leads departed, including the heroine, Norma Terris. Natalie Hall replaced her in the double role of Kathleen (in the present) and Moonyeen (in the flashback), opposite the Kenneth/Jeremiah of our old pal Michael Bartlett. Reginald Owen and Charles Winninger took the senior roles, and the second couple was Nick Long Jr. and Martha Mason. Critics blasted the book in particular, and the show closed after 20 performances. It left behind, at first, only its title song, a favorite of sopranos going crossover.

Music in the Air went over very well. Natalie Hall was in this one, too, opposite Tullio Carminati; they were the city couple. From the village, Edendorf (a paradise, one literally infers), came Walter Slezak and *Face the Music*'s Katherine Carrington, with her father (Al Shean) and a kind of Papageno called Cornelius (Reinald Werrenrath). The show was a hit in London in 1933 with Mary Ellis as the diva, and Fox filmed it in 1934 with Douglass Montgomery, June Lang, Gloria Swanson, John Boles, and Al Shean in his original role. Another classic Broadway comic got into the film, Joseph Cawthorn, and Reginald Owen was also on hand, providing yet another curious link with the otherwise unrelated *Through the Years*. Various *Music in the Airs* over the years offered now Allan Jones, now Irra Petina and John Charles Thomas, and a season at the Greek Theatre in Los Angeles in 1948 brought forth *Street Scene*'s Polyna Stoska and the 1946 *Show Boat* revival's Jan Clayton and Charles Fredericks. *Music in the Air*'s flop return to Broadway in 1951 offered a third link with *Through the Years* in the participation of Charles Winninger, but by then the show had lost its appeal, even with Edendorf moved to Switzerland and the adventure leading to Zurich. Time must truly have changed, for in 1932 Brooks Atkinson wrote "the musical drama has been emancipated," and in 1951 he wrote, "It is a shock to discover that half of the first act is wasted on some silly mumbo-jumbo about wicked city people." They were Dennis King and Jane Pickens, and King's son, billed as John M. King, sang chorus and understudied the juvenile lead. Five years later, using his middle name of Michael, he would introduce "On the Street Where You Live" in *My Fair Lady*.

By now, *Through the Years* is not much less familiar than *Music in the Air*; both have departed the stage in that terminal way in which operettas tend to depart. They don't retire: they are liquidated. Yet there is a form even more terminated than operetta—a form, I have said, that is particularly relevant to the 1930s. Okay, shoot the works!

6

FUN TO BE FOOLED: REVUE

One could argue that revue is the oldest indigenous American musical-theatre form. As the minstrel show, it was already dominant by 1850, before the book musical as we know it had appeared, and variety shows of kinds other than minstrelsy—the "olio" sequence in evenings of melodrama or old-form burlesque—proliferated into the early twentieth century.

However, when we speak of works such as *The Little Show*, we mean nothing that could be called a descendant of the minstrel show or the olio. The seeds of thirties revue were planted in 1894, in *The Passing Show*, modeled on a format pioneered in Paris: a "review" of the past year's events. This embedded in the American version a love of topical humor that has defined it ever since. The least interesting revues were no more than variety shows; but the most interesting revues were an art in themselves, and they displayed a unity within the variety that drew all the evening's "acts" into a one-of-a-kind experience, even a statement.

We have seen this in that first masterpiece *The Band Wagon*, which avoided all topical references to emphasize dance and design; and the other great thirties revues will owe more to *The Band Wagon* than to *The Passing Show*. Spoofs of trendy topics, as well as burlesques of theatre, film, and lit, will continue to supply the revue with raw material. But the thirties revue at its best looks for individual identity: in its worldview, in a theme, in a look.

The great shows, then, have broken completely with revue as it was known before *The Little Show*—yet the old style keeps popping up right through the decade. There was the big headliner presentation with a tiny bit of theme, first of all in the *International Revue* (1930), produced, co-written, and directed by Lew Leslie. It was the one time that he came to Broadway without an all-black cast. Retaining Jimmy McHugh and Dorothy Fields from *Blackbirds of 1928*, Leslie spent $200,000 on the concept of an evening of many lands—or so the word "international" suggests. In the event, there wasn't much of what we now call ethnicity, unless one counts comic Jack Pearl's Munchausen accent. Gertrude Lawrence was English; that's not very ethnic. Dancer Anton Dolin lent some Russian ballet, and unknowns with names like Radaelli and Viola Dobos were at least thematically foreign. But the score was filled with such titles as "Exactly Like You," "On the Sunny Side Of the Street," "I'm Feelin' Blue ('Cause I've Got Nobody)," and "The Margineers" (Jack Pearl's joke on stock-market traders), none of which pertains to the international, uh, community. One authentic import was a dancer called Argentinita, who came on so late in an overlong evening that most of the critics had departed to write their reviews and thus couldn't précis her performance. Just as well: Argentinita laid such an egg that by the printing of the second week's program she had departed the show, too.

Forward March (1933) had less a theme than a leftist point of view, but much of that fell away during a tryout hell that renamed the piece *Strike Me Pink*—a political title, all the same—and celebrated the doings of Jimmy Durante, Lupe Velez, singer Hope Williams, and hoofer Hal LeRoy. Durante made his entrance through the house, struggling with an impedient usher as he tried to gain the stage, and Velez did Lynn Fontanne in "Design For Loving," a burlesque of the latest Noël Coward hit. Though billed with Durante and Velez above the title, Williams wasn't as dextrous as they at imitations, craziness, and the like. But Percy Hammond of the *Herald Tribune* thought her "exquisitely Junior League," and she joined the other two for "Hollywood, Park Avenue, and Broadway." Virtually all that was left of the original socially conscious work was George Dewey Washington's "Home To Harlem," staged as an epic review of black history. As for the score, *Strike Me Pink* was another of the shows put on by Ray Henderson and Lew Brown that remind us how much more notable they were when working with Buddy DeSylva.

The Laugh Parade (1931) was the latest star-clown revue—or, more precisely, the latest Ed Wynn revue, as this comic commanded his own genre. As producer, co–sketch writer, and director, Wynn auteured his vehicles, and as performer he patrolled the stage throughout the evening, interfering with the acts, demonstrating those loopy inventions, or reviving his bicycle piano, here to accompany Jeanne Aubert. Composer Harry Warren wrote his first complete Broadway score for *The Laugh Parade* (with lyricists Mort Dixon and Joe Young), and while he got a temporary hit out of "Ooh! That Kiss" and a standard out of "You're My Everything," Warren didn't enjoy the experience. In the recipe for a show like *The Laugh Parade*, the score is the least crucial ingredient, less so even than the mostly lame stooges Wynn hired for support. After a good stay of 231 performances, *The Laugh Parade* left us with one great contribution to American culture: it persuaded Harry Warren to conquer his aversion to the business practices of movie producers and desert Broadway for Hollywood. There he created a treasury of standards for the Warner Bros. backstager, later moving on to Fox and Metro.

Many thirties revues were simply agglomerations of talent with no organization: neither old- nor new-wave, just there. *The Nine-Fifteen Revue* (1930) named twenty-six authors, and its sole point of distinction was Ruth Etting's delivery of Harold Arlen and Ted Koehler's "Get Happy." Or *The Vanderbilt Revue* (1930), so named for the theatre it played, offered a score mostly by Jimmy McHugh and Dorothy Fields and an unremarkable cast. The former show ran a week and the latter twice that. Just there.

At least Billy Rose's *Sweet and Low* (1930) got into the Barbra Streisand film *Funny Lady*, in a sequence devoted to its disastrous tryout, as *Corned Beef and Roses*. Fannie (as she spelled it then) Brice, Hal Skelly, and George Jessel offered headliner appeal that the *Nine-Fifteen* and *Vanderbilt Revue*s lacked, and among the numbers was "Sky City," dropped from Rodgers and Hart's *Heads Up!* (1929). It was dropped also from *Sweet and Low*, along with Skelly, who was replaced by James Barton, and the now vastly reworked show ran about half a year. Then Rose further revised and toured it, as *Billy Rose's Crazy Quilt*. This visited Broadway in 1931, with Brice now flanked by Phil Baker and Ted Healy. The big moment—preserved, though with a modern feel, in *Funny Lady*—was "I Found a Million Dollar Baby (In a Five and Ten Cent Store), another of the hit tunes that Harry Warren gave to Broadway before composing *42nd Street*. The song's staging put Brice in top hat and tails, reminding us that she was not at all limited to her trademark Jewish spoofs; Brice also got a contribution from Rodgers and Hart for her "Rose" series in "Rest Room Rose."

Shoot the Works! (1931) was thought up as a cooperative venture for thespian unemployment relief. Heywood Broun threw it together on a Dutch budget of $6,000, begging for sketches from such as Nunnally Johnson, Peter Arno, E. B. White, and Dorothy Parker and songs from McHugh and Fields and Irving Berlin. Broun emceed, criticizing the show as it went along; but he was no Ed Wynn.

In the matter of auteur revue, the critics preferred a now forgotten figure, Eddie Dowling, a Broadway stalwart at the time. If he is mentioned at all today, it is for his lead roles in *The Time of Your Life* and *The Glass Menagerie*, or for directing *The Iceman Cometh*—all three in the original productions. However, Dowling had established himself in musical comedy, and he put his considerable expertise to work on *Thumbs Up!* (1934). The cast included Clark and McCullough, baritone J. Harold Murray, the apparently inexhaustible dancer Hal LeRoy, the Pickens Sisters singing trio (from which Jane would emerge as a star on her own), a dance duo we've already met, Jack Cole and Alice Dudley, and Dowling himself, with his wife, Ray Dooley. Production values were high, but it was really Dowling's inventiveness that impressed. *Thumbs Up!* didn't change revue in any way, but all the choices were right—in song (Vernon Duke's "Autumn in New York," for which the composer wrote his own lyric), in dance (a Currier and Ives skating ballet, eleven years before the famous one, in *Up in Central Park*), and even in sketch ("Aired in Court," in which radio covers its first murder trial and everyone, from judge to defendant, tries to hog the mike).

Familiar as these formats were, they could be called novel compared to the bizarre attempt to reinstate a First Age genre in the arrival of *Kilpatrick's Old-Time Minstrels* (1930), complete with Mr. Tambo and Mr. Bones. Something like *Continental Varieties* (1934) may look comparatively outré, as a showcase for European talent performing in . . . well, European. The main draw, if she could be called a draw, was diseuse Lucienne Boyer, "la dame en bleu," singing such numbers as her theme song, "Parlez-moi d'Amour"; its sequel, "Parle-moi d'Autre Chose"; "Moi, Je Crache Dans l'Eau"; and titles that meant even less than these to New Yorkers. Keep in mind that Boyer's brand of song and her delivery were both almost monotonously low-key, nothing like the variety and electricity that we associate with Edith Piaf, or even the exhibitionistic *je m'en fou* of Charles Trenet. Then, too, dancer Vicente Escudero and his Sacre Monte Gypsies, a certain Carmita, a certain Raphael, and Georges De Roze as The Wonder Barman pouring all sorts of colorful liquids out of one source were curiosities at best.

European entertainments had been successfully set up on Broadway in the Russian revue *Chauve-Souris*, which emigrated from the Bat Theatre in Moscow to Paris and thence to New York in 1922, altering its program in four successive editions that racked up 544 performances. The show's title is simply the French word for "bat," and *The Bat*'s capocomico, the moon-faced Nikita Balieff, served as a deviously charming emcee for such songs, dances, and pantomimes as "Gypsy Song Intime," "The Serenade of the Deceived Pierrot," a one-act by Chekhof called "The Sudden Death of a Horse," "The Tartar Dance," and Leon Jessel's "The Parade of Wooden Soldiers" (to new lyrics by Ballard McDonald), which became a favorite encore piece for two generations of piano students.

However, *Chauve-Souris* caught on as a piquant novelty, whereas *Continental Varieties* was simply a vaudeville in the wrong languages. At least its producers secured the participation of *Chauve-Souris'* popular interlocutor. "Mr. Balieff's vocabulary," the program stated, "by Irving Caesar."

Even more unlikely were cabaret evenings put on by refugees from Nazism: *The Pepper Mill* (1937), on which John Latouche worked as translator and even performer, and *From Vienna* (1939), again with Latouche's assistance and on a more elaborate scale. Donald Oenslager and Irene Sharaff designed, and the refugees' Herbert Berghof (and our own Charles Friedman) directed. The musical's first historian, Cecil Smith, called *From Vienna* "a pathetically ineffectual collection," and it is sad to report that none of the eighteen performers and nine writers billing themselves as The Refugee Artists Group went on to notable work on American stages. Still, *From Vienna* held on for an entire summer at the Music Box, and returned with some new material as *Reunion in New York* for eleven further weeks at the Little, in 1940.

This is the minor history, of course. What we want is more work inspired by the stylish unity of *The Band Wagon*. First, however, we should consider a few attempts to create even newer forms of revue. That brings us at once to Leonard Sillman's *New Faces* series, so successful—or, arguably, relentless—that the last one came along in 1968. Sillman's concept was simple: with the exception of himself and his former vaudeville partner, Imogene Coca, who both appeared in several editions, every member of the cast would be "new" in some way, generally new to Broadway or newly promoted to principal from Broadway chorus work. Starting in California, where his show was called *Lo and Behold*, Sillman offered such faces as Eve Arden, Charles Walters, Kay Thompson, Teddy Hart, and perhaps the biggest face in the shows' thirty-four-year history: Tyrone Power Jr. Everyone except Walters was gone when the show came in as, officially, *New Faces* (1934), but Henry Fonda, Nancy Hamilton, James Shelton, and Gus Schirmer—names of varying command in years after—had joined the revelry. Both Hamilton and Shelton were writer-performers, very useful in the assembling of material. So was Sillman's sister June, though she was not to join a *New Faces* in performer mode till the 1952 edition, as June Carroll.

Producer Charles B. Dillingham came out of retirement (five months before his death) to put his name on *New Faces*, but it was really produced by Elsie Janis and Mary Pickford, who had fallen in love with Sillman's concept of the little revue as Big Break. Also, Sillman had a knack for finding the best sketches and favoring sharp burlesques, and that is lovable, too. Nancy Hamilton imitated Katharine Hepburn as she Gets Into Character for *Little Women*; the Three Little Pigs offered *The Green Bay Tree* (an extremely daring play about homosexuality, by the way), *Ah, Wilderness!*, and *Tobacco Road* in the Disney versions; and a spoof of present-day Broadway set forth Henry Fonda as Max Gordon, Sillman himself as Jed Harris, James Shelton as Noël Coward, and Imogene Coca as Gertrude Lawrence. *New Faces* went over, but Sillman's *Fools Rush In* (1934), put together by the same writing team (without Nancy Hamilton), collapsed in two weeks. Was it the empty title? Because *New Faces of 1936* did even better than the first entry, at that with a paucity of imposing faces.

Nancy Hamilton launched her own series at decade's end in *One For the Money* (1939), to focus not on newcomers but rather on gifted young journeymen. Besides Hamilton, these included Alfred Drake, Grace McDonald, Gene Kelly, Brenda Forbes, and Keenan Wynn (son of Ed), and the cast was just these and six other principals, without chorus. That alone distinguished the show; thirties musicals simply did not function without the singing and dancing ensembles. Even given the trouble it had raising its budget, the first *New Faces* nevertheless ran a small chorus besides the twenty-two leads.

Another odd thing about *One For the Money* was its subject matter: the lives and loves of the well-to-do. This was less apparent in *Two For the Show* (1940). Perhaps Hamilton simply ran out of things to say about the upper set, for otherwise she ran the most consistent of revue series, for instance retaining five players from the first work. *Two For the Show* did make a minor breakaway in producing a song hit, long a favorite with jazz musicians for its slithery chromatic chording, "How High the Moon." Hamilton wrote the words, to Morgan Lewis' music, and Alfred Drake and Frances Comstock sang it, in the setting of a blackout during the London blitz. A *Three To Make Ready* (1946), with journeymen Gordon MacRae, Harold Lang, Bibi Osterwald, Arthur Godfrey, and Carleton Carpenter and star Ray Bolger, closed out the series.

Now for the colorful children of the New Revue. Two titles of 1932 return us the tradition that can roughly be charted on: *The Little Show*→ *Three's a Crowd*→*The Band Wagon*, as we note that each of the trio has a Schwartz and Dietz score; the first two star Clifton Webb, Fred Allen, and Libby Holman and the last a comparable lineup in the Astaires, Frank Morgan, and Helen Broderick, with dancer Tilly Losch representing the new art of Broadway ballet; the last two are produced by Max Gordon, directed by Hassard Short, and choreographed by Albertina Rasch; and the set designers are major people in, first, Jo Mielziner, and then, twice, Albert Johnson.

Thus, aside from the continuity of the holdover names and an atmosphere of wit and chic, there is also an emphasis on first-division talent in all departments. So *Flying Colors*, the first of our two New Revues of 1932, falls right into the pattern, with Max Gordon presenting Clifton Webb, Charles Butterworth, Tamara Geva (of *Three's A Crowd*), and Patsy Kelly in "the new Howard Dietz revue," with a Schwartz-and-Dietz score, sets by Norman Bel Geddes, choreography by Albertina Rasch, and direction by Dietz.

In fact, *Flying Colors* was if anything too much like its predecessors— *The Band Wagon*, especially. "Alone Together" seemed rather like a second helping of "Dancing in the Dark," and its after-the-vocal dance, by Webb and Geva, may have reminded some of Webb and Libby Holman's after-the-vocal dance to *The Little Show*'s "Moanin' Low." John Mason Brown referred to "Alone Together" as "Dancing in the Schwartz." And if *The Band Wagon*'s cheer-up ditty, "Sweet Music," had an accordion, *Flying Colors'* cheer-up ditty, "A Shine On Your Shoes," featured Larry Adler's harmonica. Set on a city street, the number offered Buddy Ebsen as a shoeshine boy, sister Vilma as a customer, black onlooker Monette Moore (who introduced the number), and the kibitzing Adler. More: "Meine Kleine Akrobat" recalled *The Band Wagon*'s "I Love Louisa," and a macabre hotel sketch, "On the American Plan," recalled *The Little Show*'s "The Still Alarm." That was the one in which no one is putting out the fire; the new piece found folks checking into the Remington Arms to commit suicide. (For the blackout, a man entered, announced, "I'm a theatrical producer," and the manager handed him a gun with the words "Say no more!")

If familiar, *Flying Colors* was nevertheless cut of rich cloth, with an appealing score that has been overshadowed by that of *The Band Wagon*. The blithely elegant "A Rainy Day" was not only the perfect Clifton Webb number—it was actually a genre back then—but the kind of thing that Schwartz and Dietz excelled in, blasé and touching at once, like "I Guess I'll Have To Change My Plan" or "High and Low." *Flying Colors'* first-act finale, "Louisiana Hayride," though embarrassed by the use of black theatricalese ("All am here"), is a festive bit of regional color, and a bold tunestack found room even for "Smokin' Reefers." (Marijuana wasn't outlawed till 1937.) There was a funny sketch called "Bon Voyage," in which Patsy Kelly, sailing on the S. S. *Paresis*, gets the customary farewells from her parents, Uncle Norman, Cousin Carrie, and so on, till she tires of being seen off and attacks the lot. There was even a brilliant sketch, "The Surgeon's Debut," in which Dr. Clifton Webb treated his first job in the operating room as a show-biz debut, complete with telegrams, well-wishers, a band, and a bar. Imogene Coca played a merry nurse, Philip Loeb a sarcastic intern, and Charles Butterworth the meekly alarmed patient. He'd like to see his mother:

COCA: I told her to wait.

LOEB: You should have told her to start digging.

COCA: The anaesthetic is wearing off, Doctor!

WEBB: . . . I gave him a spinal anaesthetic, so that he is enabled to see all that goes on instead of being dead to the world.

LOEB: That'll come later.

At 188 performances, *Flying Colors* was a hit. But our other show in the new line did less well and is always given minimal attention by historians. This is *Walk a Little Faster* (1932), which opened about three months after *Flying Colors*. Its stars, Beatrice Lillie and Clark and McCullough, were saddled with underpowered material, and its songwriters, Vernon Duke and E. Y. Harburg, were not at their best. Even the show's hit, "April in Paris," is always mentioned as a footnote to the main story, in which Evelyn Hoey, who introduced it, had laryngitis on opening night, thus delaying the song's emergence because none of the critics could register approval. But surely Hoey didn't cultivate her laryngitis throughout the show's 119-performance run. Rather, a great many people must finally have heard her sing full out and remarked the music's excellence.

Monty Woolley directed and Albertina Rasch was again mistress of the dance, and we hear of some bright spots. At one point, Lillie made a brief announcement in a floor-length gown, suddenly hiked up her skirts, and roller-skated away; and she and Clark had a fine time "doing" *Flying Colors'* Clifton Webb and Tamara Geva in the number "End of a Perfect Night." But few theatre chroniclers recall how important stage design was to the thirties revue, and *Walk a Little Faster's* set designer spent decades working ahead of the curve in virtual anonymity till he joined up with Hal Prince for *Fiddler on the Roof* (1964), going on to the super-history of the five Sondheim shows of the 1970s.

This was, of course, Boris Aronson, making his Broadway debut with some of the most abstract visuals ever seen on the commercial stage. "I was fascinated with the kind of incongruities I saw on Broadway," he later explained, citing the dancing paper puppets with the invisible strings sold on the sidewalks, and the husky, dangerous-looking black men in grandly tailored suits who would croon cabaret trifles in Harlem clubs. Both these elements contributed to the bizarre look of the first-act finale, "Saturday Night," a cross between surrealism and dada. At stage right, three puppets and three black musicians occupied a constructivist dais; at stage left hung a medallion of showgirl legs against a practical curtain that rose, at first, to show more showgirl legs, real ones. Photographs of the number record its nutty observation of, indeed, the "incongruities" of mad Manhattan.

Not everything in *Walk a Little Faster* was that avant-garde. "April in Paris" was sung at café tables "under the trees" (as the lyric tells) on an odd little street of housefronts with almost no doors or windows. By no means ordinary, it was nevertheless somewhat soothing after the visual cacophony that Aronson used in so masterly a manner. Another set design built a giant player-piano's keyboard and software out of ever-changing illustrations on the roll itself and used showgirls inside the mechanism and on the keys.

That same year, 1932, saw the beginning of a second series of revues. It owed much to that first grouping of *The Little Show*, *Three's A Crowd*, *The Band Wagon*, and *Flying Colors*. But it stood out because Lee Shubert was its producer, at least nominally—and this is odd history. Shubert revues were notoriously inartistic; anyway, Lee left the making of Shubert musicals in general to Mr. J. J. It has been said that the Messrs.' tendency to sharp practice had so alienated the thespian community that Lee sought some expiatory prestige in the New Revue. But it may be also (or simply) that Lee wanted to enlarge his lifelong feud with his brother by putting on a hit revue while the other half of the Messrs. fruitlessly tried to revive operetta as Ponce de Leon searched for the Fountain of Youth.

In any case, Lee began by presenting the third of the *Americana* revues, conceived and scripted by J. P. McEvoy. Editions in 1926 and 1928 gave no hint of anything unusual in the works. But the third *Americana* was the show that introduced modern dance to Broadway. They called it "interpretive" dance then, and *Americana* helped itself to plenty of it, with both the Charles Weidman Dancers and the Doris Humphrey Dance Group, which included a future choreographer, José Limón. *Americana's* dancing was credited to John Boyle and Weidman, and the representations took in a Shaker meeting, "Amour á la Militaire," and "Ringside," a prizefight display.

Americana was not revolutionary all over, however. It had sets by Albert Johnson, one of the New Revue's most desirable merit badges. But much of the rest of it was the same old. Gordon Smith and Peggy Cartwright sang the customary Flirty Kid Duets, such as "Would'ja For a Big Red Apple?," and it turned out that, when not taking over Jack Buchanan's role in *Pardon My English*, George Givot did imitations. Francetta Malloy sang an insinuating black number, "Satan's Li'l Lamb," backed by The Musketeers; the Humphrey and Weidman gangs then took over the music. The Sue Hastings Marionettes were on hand, as so often in a thirties show. So *Americana* might have been just another revue with an ambitious dance program, but for one thing: "Brother, Can You Spare a Dime?"

Sung by Rex Weber in a breadline scene, this Jay Gorney– E. Y. Harburg classic brings us to the thirties musical that many *think* existed, in which the fun-filled stage seized the epochal moment to embrace the liberation of socialist commentary. As I've stated, this happened only here and there. But it certainly happened here, for "Brother's" status as a standard really is more political than musical. The song holds anthem rights to the age, which takes it out of the theatrical context into the sociohistorical. Hollywood turned out a number of such songs, such as "Remember My Forgotten Man" and, also by Gorney and Harburg and more upbeat, "Dusty Shoes." But "Brother" is the genre's survivor, entirely on its strength of composition. There is nothing "legendary" about the way it was staged or about the singer who introduced it, and Bing Crosby's hit record of the time is so low-tech that listeners must have had no idea of the latent power of the piece.

This derives not only from the grandeur of Gorney's melody, but from Harburg's imagery as well. The man singing the number is a former industrialist who is now a beggar; but Harburg makes him American industry in general by switching his field from railroads in the first A to construction in the second, then further widens the perspective by switching to his wartime experience in the release. By then, Harburg's protagonist is no longer a capitalist but an everyman, a good guy, a patriot, all this rooted in a devastating line about his war service just before the last A: "I was the kid with the drum."

Americana ran only 77 performances, but Lee Shubert was just getting started. Apparently, he saw great potential in the New Revue without understanding it well enough to initiate projects himself, and somehow or other he hooked up with Harry Kaufman, a stagestruck amateur who knew little of the show business but everything about the theatre. Kaufman's guidance allowed Lee to mount a series of big variety shows, presented at the Winter Garden: *Ziegfeld Follies* (1934), *Life Begins at 8:40* (1934), *At Home Abroad* (1935), *Ziegfeld Follies of 1936*, and *The Show Is On* (1936).

All five did no more than maintain the tradition crystallized in *The Band Wagon*: talent, imagination, unity. It seemed obvious enough—but then why weren't other managements doing it, too? Taking an average, we find these five titles creating a model starring Fannie Brice or Beatrice Lillie, Bert Lahr or Bob Hope, and Ray Bolger or Eleanor Powell, assisted by such as Eve Arden, Paul Haakon, and Luella Gear; with an urbane and tuneful score by one of the typifying thirties revue composers such as Arthur Schwartz, Harold Arlen, or Vernon Duke working with Howard Dietz, E. Y. Harburg, or Ira Gershwin; with Robert Alton choreographing but sometimes a taste of the New Dance from George Balanchine or Charles Weidman; and designed by *The Band Wagon*'s Albert Johnson and Kiviette or by the latest discovery, Vincente Minnelli; with John Murray Anderson or Minnelli directing. And the hit tune is the height of sophistication, "I Can't Get Started."

What is most interesting about the two *Follies* is that, though they arrived two years apart, the earlier one looked back to older forms and the later one was absolutely contemporary. For one thing, in 1934 one of the leads was Everett Marshall, the crossover baritone very closely related to the tenor who would hail the glorified girls in their theme song. You know—Roscoe. The style is a big voice making noise about rather little; one of Marshall's numbers in 1934 was "Wagon Wheels," a gala paean to ordinary subject matter, a western "Trees." Furthermore, the wooden Marshall took no part in any of the sketches, an old-fashioned way to play revue.

For another thing, though Fannie Brice did introduce her famous character of the bratty Baby Snooks* in 1934, her numbers were all of the kind that she had been doing for Ziegfeld a generation before—"Soul Saving Sadie (of Avenue A)," "Countess Dubinsky," and, about a nudist, "Sarah, the Sunshine Girl." Speaking of that, the Yiddish dialect humor of 1934's Willie and Eugene Howard—in which, for example, they made incongruous kibitzers at a cowboy campfire singalong—was nearly kaput by this time. True, Brice worked in dialect. But she also worked out of it, as when playing Baby Snooks. Besides, her versatility as a singer and comic placed her in a unique category.

The lead woman singer in 1934 was Jane Froman, another of those vocalists who couldn't do anything else. But the score was mostly by Vernon Duke and E. Y. Harburg, so Froman's numbers were at least up-to-speed

---

* This supremely impedient little girl had already appeared four years earlier in a sketch in *Sweet and Low*, but hadn't yet aquired the dangerous-when-cute name of Baby Snooks that was so much a part of her identity.

in overall style. A duet with Marshall for a Wedding Number, "What Is There To Say?," cleverly rides up on two batches of quarter notes, then floats back down on triplets. "Suddenly" takes off on a sharp downbeat before the vocal line, as the title warrants. But "Moon About Town," by Harburg and Dana Suesse, is a real curiosity, the plea of a lonely woman for advice from the moon on how to meet a man. The refrain has a useful swing, but a jazzy patter section takes Harburg into territory he clearly isn't comfortable in, with the trendy orchestral breaks, the repeated cry "Shine on, Moon!," and rhymes for New York's bon ton locales. The whole thing is so loony that Harburg doesn't even bother to fit "Plaza" and "Casa(nova)" into proper scan.

Two years later, all these problems are solved. Instead of Everett Marshall, the lead baritone is Rodney McLennan, who sings not grandiose crossover pieces but an opening number so contemporary that it's called "Time Marches On" and its point is that the age now favors wit over the glorious showgirl. Of course, its irony is that the staging fills the view with the very thing that McLennan thinks is over. "Gangway, ye platinum dollies," he cries as, behind him, and to his left and right, the stage throngs with beauty. Also unlike Marshall, McLennan can play sketch comedy; he does Clark Gable in "Baby Snooks Goes Hollywood." It would be hard to imagine Everett Marshall playing even Everett Marshall.*

Then, too, Fannie Brice's activity in 1936 gave her much less of the old Avenue A material. There was only one such number, "Modernistic Moe," the plaint of a night-club dancer seduced by an arty boy friend into the screwy world of *ballet mécanique*. Brice's opening spot in 1936, "He Hasn't a Thing Except Me," was a merry parody of the "My Man" torch song, as if finally liberating Brice from a number she had first sung in 1920: so she can get on with her new persona as Baby Snooks. The 1936 comic (and emcee of the evening) was Bob Hope, far more appropriate to the era than the Howards' First Age hangover of dialect humor. And in Jane Froman's place was Gertrude Niesen, precisely comparable but given three splendid ballads topping anything in 1934: the rhythmic "Island in the West Indies," the scalding "Words Without Music," and, in duet

* Marshall actually enacted roles in a couple of movies—real lead parts in stories—but he lacks basic thespian skills and even looks odd. Apparently, he was no big deal in opera, either. His Met career consisted mainly of the Herald in *Lohengrin*—not a small part, exactly, but one without any dramatic interest.

with McLennan, "That Moment of Moments." Eve Arden got a big promotion from her bits-and-pieces job in 1934, Josephine Baker dropped in from Paris, and there was one somewhat antique usage in Harriet Hoctor's unintegrated job as lead dancer. True, *The Band Wagon* had included Tilly Losch for the same purpose. But the one-trick pony really was becoming excrescent, and can be defended only because the intense interest in dance made the use of trained specialists like Hoctor and Paul Haakon (whom Robert Coleman dubbed "the Broadway Nijinsky") essential.

Lewis Nichols of the *Times* called Brice "the personification of the 'Follies,' " and when she fell ill the run was halted at 115 performances. Hope, Niesen, Arden, Baker, and Hoctor were busy elsewhere when Brice was well enough to resume; Bobby Clark, Jane Pickens, and Gypsy Rose Lee took over for the first three, and Baker's and Hoctor's responsibilities were eliminated. Altogether, about one-third of the show was new, and in this form it played another 112 performances.

This, then, might have been the end of *The Ziegfeld Follies of 1936*, as with virtually every revue of the time. But in 1999 Encores! brought the show back, with Mary Testa and Peter Scolari in the Brice and Hope segments, Howard McGillin for Rodney McLennan, Ruthie Henshall singing two of Niesen's songs, Christine Ebersole in an expanded version of Eve Arden's evening (including one of Niesen's numbers), and Stephanie Pope doing Josephine Baker. Some of the "extra" people of 1936, such as Harriet Hoctor and the Nicholas Brothers, were not duplicated in this streamlined version of thirties revue, throwing brighter light on the rights and duties of the stars.

What most impressed was the score. Here were Vernon Duke and Ira Gershwin at their very best, in vivid presentation by three of Broadway's greatest orchestrators (Robert Russell Bennett, Hans Spialek, and Don Walker, along with the less celebrated Conrad Salinger), their authenticity disinterred, rebuilt, reclaimed. This is the kind of music that doesn't wait for the refrain to sweep the listener away: as Karen Ziemba and the Walton Brothers chirp into the verse of "My Red-Letter Day," they are already irresistible; and Howard McGillin's zesty intro to "Maharanee" thrills us with the feeling that Everett Marshall's cape has at last been packed away for something more naturally dashing.

Some of the score has a silly side, as in the first-act finale's spoof of Warner Bros. backstagers, which climaxes in "The Gazooka." Of course, the verse warns us that this New Dance Sensation is not to be opposed and proposes to teach it to us, as did all the New Dance Sensation numbers. In the event, they gave no more then perfunctory instructions, and "The Gazooka" doesn't give any. Its repeated "And then you" is more confidently secretive than even "The Varsity Drag"'s "Stay after school, learn how it goes."

Ira Gershwin's playful smarts obviously engineer superb comic numbers, a lost art today. Modern musicals that create humor within their vocal portion tend to be either generic throwbacks like *The Producers* or shows set in the past, like the two versions of *The Wild Party*. It's all but admitting that the present is witless, that only old forms or old times require (or deserve) the application of intelligent wordplay and ironic imagery. But the Golden Age was also clever in ballad, when Ira could somersault around Vernon Duke's rich harmonic idiom and rhythmic élan. Orchestrators claimed that Duke posed their biggest challenge, because there was so much *there* in his music, and we hear it in the aforementioned "I Can't Get Started," which comes with its own book scene: Bob Hope is saying goodnight to Eve Arden (Judy Canova during the tryout, and, after the reopening, Fannie Brice) after what was apparently a terrible date. She keeps trying to dump him while he keeps rebounding. Finally, he starts the number, a list song citing his accomplishments and high cultural status. ("When J. P. Morgan bows, I just nod.")

The joke is that she finally submits to a kiss, is knocked away in awe . . . and now *he* walks out on *her*. But the music and lyrics create something far beyond a revue spot or hit tune: a paradigm of the era's value system. "I Can't Get Started" defines celebrity as a form of entitlement: the man bigger than J. P. Morgan merits the girl of his choice, and she's supposed to know that. Her opposition is incorrect, musically off-key. So Duke captures his protagonist's failure of persuasion in a melody that bangs incessantly on the seventh tone of the scale (on "I've flown around . . ."). Comparably, the release hammers on a single whole note, first in the mediant minor $^{11}\,{}^{9}_{7}$ chord, then in the supertonic major $^{9}_{7}$ chord, and last in the supertonic minor $^{9}_{7}$ chord, giving an unstable feeling to the music: because this ultra-logical serenade is falling on unreasonable ears.

Between the two *Follies* came *Life Begins at 8:40*, possibly the most comical of the Shubert Winter Garden series. Or perhaps carefree is more apt; even the torch song was a spoof, Luella Gear's "I Couldn't Hold My

Man." Gear's cohorts were Bert Lahr, Ray Bolger, Frances Williams, Brian Donlevy, and dancing Dixie Dunbar; the score allied Harold Arlen with both Ira Gershwin and E. Y. Harburg. It's not a major score but an especially happy one, as if every number wanted to enjoy itself as much as "I Couldn't Hold My Man": "Fun To Be Fooled," "What Can You Say in a Love Song (that hasn't been said before?)," the geographical list song "Let's Take a Walk Around the Block," "You're a Builder Upper," and "Quartet Erotica," for Rabelais (James McColl), de Maupassant (Donlevy), Boccaccio (Bolger), and Balzac. Lahr anticipated *The Music Man*'s "Pick-a-little, Talk-a-little" joke in a heavy accent on the first syllable of the writer's name.

That sounds like the good old Lahr of the physical comedy and urban-bum sound bites, but in fact he was already in the process of refining his identity. Experimenting with burlesques of the pretentious behavior of the tony set, Lahr nevertheless angled his point of view to that of the character he used to play. That is, Lahr was now giving the audience the bum's idea of Noël Coward, mooing out mots at tea. He's not classy: he's dainty. Thus, in Alan Baxter's sketch "Chin Up," Lahr appeared in an English drawing room, in which the mania for good show is so quietly intense that the slightest breach of etiquette demands a repentant suicide—but all in short tight phrases cleared of emotion. Lahr must dress for dinner with the duchess, but he is delayed by family members confessing their transgressions as a stonefaced butler keeps appearing with poison on a tray. Father Brian Donlevy can't pay his gambling debt, Lahr's wife, Luella Gear, is unfaithful, and mother Winifred Harris tops them both: Lahr is illegitimate. After each has taken his poison:

LAHR: Must dress.

   (The butler enters one last time with his tray.)

LAHR: For me?

BUTLER: Right.

LAHR: Late for dinner?

BUTLER: Right.

   (Lahr takes the glass. The butler leaves.)

LAHR: To the duchess.

   (He drinks, falls to the floor, and gasps out the blackout line:)
      Needn't dress.

Lahr was even more in his element in the number "Things" as a society recitalist, effete yet grand, ever aspiring to the higher eloquence and filled with clichés about "the utter, utter, utter loveliness of things." This is Lahr partway between the *Flying High* mug who confuses a slug of booze with a urine sample and the Cowardly Lion outlining his personal dream in "If I Were King of the Forest." When Lahr's son John was preparing Lahr's biography, E. Y. Harburg took some credit for this expansion of Lahr's persona: "When DeSylva, Brown and Henderson were writing for [Lahr, in *Hold Everything!* and *Flying High*], they saw Bert as . . . the patsy . . . a semi-idiotic guy who always gets things wrong. I understood Lahr in a different way . . . I saw the little man, the pathos of a human being who is stuck with his society, who is put upon and exploited by it."

Dance and design remained almost as important as *Life Begins at 8:40*'s stars. Adrienne Matzenauer (daughter of Met soprano Margarete) sang the vocal for "Shoein' the Mare," a Latin version of the New Dance Sensation, and the Cuban dance team of Ofelia and Pimento led the corps in Charles Weidman's choreography. Robert Alton worked on the show as well, for spots when the more casually hoofing Bolger and Dunbar were on; and Albert Johnson's ever-ready revolves inspired John Mason Brown to complain of the "Lazy Susan" effect. The costume plot, too, was busy, requiring the designs of not only the customary Kiviette but James Reynolds (a pioneer in design for *The Greenwich Village Follies* in the 1920s), Raoul Pène du Bois, Billi Livingston, someone named simply Wynn, Pauline Lawrence, and Irene Scharoff (later Sharaff).

A new element was added to the format in 1933, in *As Thousands Cheer* (which I'm saving for the end of this chapter): the all-encompassing "theme" that gave yet greater unity to revue. *As Thousands Cheer* took its shape as a musical newspaper, each sketch or number announced to the public in a headline. Two years later, *At Home Abroad* incorporated this device: the acts recorded a world tour taken by an American couple, the Hatricks. Mrs. Hatrick's cables to friends back home, previewing each next stop on their itinerary, were flashed like *As Thousands Cheer*'s headlines, giving a frisson of anticipation as *At Home Abroad* moved about the map, mostly through Europe but making stops also in Asia and Africa.

Subtitled "A musical holiday," *At Home Abroad* was richer in its leading women than in its men. Beatrice Lillie, Ethel Waters, and Eleanor Powell were the headliners, along with the now absolutely forgotten vaudeville comic Herb Williams. True, the indispensable Paul Haakon made a tremendous impression in a ballet called "Death in the Afternoon" as a matador getting dressed, dancing a tango with his sweetheart (Nina Whitney), and defying the shadow of death as he enters the ring. But Eddie Foy Jr. had surprisingly little to do (he left after the first month), and Reginald Gardiner was mainly aboard to present his unlikely imitations, for instance of that "vindictive, aggressive, lurid beast" the railway engine and, more famously, of wallpaper.

At Home Abroad is known particularly as the first time Vincente Minnelli served as supervising director as well as designing sets and costumes. The show was not only handsome but big, as if the Winter Garden series wished to bond the wit of New Revue with the size of Ziegfeld. Despite considerable trimming in Boston, the show opened in New York with twenty-two separate acts plus a prologue and finale. The prologue, amusingly, stylized the concept of an extremely lavish show in a single simple and painful image: a man sleeping in a cartoonishly large bed. He is suffering a nightmare, animated by the Sue Hastings Marionettes portraying the celebs of the day—Shirley Temple, J. Edgar Hoover, Mrs. Roosevelt, and even the radio-commercial page boy shrilling out his "Callll forrr Philip Morrrrissss!"

Then came the first number, "Get Away From It All." To England, for example, where Eleanor Powell and the chorus boys, all dressed as Etonians in striped pants, broad white collars, and top hats, performed "That's Not Cricket" and where, in the next episode, Bea Lillie tried to order "two dozen double damask dinner napkins" in a department store, throwing herself and three clerks into tongue-twisted tizzies, or to Africa, where Ethel Waters sang "The Hottentot Potentate" backed by The Six Spirits of Rhythm band. This was one of those "sophisticated" numbers, requiring a worldly and informed public. The allusions one had to grasp took in not only The Emperor Jones but Lulu Belle, not just savoir faire but Lalique, not to mention "camping" and "trickeration."*

---

* Worldly and informed readers please skip this footnote. Eugene O'Neill's The Emperor Jones concerned an American Pullman porter who becomes the dictator of a West Indian island. Waters, who has brought off a comparable stunt in Africa, describes herself as "the Empress Jones." Among the items she has taken along to enlighten her reign are "the script of Lulu Belle"—the Belasco melodrama about a black prostitute. Lalique was a brand of glassware and we already know triggeration (the alternate form of "trickeration"), black slang for sexual expertise.

The show also sneaked off to an unspecified locale, where Woods Miller sang "Farewell, My Lovely." One of Schwartz's most deviously haunting melodies, it is made of a constantly repeated or varied cell of two or three notes in ascending pattern. A very choice spot was "Thief in the Night," in which Waters confronted her returning unfaithful ex, one Slinky Johnson. Of course he has returned: Waters is now—as she was in *As Thousands Cheer*—the toast of Paris. After the vocal comes some spoken patter (and note the allusion to a Jerome Kern show of two years earlier):

WATERS: Boy, you lookin' mighty sharp, you must 'ave hit the numbers . . . Don't start off calling me Ruby. My name is changed— I'm now known as Madame Roberta, the celebrated courtesianne.

After she dismisses him for good:

And don't go braggin' 'round Harlem you had an affair with me. Affair with me, hell! You call *that* little thing an *affair*?

Other locales took in the Balkans (where Eleanor Powell, in "The Lady With the Tap," is a spy communicating with Control through her dancing), the Swiss Alps (for the traditonal first-act finale exhibition number, this one being "O Leo," full of yodelling and a paper snowfall), a harbor in Jamaica, where Waters sang "Loadin' Time," and Monte Carlo, where prima ballerina Lillie refuses to go on. Note a second allusion to *Roberta*, this time, of course, to the 1935 film version:

LILLIE: I will never dance again.
HER MANAGER: You won't dance?
LILLIE: Don't ask me.

Everyone's favorite number took the public to Japan, where ladies with cherry-blossom hairdos shuffle about, line up, cluster, circle, and make pretty patterns while swirling their parasols. The song, "Get Yourself a Geisha," invited naughty-boy rhymes from Dietz, who mated "geisha" with "Asia" and even "in case ya." But the number's success was based on a staging surprise: Lillie was one of the chorus girls, undetected under the heavy makeup till she got off one solo line: "It's better with your shoes off!"

The next title in the Winter Garden series, *The Show Is On*, depended on a score distributed among fifteen writers, a violation of the New Revue handbook. Still, it, too, had a unity of theme, which was the world of entertainment—the antique stage, the music hall, Shakespeare, current Broadway hits, the swing craze, the movies, opera crossover, *Uncle Tom's Cabin*, and thirties burlesque, the kind with baggy-pants comics and strippers.

The Show Is On had only two stars in the truest sense, Bert Lahr and Beatrice Lillie; they could be called the king and queen of American revue. This is not merely because both appeared in more revues than book shows. (They also appeared in straight plays, Lahr more than Lillie.) It is because the variety structure allowed writers to create ideal situations for them that might have been difficult to interpolate into narratives, as when, in *The Show Is On*, Lahr's "Song of the Woodman" suggested good old Everett Marshall in one of his crossover odes, though Marshall wouldn't have occasioned the hail of wooden objects from the wings that nightly assaulted Lahr. Or when Lillie rode a crescent moon craned out over the front two rows to sing Herman Hupfeld's "Buy Yourself a Balloon" and threw garters into the audience.

Even with all those contributors, *The Show Is On* lacked a good score. The Gershwins offered the wonderful "By Strauss" to the evening's singing leads, Gracie Barrie and Robert Shafer (later Grieg's best friend in *Song of Norway* and *Damn Yankees'* old Joe Boyd), and Hoagy Carmichael and Stanley Adams' "Little Old Lady" was popular for a while. Its melody seems to imitate the wary mincing of a fragile old soul, and the staging found the chorus girls anticipating *The Producers* by doddering around in wigs and glasses. There was a Rodgers and Hart number, too, for Lillie, "Rhythm," in which she impersonated an adherent of swing named GoGo Benuti and swelled the ranks of the show's authors with allusions to everything from "Kiss Me Again" and "I Got Rhythm" to "Rose of Washington Square" and "The Star Spangled Banner." "Up, everyone," she merrily requested.

Luckily, this was one revue with delightful sketch material, by David Freedman and Moss Hart. A takeoff on Jacques Deval's play *Tovarich* offered not Russian servants in a Parisian household but Republicans working for Democrats. This was the political sketch, all but obligatory by now, in 1936. There was social commentary, too, in "Mr. Gielgud Passes By," in which Lillie played a member of the audience (at the front of a half-dozen rows set out on stage) at *Hamlet*. Not any *Hamlet*: earlier that season, Broadway was honored with duelling *Hamlets* opening a month apart. Katharine Cornell's husband, Guthrie McClintic, directed John Gielgud's company at the Empire, with Judith Anderson and Lillian Gish; Leslie Howard's less imposing troupe, under Howard and John Houseman, took the Imperial. Howard's version lasted little more than a month. But Gielgud broke Broadway's *Hamlet* record at 132 performances.

So it was Gielgud (Reginald Gardiner) that Lillie came to see, and of course she completely disrupted the performance, arriving late, calling out to friends, reciting along with the prince. And note that Lillie is characterized not only by her outrageous bad manners but by her politics. On her entrance, she had to fight off an usher who wants latecomers to wait for the first change of scene:

LILLIE: Will you unhand me or do you want me to call Herbert Bayard
   Swope? He'll be livid, I warn you.
USHER: I'm only an usher.
LILLIE: What did you think I thought you were, the Ballets Russes?
   (The usher leaves.) That's better. There's time enough for that sort
   of thing when the revolution comes and not before.

When someone tries to shush her, she hisses at him, "Communist!" However, the blackout bit brings the usual hollow climax. An exasperated Gielgud offers Lillie a pair for Leslie Howard's Hamlet. Oh, she couldn't possibly: it was Mr. Howard who sent her here.

On a higher level entirely was "The Reading of the Play." Vincente Minnelli, again directing and designing, gave this one the sumptuous look of an old print, as the lights came up on the company posed around a table in period costumes, with one player stretched out on a huge white bear rug and Lillie ready for La Grande Jatte in gown, lacy hat, and striped umbrella. As Mlle. Léonore, Lillie objects to everything:

PLAYWRIGHT: Now, in this play, there is a man and a woman.
LILLIE: Too much plot!

Later:

> PLAYWRIGHT: Our heroine . . . comes to New York and meets a pro-
> ducer. But he will not give her a part unless she becomes his mistress.
> LILLIE: So she gets the part. Go on.

Again, the blackout isn't quite good enough, as the playwright damns his protagonist for her sins:

> PLAYWRIGHT: Beneath all the glamor and glitter she is nothing but a
> woman of the streets—a common harlot!
> LILLIE: (rising) I have never been so insulted in my life!
> PLAYWRIGHT: Why, what have I done?
> LILLIE: You know very well what you have done! You have written the
> story of my life!

Of course, the Shubert office had not given up on the other kind of revue, the one in the School of Earl Carroll. The Messrs. had dealt in this trade in the 1910s and 1920s in *The Passing Shows* and *Artists and Models*, and now they chanced upon a ragamuffin vaudeville act that suggested a Marx Brothers version of burlesque. Ole Olsen and Chic Johnson were the masters of the act as authors and stars, and, extending it to a full evening, they and the (unbilled) Shuberts introduced it to New York as *Hellzapoppin* (1938).

Famous as the longest-running Broadway musical before *Oklahoma!* at a total run of 1,404 performances, *Hellzapoppin* is less a musical than vaudeville interrupted by songs. It was the very first "musical for people who hate musicals" (to quote a regrettable PR blurb for *Rent*), a collection of stupid gags. A woman in the auditorium suddenly remembered—very loudly—that she had left her infant at the Automat and raced out of the house; laborers wandered through the aisles with equipment, forcing spectators out of their seats; sullen, fat Shirley Wayne played the violin while apparently comatose (though standing); a gorilla assaulted a woman in a box seat; a man doing a Houdini act was straitjacketed and spent the rest of the show wrestling with his bonds; and so on. That's all the work was, really. Some credit Walter Winchell for its success, because he praised it unceasingly. More likely, there was a huge audience for low comedy that found it socially prestigious to attend the theatre once in a while. *Hellzapoppin* played the Winter Garden, but it was definitely not part of the Winter Garden series.

Nor was *The Streets of Paris*, produced by Olsen and Johnson and (now billed) the Messrs., which took the Broadhurst for 274 performances. The headliners were Bobby Clark, Luella Gear, Bud Abbott and Lou Costello, and Carmen Miranda, which hardly suggests a Parisian-themed revue. Singer Jean Sablon at least was authentically French, and many of the show's acts were set in Parisian locales. But the atmosphere screamed burlesque. Though Olsen and Johnson did not appear, their names atop the posters suggested something in the *Hellzapoppin* style. However, *The Streets of Paris* was a revue with an emphasis on comedy, not at all an Olsen and Johnson madhouse. Clark had a worthy number as a tourist, "Robert the Roué (from Reading, P.A.)," and "The Convict's Return" gave him perhaps the best sketch of his career. Again, the French setting was no more than a ruse. Luella Gear played Marie, pining for her beloved Armand, imprisoned though innocent. Clark played Marie's father, then exited, changed costume, and came back as the butler. After another exit and change he returned as the escaped Armand, then raced off to reappear as the prison warden. The fun inhered in the ever increasing tempo of the exits and entrances, along with an uncooperative set of jamming doors and obtrusive curtains. And, finally, a sketch ended with a solid gag: Armand is pardoned, he embraces Marie . . . and crashes to the floor in a spectacular stupor.

For many, the high point of *The Streets of Paris* was the first-act finale, "South American Way." Toscanini's and Furtwängler's future Otello, Ramon Vinay, led off the number, which in turn went to the Hylton Sisters and Della Lind. Then out came Carmen Miranda, at that time completely unknown in the U.S., in her dizzy heels and fruity hat. We should note as well the customary political number, "Doin' the Chamberlain," in which Luella Gear introduced a New Dance Sensation for appeasers, while the chorus men all resembled England's prime minister with moustache, outlandish overbite makeup, and umbrella.

It may be that *Hellzapoppin* and *The Streets of Paris* mark an end to the sophisticated revue in favor of simple theme revues (like the populist *This Is the Army* and *Call Me Mister* in the 1940s) and Big Laugh variety shows. Olsen and Johnson starred in three more in their *Hellzapoppin* style into

1950, and even a *George White's Scandals* dated "1939–40" was suspected of *Hellzapoppin* emulation: in bathroom humor, scabrous double meanings, and a use of vaudeville flotsam instead of entertainers worthy of the *Scandals* tradition. The Three Stooges threw pies and stuck their fingers up one another's noses. The two Knight Sisters performed an acrobatic adagio dance that White would have waved away in the 1920s. The first-act finale, always something special in the classy revues, was here a salute to Tin Pan Alley, from Stephen Foster to Irving Berlin—a number so overdone it was a genre itself. White had already had at least one go at it, in the 1928 *Scandals*.

The *Scandals* style had not completely dissolved. Willie and Eugene Howard, longtime White stalwarts, were the comics, and Raymond (so billed) Middleton was the Big Baritone. Ann Miller was the dancer and Ella Logan the singer. Backed by the four Kim Loo Sisters, Logan instructed one and all in "The Mexiconga," which Miller then demonstrated. And note that Albert Johnson designed the sets.

Still, the show was, in Brooks Atkinson's words, "good looking, fleet and dirty." It must have felt odd to sample *Hellzapoppin*, *The Streets of Paris*, and this *Scandals*—all playing at the same time—in the season that hosted Beatrice Lillie in Noël Coward's *Set To Music* (1939), basically the American viewing of Coward's 1932 London revue *Words and Music* with some new material. Earlier in the 1930s, the American revue style was different from yet comparable to Coward's. But now the image of Penelope Dudley Ward and Hugh French gentling the audience down with "The Party's Over Now" just before *Set To Music*'s finale simply doesn't share any idea of theatre with the Three Stooges or even the Kim Loo Sisters.

Lee Shubert and Harry Kaufman brought in an amateur summer show, somewhat revamped, as *The Straw Hat Revue* (1939), famous as Danny Kaye's entrance onto main stages; this, too, was far from *Hellzapoppin* in style. Imogene Coca spoofed Carmen Miranda in "Soused American Way," and Kaye presented his specialty "Anatole of Paris." Alfred Drake and Jerome Robbins were in it, too. Even so, it remained an amateur night recast with pros. By the 1950s and 1960s, its format would find a home in the smaller venues of the Village and other off- places.

So the great age of revue really was over. The form remained viable in the 1940s, slowed greatly in the 1950s because of television's cooption of the genre, and met sudden death in the 1960s. But the days when virtually all the major talents wanted to write, stage, or appear in revues was ended more or less with *Hellzapoppin*'s flash success. So we can best assess the nature of thirties revue in the show that, with *The Band Wagon*, was the opposite of *Hellzapoppin* in every conceivable way. This is the second masterpiece in the form, *As Thousands Cheer* (1933).

The difference between New Revue and what happened after it is evident first of all in the personnel, for *As Thousands Cheer* called upon the established masters and a piece like *Hellzapoppin* came out of—to euphemize—independent ateliers. The earlier show's producer, Sam H. Harris, was probably the outstanding organizer of musical productions after the three known for spectacle, Ziegfeld, Dillingham, and Arthur Hammerstein: the *Follies*, extravaganza, and operetta. Harris, George M. Cohan's former partner, put on smaller, smarter shows—the *Music Box Revues*, *Of Thee I Sing*, *Jubilee*, *Lady in the Dark*. All of these works are large in scale, and some were distinctly lavish. But Ziegfeld, Dillingham, and Hammerstein dealt in big as a genre. Harris' genre was intelligence.

He was now Irving Berlin's partner; Berlin wrote *As Thousands Cheer*'s score and Moss Hart the sketches. Albert Johnson designed the sets, Charles Weidman—in his first Broadway assignment since the third *Americana*—laid out the dance, accommodating the hoofers as well as the artistes, and Hassard Short directed. This is Big Broadway, and *this* is even bigger: Marilyn Miller, Clifton Webb, Helen Broderick, and Ethel Waters.

How to classify them?: the dancer, the wit, the truth-teller, the singer? The ravishing sweetheart, the first open-secret closet case, the diva of sarcasm, the black Marian Anderson? Or how about the spirit of musical comedy, the debonair embodiment of the sheer smarts of revue, the beady-eyed embodiment of the sheer skepticism of revue, and the key symbol in the racial integration of the theatre? As Waters herself told Moss Hart when they were finagling the running order of the acts and Waters would have to follow Miller and Webb at their brightest, "I like working on a *hot* stage!"

Over at *Hellzapoppin*, the cast is vaudeville and burlesque leftovers, key credits (such as for set design and orchestration) are missing, and main songwriters Sammy Fain and Charles Tobias are not in Irving Berlin's class. After *Everybody's Welcome*—the one in which Ann Sothern went to work and Oscar Shaw minded the house—Fain went to Hollywood, where his work was ordinary. Show buffs love him for later scores, such as the melodious *Flahooley* (1951) and the crazed Indian operetta *Christine* (1960). But the *Hellzapoppin* score hits an apex of emptiness. It's not a question of the quality of each individual song. It's simply that they're irrelevant, making no attempt to mirror the enclosing chaos.

As Thousands Cheer is one of the most unified of shows; we already know of its program of headlines. HEAT WAVE HITS NEW YORK introduced a solo for Ethel Waters in "Heat Wave," followed by Weidman's modern dancers developing the notion of the torrid climate originating in a lady from Martinique. THE FUNNIES found Marilyn Miller in a little girl's fluffy frock, arriving on the Toonerville Trolley before a backdrop of comic-strip samples and a chorus in elaborate outfits and masks representing America's Sunday heroes for a song and dance. ROTOGRAVURE SECTION provided the typical Something Special to close Act One, as the lights came up on the entire cast in the black, grey, brown, and tan of ancient visual reproduction. All were frozen for the first few seconds to suggest a photograph: of a Fifth Avenue promenade on Easter Sunday, 1883. Berlin wanted an old song to match the old look, and reached back to his sixteen-year-old "Smile and Show Your Dimple," which he reworked as "Easter Parade." NOEL COWARD, NOTED PLAYWRIGHT, RETURNS TO ENGLAND unveiled a sketch in which the four stars showed how the staff of Coward's hotel has reacted to their exposure to The Master. Maid Marilyn Miller, scrubwoman Ethel Waters, and waiter Clifton Webb toss off epigrams in tight little accents, to the sardonic ripostes of housekeeper Helen Broderick.

Note the use of celebrity in the sparking of a sketch: *As Thousands Cheer* was as filled with imposing names as any big-city newspaper. Remember, the age loved imitations. So FRANKLIN D. ROOSEVELT INAUGURATED TOMORROW found Herbert and Lou Hoover (Leslie Adams, Helen Broderick) on an unhappy moving day, as the soon-to-be-former First Lady attempts to swipe a portrait of George Washington and the President foils her:

HOOVER: You want to be stopped at the train?

. . . . .

MRS. HOOVER. All right, I'll put it back. We'll just go back to Palo Alto with nothing at all to show for your having been President of the United States.

HOOVER: Nobody else in the country has got anything to show for it, either.

Barbara Hutton, Prince Mdivani, Joan Crawford, Douglas Fairbanks Jr., the Rockefellers, Mahatma Gandhi, and Aimee Semple McPherson were some of the other personalities represented on the Music Box stage, the two movie stars by Miller (in the big-shouldered lacy bodice-collar that Crawford favored) and Webb (in the aesthete's neck scarf and overflowing breast-pocket handkerchief). The headline was JOAN CRAWFORD TO DIVORCE DOUGLAS FAIRBANKS, JR: Will Hays (Leslie Adams) referees their dispute over which one gets publicity rights to the divorce, till they learn that they are both cut out entirely—Mary Pickford and the senior Fairbanks are breaking up!

The height of all this look at celebrity was the eleven o'clock number, announced by JOSEPHINE BAKER STILL THE TOAST OF PARIS. The lights came up on Waters, regal in Right Bank couture and mile-long cigarette holder, to sing "Harlem On My Mind": for all her international réclame, Baker misses the neighborhood. Berlin phrased the lament in lazy jazz building to a magnificent image: "the highfalutin' flat that Lady Mendl designed," which adores the *luxe* even while denouncing it.

It is interesting to consider the many "characters" Berlin can slip into, especially because he is thought to have worked spontaneously, tossing off his work. But in his career generally he addresses such diverse identities as those of Fred Astaire and Ethel Merman very precisely. There is no single Berlin voice as there is a Cole Porter voice or an E. Y. Harburg voice, and Berlin's ability to rove among points of view strengthens his revues by giving the audience character content. Such *Hellzapoppin* numbers as "No Wonder" and "G'bye Now" sing of nothing, and, worse, no one can clearly be heard singing them. Even "It's Time To Say 'Aloha,' " which at least implies a setting, is just another song-and-dance spot without point or pertinence. *As Thousands Cheer* and the other great thirties revues, on the other hand, expected theatregoers to be curious and educable.

True, *At Home Abroad* traveled the globe without a reference to Hitler, Mussolini, or Stalin. The show's African scene looked in on The Empress Jones, not Haile Selassie. It was *Hellzapoppin*, in fact, that recognized the world's Situations, in a filmed prologue showing Hitler ranting away in Yiddish and Mussolini mouthing Harlem hi-de-ho.

We need to make a visit through time to *As Thousands Cheer*'s first performances, when at least some of us in the audience are anticipating the newspaper frame but have no idea of the specific contents. The first act is filled entirely with such items as BARBARA HUTTON TO WED PRINCE MDIVANI, in which the Russian playboy (Clifton Webb) steals the Woolworth heiress (Marilyn Miller) from a crowd of beaux in "How's Chances." A surprising melody, it floats for five measures over G^6 till it gets restless and hits a querulous Daug^{7}_{9}. Or WORLD'S WEALTHIEST MAN CELEBRATES 94TH BIRTHDAY presents John D. Rockefeller (Clifton Webb) so outraged at his birthday gift—Radio City—that when they wheel in the cake with a little frosted model of the project on top, Senior goes after Junior (Leslie Adams) with the cake knife. By the time "Easter Parade" has run its course and the curtain fallen on Act One, we are attuned to the guiltless drollery, the diversion, the escape. So when the second headline of Act Two reads as UNKNOWN NEGRO LYNCHED BY FRENZIED MOB, what are we to think? This is surely no jest, and as the lights come up on Ethel Waters in rags, setting the table for dinner and launching the refrain of "Supper Time," we realize that she is the widow of the man in the headline, and she is wondering what to tell the children.

Curious and educable: this was the New Revue's public, and it explains why all of them, even *The Band Wagon*, ran approximately between 200 and 250 performances—a good but limited showing—while *Hellzapoppin* broke the record. *As Thousands Cheer*, one of the decade's biggest hits, lasted 400 performances. Then it vanished, as revues do, till the Drama Department mounted a very small version in 1998, with a cast of eight headed by Howard McGillin, Judy Kuhn, Paula Newsome, Mary Beth Peil, and B. D. Wong. Played in a single act, the production dropped some of the original spots (including the prohibitively grand "Easter Parade"), interpolated a song from *Face the Music*, and changed the content of the scenes. One hardly expected the original two dozen or so comic-strip figures in "The Funnies." Instead, Wong appeared alone with the Sunday comics section. But even the Barbara Hutton segment lost Prince Mdivani, presumably because his name means nothing today. Rather, Hutton's chauffeur (Kevin Chamberlin) sang "How's Chances" as a pathetic interior monologue while the flashy McGillin and Wong paid court to Kuhn.

Of course, in small quarters, this wonderful bite of Big Broadway could not possibly seem like anything more than a straw-hat revue with unusually good writing. It skews the historical perspective, because *As Thousands Cheer* was not a call to the mainstream from the powerless munchkins of off-Broadway, but rather the address of mainstream theatregoers by mainstream cultural archons. Berlin and Harris were millionaires or the next thing to it; Moss Hart could write anything he liked and see it performed. As we're about to learn, the most pungent sociopolitical statements of the 1930s were made not by the people who ran Broadway but by idealists and fanatics of independent theatre collectives, Little Broadway. And yet the important breakthroughs in the readjusting of America's sense of humanist fairness tended to arrive in such forms as UNKNOWN NEGRO LYNCHED BY FRENZIED MOB.

"I tremble to think of the fate that would await [the cast and authors of *As Thousands Cheer*]," wrote John Mason Brown, "if they had ventured to win laughs of the kind they won so freely Saturday night while living in the shadow of the Kremlin, in Mussolini's Italy, in Hitler's Germany, in Dollfuss' Austria, or even in the liberal England of George and Mary." Indeed, the latter two also were spoofed in the show, though it seems absurd to put England in company with totalitarian regimes. Noting that *As Thousands Cheer*'s jesting was "as daring as it is convulsing," Brown concluded that "America is still the land of the free . . . and . . . the Music Box continues to be the home of the brave."

Too self-congratulatory? Put another way, this is how democracy works: a free theatre promotes the notion of a free populace. The stage speaks for us, and to us, and of us.

7

A Song with Social Significance: Politics

Finally, the part of the 1930s that you thought *was* the 1930s: it starts in 1927, when the Gershwins' *Strike Up the Band* closes in its Philadelphia tryout and then, in revision, triumphs on Broadway in 1930.* One odd feature of this satire on war profiteering is a constant use of the finaletto, the through-sung ensemble scene in which plot development is carried through one little musical structure after another. Twenties musical comedy and operetta alike used the finaletto, musical comedy only to close the first act (and a second, if there were three) and operetta also to end important scenes within an act. However, the standard finaletto tried as much as possible to stay "realistic" within the ultra-musical form, while *Strike Up the Band* deliberately cartooned its finalettos, using the chorus in a goofy Gilbert and Sullivan style and gaming with the principals' interjections to emphasize the very fantasy of singing a narrative. Of course, *Strike Up the Band* is a fantasy itself—but that is irrelevant to the Gershwins' work because these same finalettos were in the 1927 version, which was not a fantasy.

George S. Kaufman wrote the original *Strike Up the Band* libretto and Morrie Ryskind made the revision; now the two collaborated with George and Ira on *Of Thee I Sing* (1931), a lampoon of party politics, viewed through a presidential election. Unlike *Strike Up the Band*, this show is very nearly plausible. Yet it uses those zesty finalettos in exactly the same way. It shouldn't work; the joke is unique, surely unrepeatable. Yet

* A full discussion of this work may be found on pages 200–204 of the first volume in this series.

at 441 performances *Of Thee I Sing* was the 1930s' longest-running book show; and the first musical to win the Pulitzer Prize. That is to say, this was the moment when the culture took notice of the musical as possibly being more than a piffle by its very nature.

This particular piffle's driveline is that election, as the show's protagonist, candidate John P. Wintergreen (William Gaxton), of an unnamed party, will if elected marry a sort of First Lady contest winner, Mary Turner (Lois Moran). In the event, Diana Devereaux (*Flying High*'s heroine, Grace Brinkley) wins the contest, by sleeping with the judges. But Wintergreen's running on a platform of love: and John loves Mary.

So the election, Wintergreen's inauguration/wedding, his impeachment, and his salvation by Mary, who announces that she's pregnant, supply the plot. One quick remark—"This country has never yet impeached an expectant father"—terminates the intrigue. Supplementary throughlines include the traditional disregard for the Vice-President (Victor Moore as Alexander Throttlebottom); the machinations of Devereaux, which eventually involve diplomatic rumblings from France (though a southern girl, Devereaux derives illegitimately from the house of Bonaparte); and, above all, the casual cynicism and rampant ignorance of the party bigwigs, such as newspaper magnate Matthew Arnold Fulton (Dudley Clements):

> FULTON: That's what we need—an issue. Something that everybody is interested in, and that doesn't matter a damn. Something the party can stand on.
> THROTTLEBOTTOM: Excuse me, gentlemen, but what party are we?
> FULTON: We've got plenty of time for that. The important thing is to get elected.

Of Thee I Sing's dialogue teems with the sound of politicians lying, posturing, conniving. The characters other than John, Mary, and perhaps Throttlebottom are caricatures, yet Kaufman and Ryskind are biting on a truth all the same. The show haunts us with its honesty even as it invents flapdoodle about the excellence of Mary's corn muffins or Diana Devereaux's bloodline.

Then, too, the William Gaxton con-man figure shows a genuine soft side in this incarnation. He'll cheat on anything *except love,* which gives the work something more to consider than satire. George S. Kaufman, who also directed, was apparently not comfortable with overt romance in the theatre, and *Strike Up the Band* was his ideal musical: a profane commentary on the evil of men, with the love stuff left to silly juveniles and ingenues that serve as contrivances rather than as people. They aren't in love. They're chirping and hoofing.

Of Thee I Sing doesn't have *Strike Up the Band*'s Jim and Joan, and Timothy and Anne. The couple who might have played such parts, George Murphy and June O'Dea, appeared in *Of Thee I Sing* as White House staffers, without a love plot. They lead the ensemble in "Love Is Sweeping the Country," the charm song as electioneering rhetoric.

But the John and Mary story is one of the more flavorful Boy Meets Girls of its day. We see the Meeting, over one of her corn muffins; we see him Get Girl. And note that, most unusually, he never Loses her. The alliance is not threatened even when his presidency is, and he gets a reprise of their duet, "Who Cares?," with a keening solo violin obbligato to keep the emotional content at the forefront.

In fact, despite the intricate vitality of the ensemble scenes, the music for John and Mary holds its place in the score, mainly because George and Ira figured out how a musical-comedy character should sound if he's not only the Boy but also the President of the United States. Certainly, nothing that Rodgers and Hart or Cole Porter wrote for William Gaxton in *A Connecticut Yankee* or *Fifty Million Frenchmen* suggests the slightly anthem-like authority of the title song. It's musical-comedy gravitas. Victor Moore had only a few scattered vocal lines and a notable business in "Posterity Is Just Around the Corner" when he laid hold of a big bass drum and led a march around the stage while pounding it. Diana Devereaux and the French Ambassador also have solos, and there's that secondary couple's "Love Is Sweeping the Country," with its curious patter section of bitty staccato eighth-note phrases and augmented (i.e., "Oriental") chords on "are taking up the Cabots."*

---

* Now It Can Be Told: the patter section ("Spring is in the air . . .") was originally composed for *Ming Toy*, a projected Ziegfeld musical based on *East Is West*, the 1918 smash about an interracial romance seen against a background of underworld crime in San Francisco. Ziegfeld abandoned the property, leaving the Gershwins to reassign its numbers. "Embraceable You" went into *Girl Crazy* and "Lady of the Moon" (as "Blah, Blah, Blah") into the film *Delicious*. Neither song sounds Asian, but the patter section referred to above suggests mandarins gadding about in a crowd scene. Its *Of Thee I Sing* lyrics tell

Even so, the bulk of *Of Thee I Sing*'s score lies in the ensembles. The first of them, "Wintergreen For President," is one of the strangest opening choruses ever: because it isn't a chorus. The orchestra sings the tunes, while the performers carry campaign signs, vocalize wordlessly, and actually utter only the song's title line and one couplet. A very long book scene follows, of pure political humor, and then comes the first genuine musical scene, for the beauty-contest girls and reporters on the Atlantic City boardwalk. It's really just two songs pushed together: the women's "Who Is the Lucky Girl To Be?," which consists of two parts sung one after the other and then simultaneously, whereupon the gentlemen of the press enter, conversing with the contestants in song till the guys reach *their* number, "Because, Because." A dance tops off the scene.

It's all very tuneful and sharp, but nothing that couldn't have turned up in many another tuneful and sharp show. Two book scenes—also long—follow, and *then* the Gershwins exploit the finaletto construct, in a great deal of plot action told entirely in song and underscored dialogue. So while the script goes for considerable stretches without music, the music can simply take over the show, almost entirely in vocal terms, for there is little dancing as such. Only five song titles could be extracted at the time for individual publication, but in that same year, 1931, Kern's *The Cat and the Fiddle*, Arthur Schwartz's *The Band Wagon*, and Harold Arlen's *You Said It* each threw off eight song sheets, the Henderson-Brown *Scandals* nine, and *Here Goes the Bride* no fewer than twelve.

Only five selections out of such a melodious evening! This tells us how integrated this score is—not into the play, but into itself. The closest thing to a verse-chorus song in more or less AABA format is the title number.* What George mostly composed in this work is a series of daffy stunts aligned with the daffy tone of the script, slipping in such academic

---

of a new peace between previous antagonists—which, ironically, is what *East Is West* pleads for, in racial terms. People are people, thus "West is East, and East is West." Best of all the *Ming Toy* numbers is "In the Mandarin's Orchid Garden," probably the closest thing to an "art song" that Gershwin ever wrote.

* This is often referred to as "Of Thee I Sing, Baby," but the first four words alone form the title. The verse is elaborate, thirteen repeated notes followed by four ascending four-note cells in E Flat Major, followed by the same thing in G Major. Ira's contribution is a lyric made of stump-speech clichés. Ironically, the verse was not used in the original production and, though published, has not to my knowledge ever been recorded.

hat tricks as a rising and falling whole-tone scale for the arrival of the Supreme Court judges, or the dainty escapade of choral counterpoint to Wintergreen's wedding solo, "A Kiss For Cinderella," or simply the quotation of *An American in Paris* to signal the entrance of the French Ambassador.

When *Of Thee I Sing*'s vocal score appeared, in 1932, it called the show "the Pulitzer Prize operetta." Indeed, it has the loaded musicality of Romberg and Friml. Still, its tone is so musical comedy that no one ever thinks of the piece as being anything else. While the original company held forth at the Music Box, the national tour set out, with Oscar Shaw, Donald Meek, Harriette "Maisie" Lake, and Betty Allen, who all extended the show's New York run with a month's visit in the spring of 1933. Later that year, *Of Thee I Sing*'s producer, its four authors, its director, and most of its original principals including Gaxton, Moore, and Lois Moran broke a cardinal rule of the musical-comedy handbook and put on a sequel, *Let 'Em Eat Cake*.

Actually, it is only such recent debacles as *Bring Back Birdie* and *Annie 2* that prove how impossible it is to retrieve a lost innocence. The First Age teemed not with sequels per se but with extensive series originating in such titles as *Humpty Dumpty* (1868), *Fritz, Our Cousin German* (1870), *The Mulligan Guards Picnic* (1878), and *The Rogers Brothers in Wall Street* (1899). Obviously, this was an antique usage. Still, producer Oliver Morosco ran a successful series starting with *Pretty Mrs. Smith* (1914), based around Charlotte Greenwood's Letty character; the line ran into the 1920s.

So the notion of a continuation of *Of Thee I Sing* wasn't preposterous. It seems that Wintergreen lost his re-election, led a revolution of "blue shirts," ran the country as a dictatorship, and demanded that the nations of Europe—not just Finland—repay their war debt to the U.S. The idea must have seemed very potential, with views of the somnolent right in the snoring chorus "The Union League" at that venerable men's club and of the hysterical left in the pleasant "Union Square." There, a new lead character named Kruger (Philip Loeb) leads a contentious middle section, "Down With Everything That's Up!"

Unfortunately, where *Of Thee I Sing* had a solid storyline, silly in nature but logically developed, *Let 'Em Eat Cake* had an even sillier storyline ineptly developed: the problem with the League of Nations is to be settled by a baseball game, with both sides demanding protection of the umpire, the perenially hapless Throttlebottom. He is nearly executed for calling a ball foul—he actually gets as far as putting his head into the crook of the guillotine before being rescued by *Of Thee I Sing*'s dea ex machina, Mary Wintergreen. She even uses the same music as before.

There are a number of musical reprises of the first show in the second. They are not clever "attachments" or puns or inside jokes. They are simply reprises, and this is never a sign of health. Moreover, the irruption into the narrative of the League of Nations is very reminiscent of the French Ambassador's irruption into *Of Thee I Sing*. Then, too, while the Gershwins at least did some excellent work, the score is in their spooferetta style, and surely three times is once too many. Victor Moore enjoyed a lovely solo in the reassuringly gentle "Comes the Revolution," and Gaxton brought down the first-act curtain with the title song, a real rouser that leaps between $\frac{4}{4}$ and $\frac{6}{8}$ as if trying to get two anthems out of one. But the show's one lasting title, "Mine," a quodlibet, is rather monotonous in both its strains, and the show failed to please critics or public and lasted 90 performances.

Of Thee I Sing was too famous to disappear. Victor Moore was to have repeated his Throttlebottom with Kaufman again directing and, not that it matters, the original French Ambassador, Florenz Ames, in 1952. Moore decided against it, so Paul Hartman stepped in, in company with Jack Carson, Betty Oakes, and Lenore Lonergan. The cast album preserves both a wonderful performance and a text much less emended than would be the case today. "Mine" was slotted in for the Wintergreens, Lonergan played in a comically cracked voice and sang in lower keys than Grace Brinkley had done, many lyrics were updated or simply changed for the usual mysterious reasons, and the chorus sang in the insistently high range then expected of a Broadway ensemble. But the original show was what the 1952 public saw, in its essence and details—even, though somewhat revised, the violin descant in the reprise of "Who Cares?"

Perhaps it was too soon for a revival, for it failed. Still, the work insistently came back—even on television, in the election year of 1972 in a garish staging with Carroll O'Connor, Jack Gilford, Cloris Leachman, Michele Lee, and "Mine" again. A 1987 concert at the Brooklyn Academy of Music under Michael Tilson Thomas brought back both shows in faithful reconstruction underwritten by Ira Gershwin's widow. *Of Thee I Sing*'s orchestrations, by Robert Russell Bennett, William Daly, and George himself, were available for reinstitution; *Let 'Em Eat Cake*'s had utterly evaporated and were replaced by Russell Warner.

Larry Kert, Jack Gilford once more, Maureen McGovern, and Paige O'Hara led the cast. To pick one example of how the years fell away, it was startling to hear O'Hara not only returning Diana Devereaux to her intended soprano range but singing her high solo line over the rest of the cast in the "corn muffin" ensemble. Freed in this concert rendering of its stupid libretto, *Let 'Em Eat Cake* came off surprisingly well, with a cut number, "First Lady and First Gent" (for Kruger and another new principal, the opportunistic Trixie) reclaimed from oblivion.

A gala occasion. But it must be said that of these three Gershwin–Kaufman–Ryskind political musicals, the only one that is really dangerous in its political observation is the *fourth* title in this group, the original 1927 *Strike Up the Band*. Kaufman's tone was not emasculated in 1930, as is sometimes said; but the emphasis was shifted from satire to star-comic fun. Even revolution, in *Let 'Em Eat Cake*, is a musical-comedy whirl; and Throttlebottom's scene at the guillotine is played for shtick. He clasps his hands above his head in the boxer's gesture, repositions the basket to avoid taking a bump, gives Trixie some coupons he's been saving, and finally says to Kruger, "Would you mind telling my newsdealer not to send any more papers?"

It was almost a rule that only extraordinary shows wanted political content; standard musical comedy did not change its tune. But here's the exception: *Free For All* (1931). This two-week flop with a score by Richard Whiting and Oscar Hammerstein and a book by Hammerstein and co-producer Laurence Schwab was determined to satirize. Psychoanalysis and "free love" were two of the targets; communism was the third. Or, really, less the leftist fascism of Stalinism or other models and more the back-to-nature ideal of the vegetarian commune.

In outline, the plot suggests a twist on the previous year's *Girl Crazy*, in which a New York millionaire's playboy son is sent west to become a man. *Free For All* found a California millionaire's playboy son (Jack Haley) sent to Nevada to learn copper mining. He gets distracted by new ideas in the appropriately named New Leaf Corners. The romances involved the usual two couples, with Haley and Vera Marsh as the main duo and a radical poet (Peter Higgins) and a Russian girl (the ever-confusing Tamara) as the cutups.

Innovative in a number of ways, *Free For All* consisted of twenty-eight roles and no chorus whatsoever, rather like *May Wine*. "There were evidences," said Percy Hammond, who tended to mistrust the unconventional, "that musical comedies are more enjoyable with chorus girls than without." But George Jean Nathan thought it "a pleasant relief to be rid of the routine ensemble dancing numbers, with their . . . concluding ejaculations of *hooray*."

There was certainly none of that in *Die Dreigroschenoper*, or *The 3-Penny Opera*, as it was spelled when first done here, in 1933. This title brings us to the handful of works of strong political purpose, all put on by forces outside the Broadway mainstream. Thus, of four stage works composed by Kurt Weill and seen here in the 1930s, *Johnny Johnson* (1936) was mounted by the Group Theatre; *The Eternal Road* (1937) was the project of a religious visionary not generally associated with the theatre; and *Knickerbocker Holiday* (1938) was produced by the Playwrights Company, a group of admittedly mainstream playwrights who had banded together in order to liberate their artistry—that is, to defy commercialism when they needed to.

So, typically, *The 3-Penny Opera* was presented by the Krimsky Brothers, John and Jerrold, Broadway freelancers specializing in oddities; their other notable credit comprises a trio of campy melodramas with songs in which the public was urged to hiss the villain and cheer the hero. *Naughty Naught '00* (1937), *The Fireman's Flame* (1937), and *The Girl From Wyoming* (1938) were all so unlike what "Broadway musical" means that they holed up in the American Music Hall, the contemporary name for the old Majestic Theatre on Columbus Circle.

The 3-Penny Opera was staged down in plain sight at the Empire, where Maude Adams had enchanted a generation with her Peter Pan. Ellen Terry played Shaw on this stage, and Ethel Barrymore Camille. Jane Cowl gave Noël Coward, Katharine Cornell an adaptation of Edith Wharton's *The Age of Innocence*.

The critics were not happy with their successors Robert Chisholm (as Macheath), Steffi Duna (Polly), Rex Weber (Mr. Peachum; remember, Weber introduced "Brother, Can You Spare a Dime?"), Evelyn Beresford (Mrs. Peachum), and Rex Evans (Tiger Brown). Though director Francesco von Mendelssohn was apparently striving for an authentic reproduction of the style of the 1928 Berlin original—at that, in sets after

Caspar Neher's designs for the premiere—the reviewers almost to a man received the piece with hostility. Bertolt Brecht got the worst of it, for it was the script (and the staging) that really galled them. Their blurbs were ready: "sugar-coated communism," "a rather collossal bore," "a dreary enigma."

They were surely unprepared for Weill-Brecht; the now famous G.W. Pabst *Threepenny* film had been screened here only privately. Indeed, some of the critics alluded to the Nigel Playfair version of the matrix of the Weill-Brecht show, John Gay's *The Beggar's Opera*. Playfair's stylish masque, seen here but five years previously, would have been a fitting followup to your Maude Adams, your Ellen Terry. But the Playfair, in the musical arrangements of Frederic Austin, is a dainty do of harpsichord and viola d'amore. Shall you take your beauty spot quite *there*, m'lud? The Weill-Brecht *Beggar's Opera* really has beggars in it, and they're the least of your problems. The blistering notices threw the actors out of the Empire in 12 performances.*

It was a bad break for Weill, who hadn't yet left Europe and was hoping for a hit with which to launch his coming career as an American composer. What brought him over was a commission for a work so peculiar it may not belong in this book. *Johnny Johnson* and *Knickerbocker Holiday* certainly do, as the only two titles that Weill actually wrote for Broadway in the 1930s; we'll discuss each separately later on. For now, then, after the importation of *Die Dreigroschenoper*, there remains of Weill in this decade only this strange assignment tendered by the Jewish activist Meyer Weisgal, to come to the U.S. to create something unique with director Max Reinhardt, writer Franz Werfel, and designer Norman Bel Geddes: an epic look at the early history of the Jewish people.

This was *Der Weg der Verheissung* (roughly, *The Way of God's Promise*), or *The Eternal Road*, which was not written for Broadway. Indeed, it's hard to imagine what venue Weisgal had had in mind, even in this age of spectacles at the Center Theatre and of Billy Rose's reclamation of the Hippodrome for *Jumbo*. *The Eternal Road* might have been right for

---

* In the light of Brooks Atkinson's intense admiration for and support of the 1954 *Threepenny Opera* off-Broadway at the Theatre de Lys, some readers may be wondering how Atkinson reacted to the piece in 1933. He didn't cover it. Lewis Nichols wrote it up for the *Times*, and Nichols gave the work its best review. "A splendid score," he said.

the old Century Theatre on Central Park West, the one built as the New to house a repertory company that gave up after two seasons. It was at the Century that Reinhardt and Bel Geddes had already presented something unique, *The Miracle* (1924), a religious pageant with music by Engelbert Humperdinck, seen in London in 1911. But the Century had been demolished in 1930, and *The Eternal Road* ended up at the Manhattan Opera House, built by Oscar Hammerstein I to compete with the Metropolitan.

Hammerstein's theatre's interior looked very much like that of the Old Met, a palace of music in red and gold. For *The Miracle*, Bel Geddes had transformed the entire Century into a Gothic cathedral; this time, the designer worked on only the stage and orchestra pit, though reconstruction of the building's interior led to expensive postponements. Evicted from their workplace, the instrumentalists simply laid down tracks on the best recording equipment available at the time, supplemented by a union-minimum band of sixteen playing in a room backstage, their material transmitted to the audience through electronic amplification.

The Miracle, however huge in scale, had told the relatively simple tale of a nun who abandons her obligations to visit the Great World, only to learn when she returns that, to save her life, a statue of the Madonna has come to life and taken over the nun's duties during her absence. *The Eternal Road*, by contrast, was anything but simple—Abraham and Isaac, Jacob, Joseph, Moses and Aaron and the Golden Calf, Ruth and Naomi, David and Jonathan, King Solomon . . . just about everyone but Ofelia and Pimento. Among the cast of about 250 were Lotte Lenya, Kurt Kasznar, Sam Jaffe, little Dickie Van Patten as Isaac, Katherine Carrington of *Face the Music* and *Music in the Air*, and even Rosamond Pinchot, who had played the nun in *The Miracle*, as Bath-sheba.

Amazingly, considering the limited appeal of the subject matter and the high running costs, *The Eternal Road* lasted 153 performances, despite a score that is difficult to love. Weill veers from liturgical recit to pure classical to his own "Weimar democracy resistance" style without once getting into those devilishly irresistible *Jazzkultur* hit tunes. There's no "September Song" in *The Eternal Road*. We find interesting string textures in the "Song of Miriam," a powerful percussive presence in the "Dance of the Golden Calf," the typical Weillian "feeling" of two woodwinds over

strings in the "Song of Ruth." Nothing that Weill wrote is without interest and presence. But this is the weakest of his American theatre scores.

Some might consider *The Eternal Road* as purely religious in nature, not
political. But it was intended as a response to Hitler's war on European
Jewry, and is thus an act of anti-fascist defiance. Its very opposite would
be an act of pro-democracy burlesque, with a basic unit set, a smallish
cast, an orchestra in the pit where orchestras belong, and a book that
unlike *The Eternal Road*'s didn't have to be translated from Franz Werfel's
German by Ludwig Lewisohn and *then* adapted into scriptese by William A.
Drake (who had done as much for *Grand Hotel*, by the way). In fact, this
other show has a book by Kaufman and Hart, a score by Rodgers and
Hart, and George M. Cohan headlining the posters: *I'd Rather Be Right*
(1937).

This returns us to Big Broadway, with one of the most intense opening-
night experiences of the decade. Oddly, the show was billed as "a musical
revue." True, the narrative is episodic. But it has a book: in Central Park,
a young couple (Austin Marshall, Joy Hodges) who can't afford to marry
meet Franklin Delano Roosevelt (Cohan) and try to persuade him to
repair the broken economy (so the Boy can get a raise) by balancing the
federal budget. Roosevelt's attempts to do so create the show's action, as
he considers levying new taxes (the Supreme Court, all made up as Chief
Justice Charles Evans Hughes, pop out from behind the scenery to forbid
it), to get American women to renounce beauty products and contribute
the money thus saved to the Treasury (American women refuse to do so),
to use the gold in Fort Knox (the stock market crashes), and so on. Other
"acts" in this "revue" comprise the arrival of various interlopers, including Roosevelt's mother with her butler, Alfred M. Landon. The former
governor of Kansas, Landon ran for president on the Republican ticket in
1936, winning 8 electoral votes to Roosevelt's 523. But Landon had balanced *his* budget back in Kansas, and Roosevelt asks for the secret. "Not
a chance!" cries Landon:

> LANDON: It's true I didn't photograph well, nor did I have that smile.
> And I will frankly admit that I was lousy on the radio. But,
> Mr. Roosevelt, I balanced my budget! So, as we say in Kansas,
> Mr. Roosevelt—try that on your ukulele!

At another point, a theatre director and a chorus line appear to announce that they're Unit Number 864 of the Federal Theatre and perform a $675,000 production number called "Spring in Vienna."*

Kaufman and Hart separately accounted for four of the decade's major political shows—*Strike Up the Band, Of Thee I Sing* and its sequel, and *Face the Music. I'd Rather Be Right* was the most overtly political of all—as 1938 saw it—because of the then unprecedented stunt of starring a sitting president in a musical. In fact, John Leacock's play *The Fall of British Tyranny*, performed during George Washington's presidency, included Washington as a character, and, more contemporaneously, revue sketches had put Woodrow Wilson and Calvin Coolidge onstage during their administrations and (in *As Thousands Cheer*, as we know) Herbert Hoover after F.D.R. had defeated him.

But *I'd Rather Be Right* promised to invest enough stage time in Roosevelt as a character to risk offense. In fact, the show's dynamic is celebration. It is a spoof of the New Deal, no question—but a loving one, and more inclined to blame the president's deputies for the country's problems than to blame the president's policies. This show worships the concept of one of the great song-and-dance men who ever lived impersonating one of our greatest presidents, which is why the production was such big news from the day it was announced, why that opening night was so crowded with anticipation, and why *I'd Rather Be Right* ran 290 performances, the decade's eleventh-longest tally for a book show.

A passionate man, seldom if ever neutral about anyone, Cohan hated Roosevelt. Thus, he in effect found himself making love to his worst enemy. Then why play the role? It was too juicy to pass up: a musical-comedy tour de force for the man who—in many opinions beside his own—*was* musical comedy. No doubt, as Cohan saw it, he wasn't playing Roosevelt. He was President George M. Cohan.

---

* The Federal Theatre (1935–39) was part of a government project to subsidize the arts in vast employment programs. The writing and fine arts communities were also supported, but thespians were the most visible beneficiaries of relief, so while most of the Federal Theatre was classic repertory, old melodrama, and the children's matinee, some of the new work aroused controversy. We'll meet up with real-life Federal Theatre projects a few pages hence. Trivia buffs long to know what *I'd Rather Be Right* did with "Spring in Vienna" when, during the show's run, Hitler annexed Austria: the title was changed to "Spring in Milwaukee." This necessitated a lyric change, for Hart had rhymed "when a" with "Vienna." The new lines are apparently lost.

The star had nothing but contempt for Rodgers and Hart as well. When all three had worked on the film *The Phantom President*, at Paramount in 1932, Cohan had been rough on the team. Now he simply ignored them. Astonishingly for a performer who was also a writer, Cohan interpolated into his eleven o'clock song, "Off the Record," lyrics of his own concoction that assaulted the president. Luckily, this was during the Boston tryout; the offending lines were expunged. But the incident made the papers, because a backstage squabble at *I'd Rather Be Right* was headline dish.

"Gilbert and Sullivan" was Cohan's sneering nickname for the songwriters, behind their backs. Was it because Cohan had seen his own writing style replaced by Rodgers and Hart's generation? How did Cohan feel about Cole Porter and the Gershwins? The last Cohan musical, *Billie*, had appeared but nine years earlier. However, nine years was a long time in the show biz that Cohan was raised in, when there was nothing on the air and only mobs went to movies. Cohan had continued to write, but he would never see another Cohan musical staged. And this was The Man Who Owns Broadway, as his show of 1909 attests. *1909?*

At least, Cohan the performer hadn't lost it. But maybe Rodgers and Hart had, temporarily. *I'd Rather Be Right* is not a terrible score; it threw off a standard, "Have You Met Miss Jones?" But only three other titles were published commercially at the time. The problem is that most of the numbers are assigned to supporting characters or the ensemble, so there is little character content. What we get instead are "A Homogeneous Cabinet" for the introduction of the Secretaries themselves, the W.P.A. workers' chorus, "Labor Is the Thing," the chorus of Supreme Court Justices and their girl friends, "A Little Bit of Constitutional Fun," and a ballad for the Secretary of the Treasury (Taylor Holmes), "A Baby Bond For Baby." Any of these—or "Spring in Milwaukee," for that matter—could be deleted without affecting the action in the least. And while that typifies the early thirties musical, it is rare by 1938 and is also not typical of Rodgers and Hart. Their identifying specialty is something more like "Dear Old Syracuse": a song that is there because the character is there.

I'd Rather Be Right has very little of such writing—in fact, just the two Cohan numbers, really more about Cohan than about F.D.R.: the first-act finale, "We're Going To Balance the Budget," and the aforementioned patter song, "Off the Record." The show almost doesn't even have a Boy

Meets Girl—not because the two already know each other, but because they are an excuse to get Cohan onstage and don't really have anything to express in music. "Sweet Sixty-Five" and "I'd Rather Be Right," duets (at first; both numbers took on extra personnel after the vocal) for Boy and Girl, are anybody's songs.

Indeed, that title number really should go to Roosevelt, because it quotes a politician: Henry Clay, Speaker of the House of Representatives in the early-middle nineteenth century, known as "the great pacificator" for his role in historic compromises, and three times an unsuccessful presidential condidate. And in fact Cohan got into the title number; how could he not have? Remember, besides making a gala return to song and dance looking very, very much like F.D.R.—a strategic part of the fun—and making his first appearance in a musical entirely written by others,* Cohan was playing one of the greatest star parts ever constructed. By rules of the day, nothing interesting could be allowed to occur onstage that didn't involve Cohan.

As it happened, the one number that truly belonged in the story, "Everybody Loves You (when you're asleep)," was cut. This was the Girl's love song to the Boy at the start of the second act, when the curtain rises on the pair, alone. The song was to have been her one solo, and, more important, it reinstates after intermission the show's trick: it's all a dream. This couple hasn't run into Franklin Delano Roosevelt in Central Park. That can't happen, even in musicals. This show isn't Boy Meets Girl. It's Boy Meets President and Asks Him To Balance the Budget. So, as we return for the second act, the show needs to reactivate the dream frame, and the second-act curtain rises on Boy Asleep. Thus her ballad, a sort of unnecessary lullaby.

The dream created a wonderful star entrance, all but essential in that age, especially for someone as touchy about his relationship with his public as Cohan was. The curtain rose on that view of the park at dusk that is all we will see for the entire evening: a moss-covered bridge at stage left, fancifully long-stemmed trees like cocktail umbrellas, and a midtown skyline of office buildings with the lights on. Once again, there is no opening number, just the music of a band concert from somewhere

---

* Cohan very briefly appeared in *The Royal Vagabond* (1919) as a scab during the first actors' strike. This show *had* been written by others, but became considerably "Cohanized" during production; and Cohan shared in the byline.

offstage, as passersby, a sanitation worker, and a cop start the script off with those chance bits that accustom us to listening and being curious about the world beyond ourselves. Others come on: two millionaires complaining about taxes, two girls, a balloon seller, an ice-cream man, two sailors:

FIRST SAILOR: I joined the Navy and my brother went into business. So what's the answer? We're *both* working for the government.

SECOND SAILOR: Okay, but how about them two dames over there?

FIRST SAILOR: All you think of is dames, you dumb cluck! (One beat) Where are they?

Next comes a young couple. It's *our* couple, Phil and Peggy. After a little exposition:

PHIL: We can't get married until they balance the budget.

He puts his head in her lap and dozes off. She strokes his hair. The show comes to a complete halt. Then George M. Cohan walks onstage in his frock coat, striped pants, and F.D.R. glasses. And the audience goes crazy.

I'd Rather be Right was the other political musical comedy that enjoyed tremendous success, though unlike *Of Thee I Sing* it did not hang on in revival. The Gershwin show has a much more brilliant score, of course, but its survival strength lies in its timeless jests about party politics. *I'd Rather Be Right* was timely, specifically referring to people and events of Roosevelt's administration—the cabinet, for instance, has vastly more to do here than in *Annie* (1977), at that in its full strength. And here's a joke that will bewilder an audience today, when the President treats Phil and Peggy to a snack from the vendor's cart:

ROOSEVELT: You know, this is the way I like to eat ice cream. At the White House, we always have to have Garner with it.*

---

* The Vice-President of Roosevelt's first two terms was John Nance Garner. Yes, *Annie Warbucks* dared a Garner joke, too: to silence in the house.

The two most overtly political book shows of the decade are very different in nature despite sharing major qualities. Each is a musical play rather than a musical comedy or operetta, cast with actors rather than singers, and lacking any choreography to speak of: Kurt Weill's *Johnny Johnson* (1936) and Marc Blitzstein's *The Cradle Will Rock* (1937). The former, though a famous title, has never established itself in revival even as a succès d'estime. The second is constantly brought back, and it has its partisans. There is this as well: *Johnny Johnson* suffered a first public performance so disastrous that one of its producers claimed the audience started leaving after "the first five minutes," and that curtain calls were taken before "no more than fifty people." *The Cradle Will Rock*'s first public performance could be called even more disastrous, because it began when its producer padlocked the theatre to keep anyone from seeing it.

Johnny Johnson came about because: one, Kurt Weill had finally come to America; two, some thespians of progressive taste owned the *Dreigroschenoper* 78s of the Berlin cast and the music thus got around; three, the Group Theatre wanted to do a musical play of that sort; four, Weill suggested an American version of a classic piece of satire on World War I, Jaroslav Hašek's novel called *The Good Soldier Svejk*. A stage adaptation had enjoyed a vogue in Berlin in the same year as *The Threepenny Opera*, 1928, with Max Pallenberg as the anti-hero, directed by Erwin Piscator and designed by Georg Grosz. And, five, Group favorite Paul Green announced—probably to everyone's surprise—that he had served in the war and thus knew military life. Green was a playwright, not a librettist or lyricist, but that was the sort of collaborator that Weill was used to from his work in Germany.

Svejk is the despair of the army, a soldier who somehow manages to do everything wrong while never actually disobeying. Green thought he could turn this character into something less ironic and European, more idealistic and American. Green's anti-hero might indeed be more hero than the heroes, an essentially simple man who is greatly radicalized by the hypocrisy and waste of the Great War into someone too sensible and noble to take a meaningful place in society. A madman: a toymaker: a pacifist.

The Group was the only successful leftist theatrical entity of the time and, in the long run, the most influential American theatre entity, period: in its naturalization of acting style. However, these adherents of Stanislafsky and Clifford Odets were not truly ready—however game—for a musical, even one as anti-handbook as *Johnny Johnson*. Moreover, the show's director was Lee Strasberg, a guru of thespian preparation and execution, but entirely lacking in musicality and show-shop smarts. If there really were so many walkouts at the first preview (the Group could not afford the expense of out-of-town tryouts), it must be because of the company's tentative vocal delivery. They had rehearsed in the Belmont, a 500-seat theatre at Forty-eighth and Sixth, but could find no booking for the actual run except the Forty-Fourth Street Theatre, a grim old barn seating three times the Belmont's capacity and ideal for *Maytime*, not a musical play nuanced in character, genre, and musical quotient.

For what Weill and Green put together was a kind of delicate epic, another of those uncategorizable works that Weill made most of his career on. For one thing, the score was as much underscoring as vocal, and the songs—as, later, in Rodgers and Hammerstein's *Allegro*—were distributed among the principals and support so that almost nobody got more than one number. For another thing, Green deliberately wrote the play's many scenes in different styles. One has the air of a vaudeville sketch, another the feeling of melodrama, and so on. It's easy for actors to emphasize the amusing antagonism of approach, but difficult for the director to maintain unity. The set designer could be useful here, but Donald Oenslager's complex constructions apparently made the performers feel dwarfed.

The critics liked Oenslager's work, feeling that he had matched the fantastical nature of Green's tale. After starting in everyday naturalism, Green reaches the impossible, when his protagonist sneaks into a meeting of the Allied High Command in his hospital pyjamas to "pacify" them with laughing gas in an attempt to stop the war. Indeed, Group Theatre memoirists make a point of praising the way that Oenslager realized certain of Green's requests for a special effect—the appearance of the Statue of Liberty at the end of the first and second acts, to simulate the view from Johnny's transport as he sails for Europe and then returns; the huge cannon barrels that slid out over the heads of dozing soldiers to intone (through the offstage men's chorus) the disturbingly elegiacal "Song of the Guns."

Only Arthur Pollock of the Brooklyn *Daily Eagle* gave *Johnny Johnson* a rave, though Brooks Atkinson recommended it on the basis of its admirable intentions. But the performance ultimately hurt the piece. All the reviews noted that too many in the huge cast simply could not put over their music, and there was high praise only for Russell Collins' Johnny and, especially, Morris Carnovsky in a one-scene role as a whimsical psychiatrist. Collins must have had a special quality even to attempt the central part, for Johnny is a naif who undergoes a harrowing journey that renders him at first numb in despair and leaves him, in the finale, vending his toys from a tray strapped around his neck. By then he is a pathetically appealing optimist, making us feel at once redeemed and appalled.

The production fairly teemed with folk who later turned their Group training into important careers—Elia Kazan, Lee J. Cobb, Paula Miller (already Mrs. Lee Strasberg), Sanford Meisner, Robert Lewis, Curt Conway, Luther Adler, Albert Van Dekker (who dropped the "Van" in Hollywood). John Garfield, then twenty-three years old and still billed as Jules, played a German sniper in granny glasses whom Johnny befriends and whose death is, at least by implication, the event that triggers Johnny's breakdown. The scene in which the addled Johnny tenderly holds the slain German's head and asks, "Feel better now?" borders on the homoerotic, as Green startles us to force us to attend to his text. Believing that brotherhood should be civilization's binding element, Johnny all but loses his reason when brotherhood is overthrown. It's the only sensible thing to do.

Green's picaresque takes his hero into so many odd corners—a peace rally that turns into a war rally with almost no change of language but the key word, an army recruiting station, the trenches and No Man's Land, a French château, a hospital for the insane—that there were fifty-eight separate roles. The huge company doubled and tripled as the hero's neighbors, comrades, and antagonists, leaving Johnny as not only the protagonist but literally the show's only leading role. Even Minny Belle (Phoebe Brand), Johnny's girl, who is very much around early in the action and makes important appearances later on, is in only four of the seventeen scenes.

Johnny is not only a difficult part but the one dependable element in a crazy play that makes a virtue of its inconsistency. "A weirdly undefinable mixture," Gilbert W. Gabriel called it, "of John Bunyan, Rabelais, and Sidney Kingsley.* So Johnny must embody qualities of not only

---

* Another Group playwright, author of the company's first hit, the hospital drama *Men in White* (1933).

wholesomeness and decency but resolve and constancy even as he so tragically loses his way. The difficulty in finding a capable Johnny may be one
reason why the work is so seldom attempted. Thirty-nine and bald
enough to need a hairpiece, Russell Collins indeed brought something
special to Johnny, for Collins later turned up in "soothing" parts in mood
pieces by Jean Giraudoux and Truman Capote and was the original
Starkeeper/Dr. Seldon in *Carousel* (1945).

Another reason why *Johnny Johnson*s have been scarce is that Green,
who lived for another forty-five years, would not let anyone cut his verbose script. Too often, a playwright collaborating on a musical refuses to
collaborate. Instead of writing a libretto—that is, the *framework* for the
score—he writes a play as if there weren't going to be any score. No doubt
this is why Green called *Johnny Johnson* "a play with music." Everything
lies in that "with": the music is allowed to accompany but never absorb
the action. Thus, many of the vocals are irrelevant tidbits, such as Minny
Belle's mother's interior monologue at the sewing machine, "Aggie's
Song"; "The Tea Song," for English soldiers; or "Oh the Rio Grande," the
nostalgic lament of a Texas recruit. At the same time, songs to clarify
character or situation are missing—something, say, to develop the resemblance between Johnny and the German sniper (who bears Johnny's
name, Johann), or something from Johnny in relation to Minny Belle
during his nineteen-year separation from her.

Ironically, the cowboy's song is one of the show's highlights, Weill's
opportunity to show how American his art is determined to become. One
might have expected him to reuse a lot of the music that he had left
behind in Europe—music that, for all he knew, would be obliterated by
Nazi culture control. On the contrary, Weill quotes himself but twice,
using *Happy End*'s "Lied vom Branntweinhändler" as the show's prelude
and, briefly, the climactic melody of "Youkali," composed in France for
Marie Galante, to cap the "Song of the Goddess"—Liberty herself—as
Johnny sails out of New York harbor.

The sound of the score, however, bears the acerbic melancholy and
commentative "objectivity" of Weill's German sound, especially in the
orchestral incidentals. True, Minny Belle's two love songs to Johnny, "Oh
Heart of Love" and the cut "Farewell, Goodbye," speak from their own
musical No Man's Land as neither precisely European nor American; in
them we can hear Weill making the transition into his American sound,

especially in "Farewell, Goodbye" 's shuffle-boogie accompaniment. People tend to divide Kurt Weill into the German writing politics with Bertolt Brecht or the expatriate doing the rhumba with Moss Hart and Alan Jay Lerner. In fact, Weill's life is defined by a relentless interest in the theatre of humanist enlightenment, and his shows with Hart and Lerner, respectively *Lady in the Dark* (1941) and *Love Life* (1948), stand among the most innovative musicals of all time.

Despite Green's unwillingness to surrender to the synoptic needs of a musical's book, he proved an eager and questing lyricist. "Mon Ami, My Friend," the solo of a French hospital nurse and one of the show's few numbers with a title instead of a description ("The West-Pointer Song," "The Psychiatry Song," "Song of the Wounded Frenchmen"), amusingly picks up the idiom of the native Francophone attempting to communicate in imperfect English. "Captain Valentine's Song" is somewhat opaque. It is all but impossible to tell exactly what happens in his narrative, which suggests that classic of hetero fantasy dates "The Lucky Burglar" but then takes a black-comic turn and ends with a hanging. The style of the lyrics veers from balladspeak to spoof, and in the show the song was broken up to be sung at intervals, making for even more confusion.

But then, Green seems to have wanted to create a work of intellectual challenge. He may wax sarcastic or poetic, even poetically sarcastic. There is as well, at times, an odd verbal construction or a wrong accent, which only adds to the work's originality. A story in which an enlisted man treats generals with laughing gas is not supposed to be rooted in the craftsmanship of the everyday.

The score's high point is the last number, "Johnny's Song," which the action has been aching to reach almost from the very first. Astonishingly, the hero of the tale has not sung before this point. With his tray of toys, physically the wreck of the young man we met in scene one—he is now, Green directs, "forty-five or fifty but looking much older"—Johnny is one notch above unemployed vagrant. Some hero.

There is no question that Green and Weill intended "Johnny's Song" as their position paper. The song is unpretentiously imposing: "When man was first created . . ." is its first line, and the melody that Weill applies to it outlines a rising major seventh, wistful yet provocative. Johnny has lost everything—stability, security, socialization. When we met him, he was the thoughtful, slightly eccentric guy who got elected class president in high school and could never figure out why the girls kept flirting with him. He was a stonecutter and a person without politics—even now, he is no ideologue. What he is, if anything, is a professional stranger. "I meet all kinds of folks who listen to my song," he tells us. At political rallies? Over the kitchen table after odd-jobbing around the house and yard?* We'll never know. As Weill's banjo-inflected music reaches its climax, Johnny wanders off crying his wares, his useless toys of peace. The hero is unbroken and his story unresolved, and there the curtain falls.

The Cradle Will Rock is Johnny Johnson's opposite in every way, most noticeably perhaps in its ultra-spoofy presentation (against Johnny Johnson's mixture of sentiment, humor, and fantasy) and the unqualified finality of its ending. As I've said, Cradle's producer tried to padlock the theatre to kill the show: because the producer was Uncle Sam—in the form of the Federal Theatre—and there were genuine fears that Cradle might ignite incendiary feelings and provoke a riot.

The piece tells of the attempt to unionize Steeltown, U.S.A., reflecting events that were unfolding just then in American labor relations. The previous year, 1936, had seen a war among unions that ended in the creation of the Congress of Industrial Organizations, in opposition to the existing American Federation of Labor. Then, 1937 saw extremely tense clashes between management and labor in the nation's biggest industries. So-called "Big Steel" made its bargain with the Steel Workers Organizing Committee in the spring of 1937 after a spectacular forty-four-day sit-down strike by forty thousand workers. This inspired comparable actions in rubber, textiles, oil, shipbuilding, and elsewhere in steel. Although the sitdown strike as a job action was finally outlawed by a Supreme Court decision in 1939, the atmosphere of violent uprising was in the air in the spring of 1937, when The Cradle Will Rock was in rehearsal. This was also when "Little Steel," led by the chief of Republic Steel, Tom M. Girdler, announced that it was unalterably opposed to unionization. Two weeks before Cradle was to open, the Republic plant south of Chicago was the scene of the "Memorial Day Massacre." According to the report in

---

* This is a lot of content for what publishers Chappell and Co. thought of as one of Johnny Johnson's few marketable numbers, so a new, out-of-context lyric for this music was run up by Edward Heyman as "To Love You and To Lose You."

The New York Times, a thousand strikers marched on the plant, where they were confronted by a police detachment. The mob threw rocks and fired guns, and the police fired back. Four were killed and eighty-four injured.

Clearly, it would have been irresponsible to risk the unknown consequences of opening so inflammatory a piece as *The Cradle Will Rock*. There were reports, as opening night neared, that cuts in the Federal Theatre's budget would target *Cradle* in particular for the obvious unstated reason. And here's a piece of the history that is almost never mentioned: on June 15, *Cradle* gave a dress rehearsal before an invited audience of important theatre people and the customary friends of the production. Like *Johnny Johnson* having skipped an out-of-town tryout, *Cradle* gave a technically rough performance, mainly because the show's director, Orson Welles, set the action atop glass wagons that were to wobble under the actors' feet at the play's climax, while lights broke screaming through the glass above their heads. (This was to suggest the storm of revolution exalted in the title song.) Apparently, the glass wagons wobbled throughout the show—but at least that audience could boast of having seen *The Cradle Will Rock* the one and absolutely only time it was presented in its original intended form.

Reports vary greatly on how that dress rehearsal was received; but let us pause to consider *Cradle*'s sole author, Marc Blitzstein, in comparison with Kurt Weill, because *Johnny Johnson* and *Cradle* are the two outstanding—in fact, the two only—subversive book musicals in the entire decade. *Knickerbocker Holiday* is certainly antagonistic to something, but everyone thought it was Nazism while its librettist and lyricist, Maxwell Anderson, said his target was the New Deal. So *Knickerbocker Holiday*'s power to subvert is, to say the least, ambiguous.

Weill and Blitzstein have a great deal in common. They were born on the same day (though five years apart), underwent classical training, and wrote classically while increasingly devoting themselves to musical theatre. Both entered into strange marriages, Weill with a femme fatale who was his soul but not sexual mate; and Blitzstein was gay. Both died childless before reaching sixty, and of course their work unites in *The Threepenny Opera*, the most famous title that either took part in, Weill naturally as its composer and Blitzstein as translator. His version, for a concert at Brandeis University in 1953, was used for the off-Broadway

revival that ran through the rest of the 1950s, reestablished Weill's reputation, and launched the stardom of his widow, Lotte Lenya, as the great
twentieth-century survivor and, incidentally, the greatest voiceless singer
in history.

The main difference between Weill and Blitzstein, besides the obvious
ones, is that Weill was vulnerably dependent on available writing partners while Blitzstein was his own writer and conceiver. A fascinating yet
ultimately incomplete talent, Blitzstein composed within a narrow
melodic vocabulary where Weill was eloquent. Both were in their twenties in the 1920s, which gave Weill entrée into the artistic liberationism
of Weimar Berlin and Blitzstein access to the New American Culture that
began to evolve after World War I. This was when the nineteenth-
century immigrant population was producing its second and third generations, to add vitality and imagination to native art. For instance, we
have already learned the lesson that "jazz" + George Gershwin = *Porgy
and Bess*. Here's another: D.W. Griffith + the Hollywood moguls'
talkie = *Gone With the Wind*.

Blitzstein intended to fit into this on a political slant, and thus may be
thought comparable to Paul Green as well as to Kurt Weill. But Green's
worldview was more humanist than political, while Blitzstein, a lifelong,
unrepentant Communist (though he left the Party itself in 1949), was
attracted only to subject matter that would Advance the Movement.
Much of his output proved more interesting than entertaining, so while
Blitzstein's work is never boring, none of it succeeded commercially
except his *Threepenny Opera* English. His people typify his Party interests:
tourist-trade workers trying to organize a union, lawlessly greedy southern
capitalists, a shell-shocked war veteran, the colonized Irish. Kurt Weill's
American subjects are more omnivorously derived: Pieter Stuyvesant, the
staff of a women's fashion magazine, the goddess of love, a time-traveling
4-F reject, Benvenuto Cellini, a good guy executed for self-defense murder, the inhabitants of a dingy brownstone, a troubled marriage, oppressed
South African blacks, Huckleberry Finn. And, as we've seen, a shell-
shocked war veteran.

Though Weill lived nine years less than Blitzstein, he got much more
done. If Blitzstein's art was to mean anything in the long view, he owed
himself a Big One, and thus accepted a commission from the
Metropolitan Opera for a work based on the Sacco and Vanzetti case.

This chance to revisit the controversy surrounding the execution of two professed anarchists for a double homicide in the 1920s of course energized the Communist Blitzstein. But the artist Blitzstein might have created something not only unique (as he always did) but deeply musical, emotional, gigantic. He could at times work fast, but on this one he daw-dled. On vacation in Martinique in 1964, Blitzstein was brutally assaulted, and poor medical care resulted in his death. He had arranged to leave his unfinished opera to Leonard Bernstein, a close associate for decades. Bernstein could not only complete the music but, a sometime lyricist, supply anything missing in the libretto. The finished piece, con-ducted by Bernstein at the Met, would have been the event of the season if not the era, a coming together of many several Americas.

But Bernstein declined. Was too much missing? Did Bernstein think the property unworthy? Did he prefer Blitzstein buried to Blitzstein revived? We'll never know; and I have dwelled at some length on all this because Marc Blitzstein's entire career is, in effect, the "thirties musical" of artistic importance and sociopolitical text that, I repeat once again, barely existed beyond *Johnny Johnson* and *The Cradle Will Rock*, the four revues in the next chapter, and *Knickerbocker Holiday*. It is an all but legendary beast—and that finally brings us to Broadway's only legendary musical. Or, at any rate, Broadway's only legendary opening night.

But first: agitprop (short for "agitational propaganda") denotes a form unique to the social climate of the Depression, when union or political meetings offered informal entertainment to dilute the monotonous cock-tail of speechmakers' harangues. Out-of-work vaudevillians would revive their acts, a small choral group might be formed to sing new go-get-'em lyrics to familiar old tunes, and short plays—sketches, really—were presented. The purpose was to rouse passion on the issues, as in the climax of the most famous of the agitprop plays, Clifford Odets' *Waiting For Lefty* (1935), which ends with performers and audience alike shouting "Strike! Strike! Strike!"

All these works are gone, but *The Cradle Will Rock*—developed out of agitprop rather than an example of it—is still with us. An ironic parable, *Cradle* is set in the kind of imaginary America that Bertolt Brecht favored, ruled by tycoon Mr. Mister (Will Geer). Mrs. Mister (Peggy Coudray) dabbles in arts patronage; Junior Mister (Hiram Sherman) and Sister Mister (Dulce Fox) are idiots. Reverend Salvation (Hiram Sherman again, doubling for an absent Edward Hemmer, and we'll see why presently) is a hypocrite, and Editor Daily (Bert Weston) and Doctor Specialist (Frank Marvel) are Mr. Mister's hirelings. In such an atmosphere, perhaps it's a relief that poet Rupert Scanscion is only mentioned, never seen. But working-class couple Gus (George Fairchild) and Sadie (Marion Rudley) are sweet and optimistic till they are murdered by Mr. Mister's thugs; the waiflike Moll (Olive Stanton) is a goodhearted prostitute, damaged but ultimately unbreakable; worker Ella Hammer (Blanche Collins) is defiant; and union leader Larry Foreman (Howard da Silva) is invincible.

The names alone warn us not to expect fleshed-out characters or naturalistic storytelling. The work's "abstract and heartless nature," wrote Mary McCarthy in *Partisan Review*, "will, I think, set up an instinctive resistance in any normal American spectator." McCarthy likened *Cradle's* intellectual appeal to "surrealist art shows" and European ism theatre— expressionism and so on. That is, the show's exaggeration and parody are not weaknesses but talking points of the one-of-a-kind genre that Blitzstein is working in. Not all of the show is as weird as that suggests. The accidental meeting of Mrs. Mister's pet artists, violinist Yasha and painter Dauber, is the kind of burlesque that might have turned up in almost any musical:

DAUBER: How's the concert business?

YASHA: Fine! How's the painting business? I had thirty concerts last year.

DAUBER: Last year! I sold twelve pictures last year. How about this year?

YASHA: This year I rely on my talent.

DAUBER: Prospects are lousy for me, too.

No, where *Cradle* challenges McCarthy's "normal American spectator" is in the score, because Blitzstein uses character songs to stake out political positions—Moll's "Nickel Under the Foot" is the classic instance— and because the music takes the element of parody to a zany level when the overall intention of the work is, to repeat, agitprop's rousing of passion. Thus, near the end of the evening, Ella Hammer sings the angrily blunt "Joe Worker (gets gypped)." How does this sit with Yasha and Dauber's duet "The Rich," whose verse is their conversation and whose chorus is an ecstatically unctuous tango? And between the two numbers comes "The Freedom of the Press," for Mr. Mister and Editor Daily, a breathless steeplechase of lies.

Again to quote McCarthy, *Cradle*'s failure to ingratiate itself generally lies less in its "abstract and heartless nature" than in its Popular Front pep rally plunked into a carnival of spoofs. Again, this isn't accidental or a miscalculation. But it creates absurd inconsistencies in the work when viewed as a whole. *Johnny Johnson* managed its contradictions more persuasively.

Then, too, the music is starved for melody. Only one title, "Summer Weather," is conventionally lyrical—at that because at that point in the action a conventional character is saying something pleasantly conventional. Another number for Yasha and Dauber, "Ask Us Again," has a haunting *non so che*. And when a real artist tackles "Nickel Under the Foot"—for example, Patti LuPone in the 1983 American Place revival—it is suddenly revealed as an intensely musical experience.

But most of the score almost isn't music. Its vitality of verbal invention keeps it spinning in the uptempo spots, and an amusing use of off-accents (as in "Ed-*i*-tor Daily") contributes to the overall fantasy-realism, as in *Johnny Johnson*. Still, that incomplete Blitzstein talent doesn't *sing* for us. "Gus and Sadie Love Song," the one spot where Blitzstein must conjure up a ballad, is supremely dreary, and the all-important "Joe Worker" is more an exclamation than a song.

But then, *Cradle* is one musical that is larger than its score, because of the historical importance of The Night It Didn't Open. Arriving at Maxine Elliott's Theatre on June 16, 1937, cast and crew and, a bit later, ticketholders found the theatre barred—literally locked up in one version, simply under federal guard in another.* Director Welles and his producer, John Houseman, decided to find some other theatre to play in. Ironically, the unions gave no support to this fiercely pro-union show. Actors Equity forbade its members to appear on any alternate stage; and the musicians were allowed to play but only at Broadway scale.

---

* Howard da Silva recalled the theatre's being locked, and he ought to know, because he was extremely fond of a blond wig he wore in the show and couldn't retrieve it from his dressing room. This reveals *Cradle*'s great link with *Johnny Johnson*: both shows cast as their hero an actor whose baldness necessitated the application of a toupee.

It was hopeless, wasn't it? Wouldn't you have given up? Yet Welles and Houseman led everybody up Broadway from Thirty-ninth and Sixth to Fifty-eighth Street and the only spare theatre they could find. This was the Venice, twice the size of the Elliott at some 1,800 seats and then the host of an obscure Italian opera troupe. As the by now surging crowd of *Cradle* company, theatregoers, and the usual "me, too" kibitzers filled the theatre, someone noticed the Italian flag, symbol of fascism, flying over one of the stage boxes, and pulled it down, "amid prolonged cheers," according to one newspaper account.

The show must go on. But the orchestra couldn't play and the actors couldn't perform. Blitzstein was prepared to deliver the piece himself at the upright piano, script and all; that isn't exactly a show. However, the actors weren't barred from performing: they had been barred from appearing on any alternate *stage*. What if they simply bought tickets to the performance like the rest of the house and spoke their roles from their seats, the boxes, the aisles? (Not everyone was willing to, which is why Hiram Sherman and Blitzstein filled in in parts they had never rehearsed.) And what if lighting technician Abe Feder ran a single spotlight by hand, swerving from actor to actor, group to group, throughout the evening? Blitzstein would bang out his music alone on the Venice's empty stage as his play rose up to join with him in the electric air of bootleg theatre.

And that's how it happened. Lucky for them all that *The Cradle Will Rock* is lean and tense enough for such a lean and tense rendition. Had Blitzstein written *The Student Prince* or *Yes, Yes, Yvette*, the evening would hardly have clocked in as a legend.

Unfortunately, that lean and tense approach has dogged *Cradle* revivals, which after all do not play in momentous defiance of theatres padlocked at the last minute. These other *Cradles* could treat us to a pictorial setting in the orchestrations that Lehman Engel had conducted at that dress rehearsal the night before. As it was, after a two-and-a-half-week run at the Venice, *Cradle* turned up at the Mercury Theatre for Sunday nights only, at the end of 1937, finally getting its "official" Broadway run at the start of 1938 at the Windsor Theatre for a total altogether of 132 performances. There were slight changes in cast, but at least now the actors had gained the deck, seated in rows upstage to step forward for their scenes and otherwise look on and react. A similar physical layout at the City Center in 1947 led to a brief reappearance on Broadway. Howard da Silva directed, with Alfred Drake in da Silva's old role and the original Mr. Mister, Will Geer, opposite Vivian Vance's Mrs. Mister. And, at last, the orchestrations were heard, under Leonard Bernstein (at that time, at least, a Blitzstein enthusiast). Even more at last, the New York City Opera *staged* the piece, in 1960—with sets! costumes! entrances and exits from the wings! Lehman Engel finally got to conduct the orchestra before the general public, and Tammy Grimes, *als Gast*, played Moll.

Still, later revivals have reverted to the piano-accompanied empty-stage approach, which seems by this time precious and convenient. Why does *The Cradle Will Rock* have so many devotees who have no interest in performing the music as its composer intended it to be heard?

At least, this work has devotees. *Johnny Johnson* could use some. It cannot compete with *Cradle*'s carpe diem launching, and Paul Green's crushed pacifism is no match for the savage war cries that Blitzstein emits. *Johnny Johnson* nevertheless is *Cradle*'s musical superior by far, artistically distinguished by its authors' wish to ask difficult questions rather than to shout easy answers. Shouting is more theatrical—and cinematic, too. Astonishingly enough, there is a movie about the making of Blitzstein's opus. Tim Robbins' *Cradle Will Rock* (1999) actually relates many interdependent tales of New York's Depression arts scene, but it concentrates on the Federal Theatre and *Cradle*'s rehearsals and first night. Verisimilitude is compromised by telescoping events into 1937, including the termination of the Federal Theatre, which occurred two years later. However, you will see them roar into the Venice Theatre and pull down the fascist flag, amid prolonged cheers. The film's viewpoint is prejudicially leftist, but a host of stars vividly recreates a vanished age. Hallie Flanagan, the Federal Theatre's chief, is portrayed by Cherry Jones, one of our most brilliant actresses in her most charming performance.

THE DECADE IN PICTURES

A PHOTO ESSAY

Marie and Louis (Adele and Fred Astaire, center) disrupt the serenity of a Parisian park in *The Band Wagon*'s "Hoops." Our shot illustrates two main developments of the 1930s—the rise of Dance (fusing elements of ballet and hoofing) and of more efficient set-change techniques, so authors no longer had to write around the décor. Look closely and you'll see where designer Albert R. Johnson cut up the stage for his double revolve; and *The Band Wagon*'s Albertina Rasch, though seldom on the short list with Balanchine, Weidman, and Limon, was the busiest of those reimagining Broadway choreography in the 1930s.

You've seen this picture of *I'd Rather Be Right* before, but we had to include it as witness to a very major star turn. "George M. Cohan as Franklin Delano Roosevelt" created the decade's biggest opening night: and here's our headliner in his eleven o'clocker, "Off the Record." Cohan's film bio, *Yankee Doodle Dandy*, preserves the number, but James Cagney struts. Cohan *pranced*. Note the Boy Loves Girl couple, Austin Marshall and Joy Hodges, in left foreground. Opposite, the *other* biggest opening night was the world premiere of *Porgy and Bess*, in Boston. At top, we present the first sight of the work after the curtain rises for "Summertime." (That is, after the Jasbo Brown blues sequence was cut.) At bottom, director Mamoulian perfects tableau for the Hurricane Scene. Note Todd Duncan and Anne Brown, left foreground.

Hooray, boys and girls!: Palgrave rings up the curtain on a *Jubilee* Featurette, including shots not seen for seventy years, if ever. First, the finale: King Melville Cooper, with Queen Mary Boland to his left, knights Derek Williams. Princess Margaret Adams and Prince Charles Walters look on, above Williams. Note the kids at right—this sextet was used throughout the show just for the fun of it. The two kids at center, however, are crucial to the plot, as their prank, mistaken for terrorism, launches the royal family on its great adventure. Fans of *Me and Juliet* will thrill to the sight of young Jackie Kelk—so memorable as the later show's candy-counter man—at left; and I hereby announce a contest to guess the identity of his older cousin, at right. Stay tuned.

"What a Nice Municipal Park." Sometimes Irene Sharaff and Connie DePinna dressed the *Jubilee* ensemble in a single style, but here they've been broken into sub-groups. The central trio seems set for the "Ascot Gavotte," and, to their left, a couple is trying out the Astaires' old number "Swiss Miss." Note Jo Mielziner's backdrop of park amenities, its trompe l'oeil perspective anticipating Bob Crowley in the brushstrokes of Raoul Dufy. What a *swell* municipal park!

Now the *Jubilee* ensemble are in matching outfits, for the Rockwell Beach Scene where Boland and Cooper (left foreground) sing "Me and Marie." Scope out the guys' headgear, the six little kids, and the quaint lighthouse beach toy in their midst. Answer to contest from two pages ago: that's a precocious Montgomery Clift, as Prince Peter.

Jubilee's first-act finale is set at a Greek–themed masquerade ball, and we can see all eight principals. From left to right: "Mowgli" (Mark Plant) is Cupid, near Margaret Adams and Mary Boland. Jump past the party entertainment to a bearded Melville Cooper, hostess May Boley (holding the harp), then Derek Williams, American *vedette* June Knight (in the huge diaphanous veil), and Charles Walters.

A closer look at Plant and Boland gives us what we might call the Palgrave Pose: a torrid hunk vamping a grande dame (cf., the shot of *New Faces of 1962* in Volume Five of this series). Plant's character, Charles Rausmiller, is patterned on Johnny Weissmuller, and Mowgli, of course, is Tarzan. *Jubilee*'s book writer, Moss Hart, saw celebrity as the essential element of American show biz, not only in its personnel but in its content. No cursed power rings or glass slippers for Hart: his storybook told how the famous have fun.

8

It's Better with a Union Man: The Leftist Revue

Those in search of a "real" thirties musical besides *The Cradle Will Rock*—so familiar that its legend has passed into cliché—need look no further than *Parade* (1935). This show is what happens when a producer thoroughly unversed in musical technique decides to produce a musical. *Parade* was the Theatre Guild's first attempt to fly from its eyrie of Shaw and the Lunts and go into its dance on The Street.*

With music by Jerome Moross and sketches and lyrics by Paul Peters and George Sklar (along with contributions by a few others of the usual suspects, including Marc Blitzstein), *Parade* was a revue unified by its outlook. There were no spoofs of plays or movies, no imitations of Joan Crawford or Noël Coward, no concept of headlines or world travel. There was, however, a binding irony, introduced in an opening sketch, set in a cop shop, where the officers are too busy playing tic-tac-toe to fight crime. They ignore complaints of robbery and rape, even a gun battle. Then they hear of a peaceful parade being held without a permit! Donning gas masks and arming themselves with machine guns, they march off goosestepping as the orchestra takes up their rhythm to cue in the first number, "On Parade," sung by Edgar Allen as a kind of anthem of the Popular Front.

The parade becomes a structural element, as the cops march across the stage to cover set changes or punctuate the continuity. It's an arresting idea, and whatever one thinks of *Parade*'s political stance, the show did

* *The Garrick Gaieties* doesn't count, because it was originally devised by Guild staffers as an informal two-performances-only benefit show. The Guild simply inherited it, sequels and all.

strive to present it with imagination. For instance, the big dance number, choreographed by Robert Alton, was "Sugar Cane," in which an overseer abuses West Indian cane cutters, who finally rebel. Pure agitprop—except the lights up found the cast frozen in a simulation of a Diego Rivera, and two marines enforcing the overseers' treatment of the workers moved in a time and rhythm different from those of the other dancers, apparently to suggest the inhuman nature of the oppression. Another number, "Dancing on the Mall," offered a strange gloss on the "couples in the park" number typical of many another musical: here the action seemed full of anxiety, even near to violence. The typical Boy sang a ballad with the Girl, but with lines such as "Tomorrow is the fear in my heart."

Even some of the sketches were creative. One of Peters and Sklar's most original ideas was "The Joneses," played by two couples simultaneously. One is clearly rich and the other poor, and all the lines are spoken by both husbands or both wives or all four players together. For instance, when the two men said, "No luck. Couldn't land a thing today," the rich husband showed his fishing tackle while the poor husband held up the want ads. Later, the men morosely asked, "What have we got to look forward to?" Both wives answered, "This," the rich wife holding up a cocktail shaker and the poor wife a baby dress.

On the other hand, "The Joneses" is wry compared to most of *Parade*. "The Tabloid Reds" was the left's view of how they are demonized in the mass-appeal papers: they "eat little children with gunpowder sauce" and "make little bombs which we love to toss." When Stalin phones to ask what's new, they brag of sinking the *Morro Castle*, closing banks, creating drought in the west, and kidnapping the Lindbergh baby.

The savage tone was suitable to the Theatre Union, the most leftward of all the major thirties thespian groups, not to the Theatre Guild. And indeed, it was the Theatre Union for which *Parade* was conceived. Adhering to the classy intellectual's pink rather than the street-brawl red that colors most of *Parade*, the Guild did tame the show in spots. For instance, somewhere between the show's composition and its New York opening, "The Joneses" was dropped, despite its relative mildness. But a piece of agitprop called "Newsboy," in which the mainstream press is shown to be hooked on crime and scandal and the *Daily Worker* is touted as the only dependable source of news, made it as far as the Boston tryout, to be dropped after a single performance.

This caution may explain the presence of one sketch, "Home of the Brave," because its sardonic irony reminds one of the kind of thing George S. Kaufman or David Freedman would devise for the political spot in the Big Broadway revues. Could it have been written at the Guild's request? Alone of *Parade*'s contents, "Home of the Brave" targeted nothing American, but rather the ongoing "Aryanization" of German life. What if something similar happened here, and everyone had to be . . . an Indian? As Mr. and Mrs. John Smith, C. D. Brown and Eve Arden have had to erect a wigwam in their apartment, now called "Teepee 8A":

> ARDEN: You're the worst brave in the building. We never even have fresh meat.
> BROWN: I'd like to see you take that bow and arrow and hit one of those damned little rabbits.

Of course, identity politics creates new myths:

> ARDEN: The white man never really overcame the Indian. That's just vicious pilgrim propaganda.

Mr. Smith troubles to remind his wife that he himself claims pilgrim ancestors:

> ARDEN: (A hand over his mouth) You promised you'd never tell. Keep quiet or we'll have a pogrom down on our heads.

"A prolonged twanging on a single string," Richard Lockridge called *Parade*, and Burns Mantle had ready not only his blurb but a kind of Leftist Revue 101 précis: "Take cracks at practically everything the government is doing, or trying to do. Shoot a few Brain Trusters. Show up the fallacies of relief. Make sport of the hysteria every Communistic parade is likely to stir up. Belittle [higher] education. Capitalize on apprehension. Ridicule Peace Conferences."

Virtually every critic razzed *Parade* to bits while very much liking its star, Jimmy Savo, another in the line of tramp comics given to pathetic mime sequences. (*Parade*'s found him starving between a hot-chestnut stand and a hot-dog wagon.) Savo's was an odd career, less suited to musicals than to the autonomous arts of vaudeville. Of Savo's seven Broadway appearances, only two were in book shows, although they are arresting credits—*The Boys From Syracuse* (which will be along presently) and that first piece by Alan Jay Lerner and Frederick Loewe, *What's Up*. Indeed, one wonders how Savo got into *Parade* in the first place, for he was if nothing else a delicate being and *Parade* is hard-edged.

Even more anomalous was *Parade*'s ticket scale, to a $4.40 top, standard for musicals but surely too demanding for *Parade*'s intended working-class audience. *The Cradle Will Rock*, as a Federal Theatre project, could announce a top of fifty cents—twenty cents in the balcony, at that of a smallish house. Whom exactly did the Theatre Guild hope to reach with its high-priced spread—the beautifully tailored foursome that blundered into seats down front at *The Cradle Will Rock*'s official first night at the Windsor Theatre in 1938 and walked out during the first act, to the public's vocal scorn?

So at least *Sing For Your Supper* (1939), another Federal Theatre project, was able to scale down its tariff to admit potential enthusiasts. Unfortunately, this particular show exemplified much of what Republican legislators hated about the Federal Theatre—not merely the propaganda for the New Deal and points leftward but the waste of taxpayer money. For reasons that no one has ever explained, *Sing For Your Supper* rehearsed for eighteen months. This was so infamous a piece of news, from Capitol Hill to the Astor Hotel Bar, that *Sing For Your Supper* actually programmed a choral number about it called "At Long Last." Ironically, on opening night the curtain went up twenty-five minutes late. You're *still* not ready?

What was finally unveiled that day was no *Band Wagon*. John Mason Brown's "dull," "amateurish," "feeble," "poorly sung and inefficiently danced" typify the terrible reviews. With *Parade*, the critics found the soapbox badgering tedious, but *Sing For Your Supper* sweetened its Message by observing revue conventions—a spoof of *The Cradle Will Rock*, a sketch showing Grover Whalen getting lost on the grounds of the World's Fair out in Queens,* and an updating of *Romeo and Juliet* that mated Boy (in the C.I.O.) and Girl (on the strikebreaker side) in the

---

* How does one explain who Grover Whalen was? Today, we have celebrities "famous for being famous"; Whalen was, perhaps, prominent for being prominent, as a kind of professional New Yorker, the official top-hatted greeter of the visiting great, and, relative to the point of this sketch, the spokesman for the Fair, known as the World of Tomorrow.

ballad "Her Pop's a Cop." The show's tone varied from hardcore to left-liberal. But it did at least vary.

Three numbers stood out. "The Last Waltz," choreographed by Anna Sokolow, offered Hitler barging in on a ballroom fit for Johann Strauss: in time with the music, the dancing became severely regimented till a cloaked figure with a vast right hand raised it in the Nazi salute. Far more congenial was "Papa's Got a Job," set in the backyard where the neighbors congregate, to share in Papa's joy, for his family was just about to be evicted. Credited to composer Ned Lehac, lyricist Robert Sour, and one Hector Troy, the number has the exultant proletcult feeling that Harold Rome more or less invented—and, indeeed, Hector Troy turned out to be Rome's pseudonym, based on his nickname ("Heckie") and the substitution of one ancient city for another. It is tempting to speculate that *Sing For Your Supper*, desperate for a solid number, brought in Rome to write his unique version of an idea that Lehac and Sour couldn't quite pull off.

In the end, *Sing For Your Supper* did have a solid number, the finale, "Ballad of Uncle Sam," an ensemble for bass and speaker Gordon Clarke and the full chorus. Written by Earl Robinson and John Latouche, the piece is very much of its time: populist, patriotic, and sentimentally utopian. Corny. Making constant references to events and people of the American past, the soloist keeps teasing the chorus about his identity. Finally, he claims to be a person of every profession, ethnicity, and religion. In short: America itself. The music is rousingly tuneful, and the somewhat intricate choral arrangements are the kind to delight the naive ear unfamiliar with classical sophistication. When, later in 1939, Paul Robeson headed a performance of the work on radio under the title *Ballad For Americans*, the response was tremendous, and one wonders if good word of mouth for the finale alone kept *Sing For Your Supper* going as long as it did. *Parade* eked out its 40-performance run because of the Guild subscription arrangement, but *Sing For Your Supper* was still playing after two months when, by Act of Congress, the Federal Theatre was terminated and its every activity, down to the last children's puppet show, was shut down at midnight on the very day the law was passed, June 30, 1939.

Sing For Your Supper's cast was typical New York Federal Theatre level, essentially unemployed or just-starting performers who qualified simply because they weren't already in commercial Broadway fare. Besides Clarke, we note the young Paula Laurence, Bowen (later Sonny) Tufts,

Peggy Coudray (Mrs. Mister in *The Cradle Will Rock*), and a rather large number of people never heard from again.

The biggest hit among the leftist revues put forward a cast even more unknown. The Federal Theatre took only professionals into its ranks, however lowly their standing, but *Pins and Needles* (1937) was literally an amateur night. It came into existence by fluke, one that coincidentally involves a major piece of musical-theatre history: the Princess Theatre. Built in 1913 to feature evenings of one-act plays on ghastly crimes and spirit-world visitations in the style of Paris' Théâtre du Grand Guignol, the Princess was at first known as "the theatre of thrills." But the public would not support more than a single such season, and the 299-seat house went over to small-scale musical comedy. Some of these, of course, were the masterpieces of Jerome Kern, P. G. Wodehouse, and Guy Bolton.

However, by the mid-1930s, the location, on Thirty-ninth and Sixth, just across from Maxine Elliott's Theatre (where *The Cradle Will Rock* didn't play) was antiquated, a part of the Old Broadway that had been swept away with the change in styles that followed World War I. This is the fluke: the International Ladies' Garment Workers' Union took over the Princess building as a recreation center, possibly only because it stood mere blocks from the garment center where the union members worked. But for the fact that there was a perfectly utilizable auditorium downstairs, it seems unlikely that the union would ever have considered mounting a show, selling tickets, becoming famous, moving to Broadway, and breaking Broadway's long-run record for musicals.

True, back then "theatre nights" were a feature of almost any organization. But these tended to occur in a large room with folding chairs. Surely it was that once celebrated (and quite beautifully designed) house sitting vacant in the union's very quarters that inspired somebody with the idea of making something special out of theatre night—something the general public might wish to partake of. With Harold J. Rome (as he was then billed; the "J." is for Jacob) writing the score and playing the two-piano pit with Baldwin Bergersen, and with sketches by five men, including Marc Blitzstein and Emmanuel Eisenberg, the I.L.G.W.U.'s press agent, *Pins and Needles* underwent a prolonged rehearsal period, not because of a federal budget in the *Sing For Your Supper* manner, but because it was limited to evenings, when the cast of cutters, pressers, dressmakers, one Bonnaz embroiderer, and so on was free.

On November 27, 1937, *Pins and Needles* opened at what was now called the Labor Stage. It played only weekends at first, then took up a full week's schedule. After about a year and a half, the show was still so successful that it moved to the Windsor Theatre, which accommodated three times the size of a Princess audience. Meanwhile, the weaker (or outdated) acts were continually replaced, till the show claimed four editions when it finally closed, at 1,108 performances.*

What distinguished *Pins and Needles* from not only *Parade* and *Sing For Your Supper* but such shows as *Johnny Johnson* and *The Cradle Will Rock* was the good humor in which it cloaked its commentary. In the *New York Times* review two days after the opening, stringer Jack Gould wrote, "The leftwing theatre may take pride in the delayed descent from the usual soap box." But that isn't quite correct. Some of *Pins and Needles* was as ideological and edgy as anything in *Parade*, such as "Doin' the Reactionary," a New Dance Sensation that actually tells you how to perform it, with such admonitions as "Close your eyes to where you're bound" and "Move to the right." More specifically targeted, "Four Little Angels of Peace" presented winged replicas of Anthony Eden, Hitler, Mussolini, and an unnamed Japanese warlord, all bragging of the enormities they've committed.†

What was different about *Pins and Needles* was its interest in not just workers' politics but their personal lives. Bespectacled Millie Weitz had a completely apolitical comic lament called "Nobody Makes a Pass At Me," in effect a satire on the use of cosmetics and other aids to romance. In "Chain Store Daisy," Ruth Rubinstein told of her job in the lingerie department of Macy's despite having been graduated from Vassar. In a patter section, she gave an impression of a day on the sales floor, seeing

---

* *Hellzapoppin*, which would eventually surpass *Pins and Needles* at 1,404 performances, was at that time still running but some 350 repetitions behind.

† As testament to the organic growth of *Pins and Needles* as a whole, this number was constantly overhauled to keep it abreast of international headlines. Sometimes a few lines were changed; Eden was replaced by his successor, Neville Chamberlain. However, the English character was dropped altogether after September 1, 1939, in sympathy with an England at last at war. Then the number itself was cut, replaced by "The Harmony Boys (from Demagogue Lane)": radio bigot Father Coughlin, American Nazi leader Fritz Kuhn, and reactionary senator Robert Reynolds. (Compare this to a trio in *Parade* called "Bon Voyage" and sung by Coughlin with Louisiana's governor, Huey Long—in the year he was assassinated, incidentally—and the big business–loving head of the N.R.A., General Hugh S. Johnson.) Meanwhile, the *Pins and Needles* angels returned soon enough, if only to express the show's disgust with Stalin (who now had his own wings and verse) for making his pact with Hitler, in August of 1939.

to a naggy customer and cursing her out in undertone. "When I Grow Up" found Bernie Gould in a Buster Brown outfit with a cap gun, expressing his wish to become a G-Man. And an ensemble number, "Sunday in the Park," showed the working class simply relaxing.

The *Times'* critic is right in one sense, for most of *Pins and Needles'* political remark was amusing rather than preachy. Lynne Jaffee had a funny number as a Park Avenue matron rebuking picketing workers for their lack of fair play, getting more and more heated in her sermon till a cop had to drag her off as a public nuisance. A sketch called "Papa Lewis, Mama Green" made a black-and-white comic strip out of the enmity between John L. Lewis of the C.I.O. and William Green of the A.F.L., a tight unit of organized labor today but, as we learned in the last chapter, bitter rivals in the late 1930s. In the sketch, two "children" wearing signs reading "Rank" and "File" tried to create peace between Papa, in checked flannel and overalls, and Mama, a drag role in giant white apron, flowered top, and Hippodrome bust.

Pins and Needles' staging in general was frankly almost cheesy, with the players mainly in street clothes and many numbers sung in one before a drop. However, after the move to the Windsor, numbers and sketches were added to put on a bit of the dog. In 1939, when *The Swing Mikado* and *The Hot Mikado* appeared within the same month, *Pins and Needles* sensed a cycle and joined in with "The Red Mikado." The stage was decorated with posters announcing other spin-offs: Minsky's *Strip Mikado* "with 20 gorgeous Titipu girls," a *Flea Mikado* (someone's blurb was ready: "biting"), and a *Hollywood Mikado*. In fact, there really was one that year, made by MGM in England with the D'Oyly Carte troupe and our own Kenny Baker. But in *Pins and Needles'* *Hollywood Mikado*, of course, "Gable loves Crawford." "With bingo," the poster promised.

It would appear that "The Red Mikado" was inspired not only for the usual reasons of burlesque, but also to skewer the Daughters of the American Revolution for refusing Constitution Hall to black Marian Anderson; it had occurred shortly before the spoof went in.* The second

---

* Mrs. Roosevelt saved the day. She resigned from the D.A.R. and welcomed Anderson to the steps of the Lincoln Memorial, quite a place for a concert by a black contralto. The D.A.R. are parvenus, anyway. To be eligible, one must be able to claim an ancestor who fought in the War of Independence. Who can't? The Truly Social Lady will belong to the more exclusive Colonial Dames.

line of "Three Little D.A.R.s (are we)" ran "Full to the brim with bigotry." "I've Got a Little List" targeted debutantes who spend fifty thousand dollars on their coming-out balls, along with café society, Lucius Beebe, the "filibusterist" in Congress, and ex-presidents who ceaselessly complain about their successor. No name was mentioned, but it was unmistakably Herbert Hoover, called "the distinguished pessimist."

The Mikado himself was played as an imitation of Bert Lahr, and his version of "My Object All Sublime" was witless. "Tit-Willow," too, was vexed, by a refrain of "Oy, Munich." Worse, the *Pins and Needles* singers, while adequate for the ballad "One Big Union For Two" or the jaunty anthem "Sing Me a Song With Social Significance," were not up to Gilbert and Sullivan. One tends to forget why their works were always referred to as "operas" when they were new until one hears amateurs take a crack at them. Indeed, the two authors themselves appeared at the end of "The Red Mikado" (in their nightshirts) to picket the proceedings with "Unfair" signs, in sound Wagner Act technique.

How would *Pins and Needles* do in revival? So much of it deals with attitudes that precede and survive the 1930s that an evening's selection of its many songs and sketches might well prove timely today. "It's Better With a Union Man" unfolded the cautionary account of Bertha, the sewing machine girl, and of the fatal peril that befell when she dated extramurally. Even the overtly political pieces may favor the universal over the immediate, as in "Mene Mene Tekel," a retelling of the fifth chapter of Daniel. This relates God's warning, at the Feast of Belshazzar, that (in Rome's version) "The Lord don't like dictators or dictators' ways." No *Pins and Needles* film was ever made, but television played host to the show in 1966, with Bobby Short, Josephine Premice, Bob Dishy, and Elaine Stritch, brisk and uncrushable in "Nobody Makes a Pass At Me" and scalding in "Chain Store Daisy."

Not only *Pins and Needles* moved uptown: Harold Rome took his proletarian joie de vivre into the Music Box, in the company of such mainliners as Max Gordon, Kaufman and Hart, Jo Mielziner, and a full orchestra playing Hans Spialek's charts: *Sing Out the News* (1938). The cast lacked éclat. There wasn't a single genuine star, and among principals Hiram Sherman, Philip Loeb, Dorothy Fox, Will Geer (*The Cradle Will Rock*'s Mr. Mister), and Mary Jane Walsh, only Walsh is of historical note, for her stylish vocals in shows by Cole Porter and Rodgers and Hart and for her mission impossible of taking over the title role in *Annie Get Your Gun* during Ethel Merman's six-week vacation.

All the same, this *was* a Max Gordon show, and the first production in the last five we've discussed—*Johnny Johnson, Cradle, Parade, Sing For Your Supper*, and *Pins and Needles*—to be the work of Big Broadway powerhouses. John Mason Brown devoted his entire review to a comparison of *Sing Out the News* with *Pins and Needles*, claiming that the little show had "opened a charge account at Cartier's" without having "sold out" or "lost its youth." In other words, the big show retained the little one's interest in how ordinary people live their lives. So the main ballad was "How Long Can Love Keep Laughing," which explodes the classic clichés about love's power to overwhelm all obstacles: because poverty conquers all. And the big number was "F.D.R. Jones," set during a black block party for a newborn named after the president and so engaging that it stopped the show on opening night.

Sing Out the News was not unlike a mating of the Shubert revue with the insurgent revue: the sheer gala of the one supporting the worldview of the other, so that a takeoff on *I Married an Angel* is "I Married a Republican," with Hiram Sherman floating down (as Vera Zorina did in the Rodgers and Hart show) to learn the human art of duplicity. Or the first-act finale, the "Congressional Minstrels," featured the battles between Roosevelt and Congress. In other words, the structural format was that of Big Broadway while the philosophy was that of an I.L.G.W.U. theatre night. Though Kaufman and Hart were billed as Max Gordon's associate producers only, they wrote the sketches, going rather *Pins and Needles* in "The F.L.O.P. Plan," a spoof of Dr. Francis E. Townsend's crackpot scheme to finance old-age pensions with a two-percent national sales tax. The Social Security Act was passed partly in response to the so-called "Townsend Plan," yet Townsend continued to attempt to influence American affairs by going with some of the more apparent right-wing nuts into the Union Party. They actually fielded a candidate, Republican congressman William Lemke, in the presidential election of 1936. (The party polled nearly 900,000 votes.) Townsend was exactly the sort of figure that a Shubert revue would not have looked at and a leftist revue couldn't resist. Kaufman and Hart dispatched Townsend's Plan by having it explained by actors representing the Marx Brothers. Mrs. Rittenhouse was in it, too.

So, yes: there was a political presence in the musical in the 1930s, but not nearly as extensive a one as some might have expected. The spoken political stage was much more active, for two reasons. The obvious one is cost: straight plays for a small cast in street clothes could still get on for something like ten or fifteen thousand dollars; a full-sized musical ran ten times as much. The other reason is an artistic conundrum: what kind of music accompanies political theatre? If it's Gershwin or Berlin—in other words, *Of Thee I Sing* or *Face the Music*—then it isn't political theatre in any real sense. On the other hand, if it's *Johnny Johnson* or *The Cradle Will Rock*, then Kurt Weill and Marc Blitzstein seem to feel the need to invent a new style of "song" to bear the weight of the material. And both men did that—but how many others could, or would wish to? *Pins and Needles* pulled it off because the show's congenial tone welcomed traditional Broadway carolling. But surely one of *Parade*'s problems was that it wasn't clear what style of music suited an entertainment originally written for the angriest of the major leftist theatre groups.

There's an irony in that, because Jerome Moross' musical theatre works after *Parade* found ways to employ traditional song in untraditional scores, reaching an experimental apex in every musical buff's favorite hidden classic, *The Golden Apple* (1954). Perhaps some messages simply aren't meant to be sung.

9

LIFE'S A DANCE: THE CHOREOGRAPHY OF THE 1930s

In his review of *Parade*, *Variety*'s critic, who signed as Ibee, complained that there was "too much group dancing of the modernistic type." That phrase could serve as a definition of what the 1930s gave to the history of choreography in the musical; and Ibee's wording is vague because no one knew what to call "it." They knew it when they saw it: it involved the ensemble rather than a few soloists, it had a theme or was at least "expressing" something, and, most important, it was more "artistic" than hoofing yet more "fun" than ballet.

For instance, in *The Ziegfeld Follies of 1936*, Josephine Baker had a number called "Five A.M.," the reflections of a worldly woman, apparently a high-priced prostitute. She is free of her workplace of "cafés" and "jazz rhythms"; reclining on a sofa in a gown of silver sequins, she summons up a world of more genuine erotic power. "No white tie is facing me" ran one line of lyric; and, indeed, choreographer George Balanchine filled the stage with the opposite of white tie, as his dancers went as far as 1936 would allow in presenting the sensual. Here was another Dream Ballet, addressing the audience in the vocabulary of both classical and modern dance but also of popular dance. It was "highbrow" yet entertaining—or was that an interior contradiction? Though Baker danced elsewhere in the show, in "Five A.M." she strode pensively through the ballet, apparently considering its message, dragging her ostrich-feather cape behind her as she returned to the couch to finish off the scene by repeating the song—which now, of course, bore the ironic content that it lacked the first time. To explain Baker's character's distance from all eros, the dance needed the song as much as the song needed the dance.

Some of these set pieces would take off from the imagery used in song lyrics, as in "Five A.M." Sometimes the dancing was autonomously pictorial, as in *The Band Wagon*'s "Beggar Waltz," which offered no vocal before embarking on Fred Astaire's "dream" of Tilly Losch. Still, the choreography was consistently "modernistic"—but what does Ibee *mean* by that word? Remember Fanny Brice's "Modernistic Moe," in *Ziegfeld Follies of 1936*? An artistically ambitious impresario who quotes Gertrude Stein and affects radical politics, Moe is really a guy from the neighborhood flying toward the higher reaches of art. For some, "modernistic" was simply a description; for others, it was a derogation. ("Integrated" would be like that in the 1940s, depending on what one preferred—*Oklahoma!* and *Carousel* or something with Bobby Clark.) Still, whether one liked one's dance modernistic or not, everyone seemed to be referring, by that word, to the same concept: a blend of traditional American show-biz motion with some other style that was sort of European, perhaps elevated, and surely prestigious.

Did they but know it then, the modernistic movement probably was derived mainly from Fred Astaire, because his dance was artistic fun. And note that Astaire, whether partnering his sister or making his stage farewell alone in *Gay Divorce* (1932), was the opposite of a guy from the neighborhood: the New Dance lent elegance to the Moes. It is no accident that all the choreographers who created dance style in the 1930s on Broadway came from the ballet world: Albertina Rasch, Agnes de Mille, Charles Weidman, José Limón, and, most influentially, George Balanchine.

In order to appreciate how they and the New Dance affected the thirties musical, let us examine a typical choreographic layout in a show that precedes modernism. What better sample than this same *Gay Divorce*? Though not an Aarons-Freedley piece, it adheres to that style: an original story* filled with masquerade and comic kibitzers. The star, as

---

* Technically, the libretto, by Kenneth Webb and Samuel Hoffenstein, is drawn from a script by Dwight Taylor that was adapted from an unproduced play by J. Hartley Manners, who was Laurette Taylor's second husband and Dwight's stepfather. *Gay Divorce* was all the same an "original" in that it was not based on an existing work that the public might have been familiar with, in the manner of such Second and early Third Age musicals as *Leave It To Jane* (from *The College Widow*), *Going Up* (from *The Aviator*), *No, No, Nanette* (from *My Lady Friends*), or *The Vagabond King* (from *If I Were King*).

said, is Fred Astaire; the star score is by Cole Porter. Assistants include heroine Claire Luce, wisecracking confidante Luella Gear, soubrette Betty Starbuck, and three stock clowns: the Silly Brit, in this case an attorney (G. P. Huntley Jr.), the zany waiter (Eric Blore), and the Italian gigolo (Erik Rhodes).

Gay Divorce is actually something of a play with songs. There are only ten vocal numbers, along with reprises, underscoring, and a great deal of dancing that pushes the work into the musical-comedy category. But there is no opening number. The curtain goes up, during the overture's final bars, on a prologue of exposition for novelist Guy Holden (Astaire) and his lawyer pal (Huntley). This leads into Astaire's solo "After You, Who?," with a followup dance to some jazzy new music and then the typical plugging of the song's chorus.

Naturally, Astaire has laid out his own choreography. Not till the view changes to the exterior of an English seaside resort and Betty Starbuck leads the girls in "Why Marry Them?" and another consequent dance do we see the work of the show's credited choreographers, Carl Randall and Barbara Newberry. (We met them joining Pardon My English during its tryout.) Huntley and Starbuck now enjoy a rousing though narratively irrelevant number, "Salt Air," which is duly followed by a dance.

A pattern has emerged, hasn't it? Characters sing, then dance. Even: characters sing, then leave while other characters come in and dance. So if the number is keyed to character, as with "After You, Who?"—in which Boy pines for Girl, whom he has barely Met—and if that character executes the dance, the choreography expresses something substantial. If not, then the dancing is merrily extraneous, as with "Why Marry Them?" and "Salt Air."

Luella Gear's first comic number is next. This is "I Still Love the Red, White and Blue"; musically lumpy, it deserves and gets no dance. But the stage is heating up for Boy and Girl's second Meeting. She is Mimi Pratt, an Englishwoman hoping to divorce a stuffy geologist by being caught in a staged "adultery" with the Italian—what they used to call a "hired co-respondent." The romantic tone is reinstated with Astaire's reprise of "After You, Who?" and his second dance solo. Then comes the Meeting: he hypnotizes her with "Night and Day." Here, above all, dance will essentialize action, as Astaire uses the pas de deux to deepen the meaning of the love plot virtually to Boy Fucks Girl. Certainly, the look of wonder on Luce's face at dance's end, preserved in a photograph, suggests that she has undergone more than a turn around the ballroom.*

Now it is time for the Italian to join us. His number is "How's Your Romance?," sung with the girls; this, too, leads to another pointless dance. But we have reached the end of Act One, as Girl mistakes Boy for Co-respondent. Worse, he thinks they're talking about his novels when she's talking about his experience as a gigolo, and he blithely tells her that he's made thousands happy that way. Well, that does it:

> MIMI: Here, take my key. Come to my room at ten o'clock. And bring
>   your own pajamas.

She stalks off as he gapes at her, the orchestra plays five seconds of dramatic punctuation, and the first-act curtain hits the floor.

It turns out all right when Luce's husband shows up and is unmasked as a real adulterer. But meanwhile, eight of the show's ten songs take a succeeding dance "illustration," sometimes a lengthy one. Only Luella Gear's two numbers—the other one is "Mr. and Mrs. Fitch"—consist entirely of vocal material. That's an awful lot of dancing about nothing. True, Astaire's movement illustrates his singular blend of wise guy and lover—once again, that modernistic wedding of pop and art. But most musical comedies offered much less substance in their Boy, whether the giggly Oscar Shaw, the goofy Jack Haley, the seedy William Gaxton, or even the juvenile most people seemed to prefer, Jack Whiting. So most musical comedies really had nothing to dance about in any meaningful way.

But see how quickly this changes; and let's control our comparison by looking in on another Cole Porter show. We've got *Jubilee* under our belts already, and we can see important distinctions between it and *Gay Divorce* already: *Gay Divorce* contains only its central couple, the attorney and his date, and three other jesters. Even the chorus is limited, to women only. *Jubilee* is an adventure, following four couples of more or less equal weight. More: *Gay Divorce* could have been a spoken play; indeed, it started out as one. *Jubilee*, on the other hand, is too campy and

---

* Ginger Rogers looks downright deflowered at the same moment in the screen version, retitled *The Gay Divorcee* and featuring a replica of the original "Night and Day" dance. Ironically, the song is the only one retained from Porter's stage score.

sophisticated to exist except as a musical—a very thoroughly musicalized one, at that.

Jubilee arrives three years after *Gay Divorce*, yet already Albertina Rasch has more to do than set everybody hopping and stepping in response to the vocal. The New Dance has made that method of structuring a number seem like so much prancing. Now one has to have a reason to dance, something to communicate that the vocal can't, at least for part of the evening. Two of *Jubilee*'s numbers, "What a Nice Municipal Park" and "Me and Marie," grew into big ensemble dances just because they wanted to, true enough. And *Jubilee*'s dancing leads, Charles Walters and June Knight as the Prince and Karen O'Kane, naturally danced after their two duets. Their beguine was of course *Jubilee*'s dancing centerpiece, as the two commanded the floor of a nightclub backed by a curtain of thin wooden slats, the bandstand surmounted by a gigantic metal palm tree. But note that "Begin the Beguine" really introduces a plot dance, a Boy Meets Girl. It seems odd that Rasch was willing to surrender this plum to Tony De Marco, for it was clear that the dance would become one of the memories of the age, choreography in art deco. Is it possible that the song did not become immediately popular because the public was too entranced with the characters' emotional transaction to absorb the music?

The social gala at the end of *Jubilee*'s first act introduced two numbers more danced than sung, the Greek masque called "The Judgement of Paris" and "Swing That Swing," another plot number, as Eva Standing invites her guests to figure out which of them are the royal family. And we notice that short dance breaks are slipped into what should be purely vocal numbers here and there in the show, a trick popularized if not invented by George M. Cohan in the 1910s and 1920s. For example, when the four royals launch a last chorus of "We're Off To Feathermore," they suddenly stop singing after the second line, to create a daffy dancing exit. Comparably, the second-act opening, "Sunday Morning Breakfast Time," finds the servants dropping their vocal in mid-line to go into a strutting syncopated cakewalk.

"I didn't think anything of her work," Agnes de Mille told theatre historian Foster Hirsch, of Albertina Rasch. "She sent rows of girls spinning. She moved her dancers from one edge of the proscenium to the other, as if they were in *Swan Lake*." But Rasch's Hollywood work, all within the first ten years of the talkie, preserves a more imaginative talent, and, for all we know, some of *Jubilee*'s integration of dance may have been made at her suggestion. Certainly, the opening of the Rockwell beach scene was stunning: after the "Six Little Wives" sextet in front of the traveler, the full stage was revealed, with the ensemble in beach togs consisting of elaborate suit-jacket tops over obscenely high-cut shorts. And, as they shag and shuffle along, everyone's in a madcap hat, the men included.

De Mille herself did not have Rasch's success at this time, and she was stuck in musical comedy instead of the musical play in which she was to make her history. *Hooray For What!* (1937) seems an extremely odd career choice for de Mille, as an Ed Wynn chowder into which so many variety specialists were stirred that it had the taste of a revue. Al Gordon's Dogs; the Briants (mime tramps); Will Ferry (a contortionist); the Modernistic Moe of the day, Paul Haakon; and the decade's inevitable puppet act, the Sue Hastings Marionettes, all got a look in. The plot as such concerned heavily accented spy Vivian Vance's attempt to steal horticulturalist Wynn's formula for poison gas while trying to muscle in on June Clyde's romance with Jack Whiting. There really was a script, by Howard Lindsay and Russel Crouse; and Lindsay directed. The score was by Harold Arlen and E. Y. Harburg. It surely sounds like a book show, though only Harburg's first and Arlen's second. Still, with the Messrs. Shubert producing and Vincente Minnelli and Raoul Pène du Bois designing, it struck some as an especially funny entry in the Winter Garden revue series, just after the two-week return engagement of *The Show Is On*.

Hooray For What! had a raucous tryout, as all the leads but Wynn were replaced. Kay Thompson had been the spy, Roy Roberts (later the perhaps somewhat beloved Captain Huxley of Gale Storm's fifties sitcom *Oh! Susanna*) the hero, and Hannah Williams his sweetheart—and Agnes de Mille had been the choreographer. As with a later Arlen-Harburg show, *Bloomer Girl* (1944), de Mille dared a serious set piece amid the dizzy hoopla. But the later show's Civil War Ballet is romantic, and *Hooray For What!*'s Hero Ballet was dark and ironic. With the international situation having grown so volatile, a musical about spies and secret weapons was perhaps bound to make some concession to reality. And a Hero Ballet did lend the foodledooing Wynn carnival a touch of dignity.

Still, something went wrong, for while the Hero Ballet came in with the show for the New York opening, the name of Agnes de Mille was taken off the hoardings. Robert Alton joined the production out of town to bring on the girls, so to say, making an odd mix with the Hero. In the end, Vance copied Wynn's formula down in her compact mirror, reversing its effect. So, like Johnny Johnson, Chuckles—the Wynn role—has a chance to save the world from itself with happy gas. Despite rave notices, *Hooray For What!* achieved a merely acceptable 200-performance run.

De Mille's next one closed after 13 performances; luckily, her fourth show (remember, *Nymph Errant* was her first) was *Oklahoma!*. But *Swingin' the Dream* (1939) has to be one of the most fascinating bombs of all time. The last of the Center Theatre spectacles before the house went over to ice shows, *Swingin' the Dream* was a mixed-race jazzup of *A Midsummer Night's Dream*, with the Benny Goodman Sextette both onstage and in the pit, Louis Armstrong as Bottom, and Butterfly McQueen as Puck. (Instead of a magical flower, she employed a pump of her Flit gun to enchant her victims.*) The décor was in the style of Walt Disney, and, in the manner of the two jazzings of *The Mikado* earlier that year, the idea was to razz a classic with new art, especially jitterbug, swing, and anything else that might inflect Shakespeare with the flavor of now. For example, Titania (Maxine Sullivan) navigated the stage in a chair on wheels just like those at the World's Fair.

The nobles were white (Dorothy McGuire played Helena) while the fairies and *Pyramus and Thisbe* troupe were black. *The Great Waltz's* Erik Charell produced, showing an astonishing comprehension of that American thirties show-biz obsession, the merging of art and pop. *Porgy and Bess* is its best-known example and *Swingin' the Dream* the least. It's hard to know what exactly went wrong, for even the critics, while disapproving, thought the dancing—the work of de Mille and Herbert White—was excellent.

Charell not only produced but co-wrote the book (with Gilbert Seldes, author of *The Seven Lively Arts*, a seminal collection of essays on the fine art of, for instance, *Krazy Kat*), and co-directed (with Philip Loeb).

---

* Flit was insect repellent, extremely common in American culture at the time. It was a buzz term; Harold Rome refers to it in *Pins and Needles'* "Nobody Makes a Pass At Me."

So Charell is the one who erred, perhaps in putting too much confidence in the slanging up of Shakespeare; and the exploitation of familiar lines from other of his plays; and spending too much book time on the lovers. The setting had been moved from Athens to "New Orleans, the Athens of the Southland," and the time was now "1890 at the birth of Swing." Fine; and with a production filled with personal microphones disguised as forest animals and with hats resembling watermelons, there is no question but that Shakespeare had been fully "colored in" by the Disneyland Harlem of it all. *The Daily Mirror*'s Robert Coleman thought it "swell when it loses the book and shags and jives"—but should there perhaps have been more of a score? Jimmy Van Heusen and Eddie de Lange were credited as composer and lyricist, but in fact there were few new numbers. The high point was "(I was) Swingin' a Dream," introduced in close harmony by the Dandridge Sisters, Dorothy, Vivian, and Etta, the first of whom went on to a solo career in film. There were few other original vocal spots at all, for the performance built up to a *Pyramus and Thisbe* opera made of "Ain't Misbehavin'," "Hold Tight," "I Can't Give You Anything But Love," "Sugarfoot Stomp," and other standards. Mendelssohn's Wedding March got a look in, and his twittering "Spring Song" was used as well, for the first vocal number, by the Deep River Boys.

Hooray For What! and *Swingin' the Dream*, obviously, were detours on the road of de Mille's career; her contribution comes in the next decade. The main player in the 1930s is George Balanchine. Oddly, he brings us to not only the very center of modernistic dance but to Rodgers and Hart, because they brought Balanchine importantly into the creation of four of their best shows—even, by common consent, their four best in this decade: *On Your Toes* (1936), *Babes In Arms* (1937), *I Married An Angel* (1938), and *The Boys From Syracuse* (1938).

As stated, Rodgers and Hart form the other half of the great thirties songbook, opposite Cole Porter. The two sets may seem similar, for unlike Jerome Kern and Vincent Youmans they did not venture into the heady emotionalism of operetta, and unlike Kurt Weill, Harold Arlen, and E. Y. Harburg they were not associated with work of sociopolitical import, and unlike Irving Berlin they didn't run a busy shop in self-contained pop tunes, and unlike the Gershwins they never wrote an opera. Then, too, Rodgers and Hart and Porter alike worked in what would appear to be standard-format musical comedy in contemporary urban settings and a "sophisticated" worldview.

It's not that simple. Porter always worried about how well he addressed the market; Rodgers and Hart were comfortable with their gifts. There is also the odd realization that, unbeknown to possibly everybody but himself, Rodgers must have been nursing dreams of writing . . . well, *Oklahoma!* and *Carousel*. The kind of show that didn't exist in the 1930s.

Then, too, a Cole Porter score is an Ethel Merman score. She played leads or utterly starred in five Porter shows, and it was Porter who invented the Ethel Merman Number—the "Blow, Gabriel, Blow" raveup, the "I Get a Kick Out Of You" torch song, the "Anything Goes" *gangway!* anthem. No one played leads in five Rodgers and Hart shows. True, Helen Ford, Ray Bolger, and Vivienne Segal each appeared in three, but Ford is not identifiable in any important way; Bolger's appearance in *Heads Up!* is hardly a stylistic foundation for loyalty to the firm; and there is no such thing as a Vivienne Segal number.*

Most important, Rodgers and Hart's thirties shows are far more various in type than Porter's. Yes, Porter's *musical* approach is very changeable: but the overall tone of his shows is not. One couldn't imagine Cole Porter doing a *Babes In Arms* or *Too Many Girls*—kids and college students? Porter doesn't write for innocents. Nor would Porter have done *The Boys From Syracuse*, the first modern musical to adapt Shakespeare. Yes, of course Porter did get to *Kiss, Me Kate* ten years after the earlier work— but surely only because the backstager frame accommodates Porter with the self-dramatizing or raffish folk he is comfortable with. It would be hard to picture Porter tackling *The Taming of the Shrew* all by itself. Anyway, aren't his *Shrew* numbers character songs for the real-life actors within the story? Isn't "I Hate Men" Lilli Vanessi's song? Doesn't "Where Is the Life That Late I Led?" illustrate Fred Graham's little black book? This is more of the Porter we already know, hymning the disenchanted woman and the randy male.

---

* Segal left souvenirs of two of her Rodgers and Hart shows; her "Bewitched" suggests a matchless Vera and her "To Keep My Love Alive" in the revival of *A Connecticut Yankee* alerts us to a definitive Morgan Le Fay, if such were needed. However, the very concept of a genre of number wedded to the performer who inspired it means that that performer will, if only slightly, haunt that genre and its examples ever after. One cannot argue that Vivienne Segal haunts "Bewitched" the way Ethel Merman does "I Get a Kick Out Of You."

Rodgers and Hart looked for many different characters to sing of—Arthurian knights, fairy-tale folk, ancient Chinese mandarins, people of Hollywood, the circus, the ballet, the after-hours underworld. Porter the lyricist would have been comfortable with only the last group. Harold Clurman called Hart "a sort of honky-tonk Heine," but that is misleadingly simplistic. Yes, Hart's more worldly utterances locate poetry in a rude place of wistful confusions and shattered dreams—but "honky-tonk" suggests a collector of "knowing" figures, those who willingly show up at the house of pleasure. On the contrary, Hart writes far more about the unknowing, the innocent taken for a ride. The honky-tonk, really, is the house of Porter, not Hart. True, Vivienne Segal's three Rodgers and Hart characters have been around the block; but she is exceptional. The babes and college kids are more typical. Porter writes of mankind after the Fall. Hart writes of individuals still chaste, on the verge of sin.

Rodgers, too, is very different from Porter the composer, avoiding the country spoofs and only occasionally trying Latin rhythm. Nor is Rodgers interested in Porter's obsessive use of triplets in a line of quarter notes, that effect of the melody floating over the accompaniment. Rodgers prefers tunes locked into a solid $\frac{4}{4}$ beat, possibly syncopated but never ambiguously accented with triplets: "Blue Room," "Mountain Greenery," "My Heart Stood Still," "I Still Believe in You," "I've Got Five Dollars," "There's a Small Hotel," "Where Or When," "Sing For Your Supper," "I Like To Recognize the Tune," "Zip." Then there is the "Rodgers waltz," so singled out because none of his contemporaries sounded as fresh as Rodgers in $\frac{3}{4}$, as ready for this week's hit parade: "I Blush," "Nothing's Wrong," "Lover," "Over and Over Again," "The Most Beautiful Girl in the World," "Falling in Love With Love," "Nothing But You," "Wait Till You See Her." By contrast, Porter wrote few waltzes—and those mainly as pastiche, to suggest a different timeplace—*Anything Goes*' cut operetta spoof "Waltz Down the Aisle"; the Noël Coward imitation in *Jubilee*, "When Love Comes Your Way"; *Kiss Me, Kate*'s operetta spoof, a new evolution of the melodic germ of "Waltz Down the Aisle," "Wunderbar"; *Can-Can*'s belle époque evocations in "Never Give Anything Away" and "Allez-vous-en."

Considering Rodgers and Hart as a unit, we find another important difference from Porter's art, a joyful self-confidence that Porter doesn't believe in. He can strike that pose when he needs to treat a character so, but it won't inspire his best work. A typical Porter number is a lament; a typical Rodgers and Hart number is a piece of advice. "Love one time," they urge us in "The Heart Is Quicker Than the Eye": "look at the Lunts." Only Hart of all in this age—except possibly Ira Gershwin—would think of condensing the life and work of Broadway's great acting duo into a seven-word guide to healthy living. Only a Rodgers and Hart show (*On Your Toes*) would feature a song (this one) about love's pitfalls that makes love attractive. What this team does is readjust the essential sunniness of musical comedy to the wisdom of the honky-tonk Heine—or, perhaps a little more precisely, the playground Voltaire.

Was it both men who kept modifying convention to suit their story-telling? For Hart often seemed less impelled than Rodgers by the concentration needed to write and produce theatre. When working, Porter meticulously plodded and perfected. In Boston for the tryout of *Red, Hot and Blue!* (1936), Porter had to replace Ethel Merman's first number, the keening "Goodbye, Little Dream, Goodbye," which was depressing the public. We've already had a footnote on "Dream" and its later history, but right now I want to emphasize an aspect of the respective work habits of Porter and Hart. At the time that Porter was in the process of creating "Dream"'s successor, Russel Crouse, co-author of the *Red, Hot and Blue!* book, found Porter cutting him dead during rehearsal, repeatedly wandering past Crouse without even a nod. Suddenly, Porter's face broke out in a sunbeam of animation as he triumphantly called out to Crouse, "In my pet pailletted gown!" Unable to round off a couplet, Porter had in effect gone into a trance in search of the needed rhyme.

Hart never went into trances. Facile in the best sense, scribbling perfect couplets onto paper scraps held against the wall, Hart was all the same often unavailable, even during rehearsals. Yet the Rodgers and Hart shows of the late 1930s keep trying out new things as if determined to enlighten formula with alternatives. Most thirties musical comedies begin in one of only two ways: with an opening chorus (or musical number of some kind), then an expository book scene, then an "explaining" number such as the Heroine's Wanting Song or something from the second couple; *or* the same thing *without* an opening number. Yet, for starters, each Rodgers and Hart show of the late 1930s begins in its own special way. Had Hart not cared about what he was doing, wouldn't he have taken the easy line and chosen all the obvious options? Moreover, on four

of their shows, despairing of getting good librettos, Rodgers and Hart
wrote not only the score but the script as well. Isn't that dedication?

On Your Toes in fact claims one of the few amusingly mystifying first
four minutes in the entire decade. After two Broadway revivals, including the one with Natalia Makarova in 1983, we know what On Your Toes
is concerned with. Some may know its songs and their purposes. But, in
1936, the curtain rose on one of those break-the-rules numbers, "Two-a-
Day For Keith," a three-person family vaudeville act. It's jaunty and
charming: but why is it there? Who are these people? Indeed, after the
number and the following book scene, the three actors playing these roles
all but disappear. (The two oldsters return briefly at the end.) Their purpose lies only in establishing the hero's background as a hoofer; the show's
third scene, when he is an adult, reveals his interest in classical music.
Thus, the work's theme of pop vs. classical dance is given us partly in
musical code, a brilliant stroke.*

Babes in Arms opens more conventionally, in an expository book scene:
the babes' parents are taking jobs on the road, leaving their children vulnerable to time on the county work farm. We meet some of the youthful
principals, and also a newcomer among them, a vagabond lass who finds
herself drawn to the lead kid, as he to her. This brings on a kiss and a
ballad—but an odd one, on déjà vu. We keep hearing how the more
resourceful writers seek variations on "I love you" to avoid cliché, but this
is truly arcane. One wonders how many admirers of "Where or When"
simply enjoy the music without considering the paranormal nature of the
subject matter.

That's not a problem over at I Married An Angel, with the suavest of
these four opening sequences—as befits a continental piece based on a
Hungarian play. Waltzy underscoring accompanies a book scene of guests
arriving for a party, a surprise birthday bash for the protagonist. But he
bustles in unhappily, in no mood for socializing. Soon enough, alone with
his worldly sister and his cute-young-dancing-guy secretary, the protagonist starts "Did You Ever Get Stung?" with a conversational abandon.

---

* For the first revival, in 1954, the director of all three Broadway On Your Toeses (though
unbilled the first time), George Abbott, suddenly feared that a public weaned on the
explicatory openings of the Rodgers and Hammerstein shows and their imitators might
miss this subtlety of gesture. Just after the opening, Abbott fired the three actors and cut
their scenes. He was wrong, and he finally knew it: in 1983, song and characters were
reinstated.

It's an outburst, in fact: "Every woman is a cheat!" This leads to a brisk refrain that tells us all we need to know for now: the hero has been badly hurt by womankind and can't wait to try his luck again, protest though he may.

The Boys From Syracuse, whose Shakespeare is the plot-driven *The Comedy of Errors*, has the most unusual of this quartet of openings, one of the most unusual of the decade. Few shows crowd so much exposition into an opening number; one thinks of *Wonderful Town*'s "Christopher Street," *Li'l Abner*'s "A Typical Day," *Goodtime Charley*'s "History," *Pacific Overtures*' "The Advantages of Floating in the Middle of the Sea." *The Boys From Syracuse*'s "I Had Twins" has to tell of far more than local culture or chapters of European chronicle. This tale is the sad family history of Aegeon, a merchant of Syracuse, who—just as in Shakespeare's Act One, scene one—recounts to the Duke of Ephesus the tragic sea voyage that parted him from his wife while also parting his twin sons and their twin slaves. It's a heady report to take in; Shakespeare simply throws the scene to Aegeon in what is virtually a vast soliloquy.

That's no way to run a musical, so Rodgers and Hart set the Duke and Aegeon apart from the onstage chorus, conversing in the Duke's authoritative bass clarinet and Aegeon's high-tenor, Victor Mooreish E Flat clarinet. Another character, following the two men's dialogue, repeats it to the chorus people, so every line of the complex backstory is twice musicked: first on Aegeon's clarinet and then verbally, in human song.

Ephesus has issues with Syracuse, so Aegeon faces death. Yet the melody of "I Had Twins"—once the actual storytelling begins—is perversely frivolous, partly because this is after all a musical comedy and because the driveline of the reuniting of Aegeon's family will find fulfillment by evening's end: unbeknown to Aegeon, all five of his missing people are in Ephesus as we speak. The number is astonishingly progressive considering the generic choral dumdum so common just a few years before.

Let us consider, too, how differently each of these four shows originally played. *On Your Toes* had a typical thirties musical-comedy breakdown: hoofer lead (Ray Bolger), amorous ballerina (Tamara Geva), hoofer's faithful girl friend (Doris Carson), sarcastic society lady (Luella Gear), big noisy comic (Monty Woolley), jealous ballerino (Demetrios Vilan). With George Abbott presiding, farcical playacting will be the vogue, not character motivation. But all the jokes will land and the pacing will never falter.

Babes In Arms of course claims a famously fledgling cast; the two lead women, Mitzi Green and Wynn Murray, were sixteen. Duke McHale was nineteen, Alfred Drake twenty-two, Ray Heatherton a Gandalf at twenty-five or so, and the Nicholas Brothers (whose managers concealed their age to prolong their infant phenomena status in vaudeville and the movies) apparently adolescent. Kids playing kids have a different quality than people like Ray Bolger or Doris Carson do, not to mention the precious caricature that Monty Woolley indulged in. Of course, you reply— but what happens when those kids sing grownups' songs like "I Wish I Were in Love Again" or "My Funny Valentine?" There's an arresting tension in a sixteen-year-old singing so deeply and honestly of love for her Valentine. (This is in fact the character's name.) Whereas when *On Your Toes'* Bolger and Carson sing "There's a Small Hotel," we hardly notice that the hotel deals in "marriage trade" and these two seem to be contemplating a pre-marital tryst.

I Married An Angel was directed by Joshua Logan, who was much less inclined than George Abbott simply to steer actors around and give line readings. Then, too, the cast was drawn mainly from talent able in "adult" comedy of double meanings and the Higher Wisecrack. Dennis King played Count Willy Palaffi, the "I" of the title, and the enchanting Norwegian ballerina Vera Zorina was his Angel. Vivienne Segal played an odd role, for with her womanly charm she ought to have been the romantic lead. Instead, she was King's sister, Peggy Palaffi. This made for an extremely strange singing of the show's main ballad, "Spring Is Here." A duet of elegiacal rue, it surely belongs to the senior version of Boy Meets Girl—but King sang it with sister Segal. No doubt it was meant to show how well each comforts the other: but it bears an incestuous undertow.

The other leads were cutups—Walter Slezak as banker King's main creditor, Audrey Christie as King's troublesome ex, and the decade's favorite juvenile, Charles Walters, as King's secretary. But the surprisingly talky book (by Rodgers and Hart) really centers on this heavenly creature and her effect on the imperfect human world. The project was originally to have been filmed, for Jeanette MacDonald during Rodgers and Hart's final days in Hollywood, at MGM, and perhaps for that reason only

Angel has a character agenda. The others just joke, and Rodgers and Hart weren't the sharpest writers of joke books. Still, they had worked with Herbert Fields and Guy Bolton, who more or less invented the Third Age joke book, and the players of that time were skilled in the timing and inflection that makes the humor land beyond its right to. Try this sample, when King finally tells Segal that he has married out of species:

WILLY: She's an *angel*!
PEGGY: I know she's an angel, she's got a cute figure, but where does she come from?
WILLY: From *heaven*!
PEGGY: Oh, shut up!

Finally she gets it. Zorina isn't just an "angel." She's an *angel*:

WILLY: Angel . . . came down from heaven and married me.
PEGGY: (waits for seven beats) Ooh, how perfectly *disgusting*!

With so much book, *I Married An Angel* has the smallest score in this quartet, just eight numbers. At that, "The Modiste" and "Angel Without Wings" are largely made of the rhythmic dialogue that Rodgers and Hart developed in their first years in Hollywood. "Angel Without Wings," in which Angel is visited by her sisters, is entirely spoken till it turns into a close-harmony septet. More elaborate in structure, "The Modiste" starts as a reprise of the title song, then goes its own way as Angel makes her first aquaintance with a modern woman's attire. Near the end, she leaves to try everything on and, for a sight gag, returns wearing it all in the wrongest possible way, from bra to chemise.

Leaving further discussion of *The Boys From Syracuse* for dessert later, let us consider the music of these shows and why Rodgers and Hart thought they needed so strong a helping of dance. *On Your Toes*, obviously, could only have been conceived as a dancing musical: what better art to illustrate the hero's bigamous romance with high and low culture? But *Babes In Arms* is the simplest of musical comedies: born yesterday, unaware of culture, and hot to hoof. And *I Married An Angel*, at least as written, is the next thing to a play with songs, the kind of show that usually lacks an ensemble and a choreographer.

The explanation must be that Rodgers and Hart saw their creative outlet as inhering not only in songs but in entire shows, each unlike all others. Cole Porter nourished a platonic concept of the Cole Porter Show; Rodgers and Hart had no idea what a Rodgers and Hart Show was, because their art was not fixed. It may simply be that they loved the New Dance because it kept their storytelling fresh. In today's age of revivals and stagings of movies, we have lost the idea of each musical comedy as being, in part, a surprise.

At the same time, the pair knows as much as anyone about holding a show together logically. In *I Married An Angel*'s second act, it becomes clear that the perfect Angel is a perfect terror because she is rooted in truthtelling. She actually wrecks a restaurant (offstage) because a waiter promised her that the goulash was "delicious": and it wasn't. So the all-knowing Peggy must give her divine sister-in-law a course in female deceit—sorry, *charm*—thus to accommodate the quotidian dishonesty of humankind and fare well in the world. Note how suavely our boys cue in the next number, "A Twinkle in Your Eye," as Peggy gets Angel to join her for a night out:

ANGEL: But who's going to be at the party?
PEGGY: Men, darling. Men.
ANGEL: (as the orchestra starts the intro) Could you tell me what to do?
PEGGY: (singing, as she launches the vocal) It's not what you do . . .

With the narrative so firmly ruled as it moves between dialogue and song, dances comes as the exception to the rule, a wonderful abstraction: a surprise. Dance lifts the spirit, lends beauty to the account, and even partakes of humor. In New Revue, dance was arty prestige, especially as most of the soloists—Tilly Losch, Paul Haakon, José Limón—were all European or otherwise exotic. But in musical comedy, dance was a novel source of fun.

The usual plan was a Big Ballet in each of the two acts, often listed in the program by its own title, along with extra helpings of dance slotted in after the more rhythmic numbers. Audrey Christie's first-act spot, "How To Win Friends and Influence People," is a jazzy fox trot full of Rodgers "wrong" notes that begs for the dancing boys and girls to rush in on and bang out their combinations to. And of course the orchestra simply plays the refrain over and over for them, giving the public a chance to collect it.

That is the very spirit of musical comedy, for hoofing attended its first parties, way back in the mid-nineteenth century; and what could be more natural than to plug a good tune, as we saw them doing in *Gay Divorce*? However, Big Ballet is special and calls for special music. Themes from the score could be used, but they were most often twisted to dramatic commentary. *I Married An Angel*'s first-act entry is the "Honeymoon Ballet," which reveals the itinerary of Willy and Angel's marital bliss in ways that book and score cannot. Amusingly, the orchestra draws on familiar tunes to describe or pun on what the dancing shows us, quoting Anna Held's hit (she also wrote the lyrics) from *A Parisian Model* (1906), "It's Delightful To Be Married"; the famous tune from Glière's ballet *The Red Poppy* (which in those days was a musical buzz-term for "Russia"); "The Campbells Are Coming"; then some crazy Middle Eastern pastiche; and finally a rustic tune, for The Palaffis in the Country. This accords with the show's overall tone, which is mocking rather than romantic.

It was the second-act ballet that had the town talking, a spoofy tribute to the kind of stage show that accompanied the feature film at the Roxy or Radio City Music Hall. Completely unmotivated, it slipped into the narrative when Willy, facing financial ruin because of a whisper campaign against his bank, envisions fleeing Budapest. How about New York? And when one is in New York, one must see the Roxy, no? That cued in Christie's second number, "At the Roxy Music Hall," which inspired Balanchine to put on his own version of those stage shows. Somehow or other, the tale of Othello got into the mix, and Walter Slezak played a walrus to Zorina's sea nymph, and Segal and Christie were the Rockettes. Every critic reveled in it.

So we notice that Big Ballet, in its youth, did not necessarily attempt the psychological analysis we associate with *Oklahoma!*'s "Laurey Makes Up Her Mind," or the feminist romanticism of *Brigadoon*'s "Come To Me, Bend To Me" ballet, or the pageant-with-a-subtext in *The King and I*'s "The Small House of Uncle Thomas," or the erotic comedy of *Can-Can*'s "Garden of Eden." Sometimes Big Ballet was just silly fun.

One might say that particularly of *On Your Toes*' first-act ballet, "La Princesse Zenobia." An ideal assignment for Balanchine, it is in effect a re-creation of classic Russian dance, neither academic nor altogether spoofy. It does contain a joke: having gone on at the last minute in a topless costume, Ray Bolger doesn't know he's supposed to don dark body makeup, and he nearly wrecks the performance. Not only the choreography but the music, too, gets humorous here, suggesting the pseudo-oriental tone poems of Albert Ketèlbey, such as "In a Chinese Temple Garden" or "In a Persian Market."

The thematic center of On Your Toes was the dancing of the title number, by duelling corps of hoofers and ballet people: sweet or hot? But the high point—and possibly the most famous single ballet in the musical's history—is "Slaughter on Tenth Avenue." It calls for three principals, Hoofer (Ray Bolger), Strip Tease Girl (Tamara Geva), and Big Boss (George Church), and narrates autonomously, without even subtextual reference to the larger work. In fact, "Slaughter" has a reputation as an "integrated" dance that is entirely unmerited. On Your Toes' plot intrudes on it in that Geva's jealous boy friend has put a hit on Bolger, and he keeps dancing at the climax to avoid being shot. Like "La Princesse Zenobia," "Slaughter" is a self-contained performance piece, shown to us in real time as it is seen on the stage of the Cosmopolitan Opera House. It is the culmination of On Your Toes' culture war: Bolger's student has written this "jazz ballet" the way George Gershwin wrote a concerto, a tone poem, an opera.

One of the great things about "Slaughter" is that it is very much a part of its score, for Rodgers composed it (and "Zenobia") himself. This was rare. A polished musician such as Victor Herbert wrote the dance music for his shows, but, generally, the genre was assigned to some unbilled assistant. By the 1930s, this was all but inevitable especially because the choreographer became not just illustrator of the dance but author of it, and only a subaltern could be expected to hang around a rehearsal hall tailoring music for the fit. However, Balanchine was obviously used to making his art on already existing music, so Rodgers saw no reason not to try his hand at the ballet pastiche of "Zenobia." As for "Slaughter," this was the historic moment when pop's love of amusement and art's love of meaning were influentially to mate. Why wouldn't Rodgers want to be the first on the block to marry them?

As with "Zenobia," Rodgers used nothing from On Your Toes' vocal score in "Slaughter," straining into unstable harmonic territory from the start to suggest the volatile life of the criminal quartier. The set is a

barroom, and the music, after four bars of grand ceremonial intro, kicks
into bustling city music with a melody slithering over chords of $B^b{}^7_6$ and
d^7_4, an extremely distinctive sound. The view gives us thugs and whores.
Big Boss shoots a bum, and employees sweep the corpse offstage. Then
comes Bolger's first dance with Geva, to the ballet's big romantic theme,
one that, one imagines, Rodgers and Hart's publisher begged them to turn
into a pop tune in the "Blue Moon" manner; to no avail, if so. "Three
Blind Mice" and whistles herald the entrance of three cops pursuing
the murder case, but the girls distract them, and Bolger again pairs off with
Geva, now in a stamping rhythm that finds Bolger frantically tearing up
the place till Big Boss shoots at him and hits Geva. The two men fight for
the gun; Bolger kills Big Boss and keens *with* Geva's lifeless body to the
big romantic tune. From the sublime to the grotesque: Bolger dances
around Big Boss' corpse to music at once dark and sprightly, leading to a
shattering climax of the romantic tune, fortissimo, in *Alla breve maestoso*.

This is the musical's first great narrative ballet, and it allied the music
of thirties Broadway to the decade's discovery of dance. Did Rodgers have
to compose it because it was a major event, or was it a major event
because Rodgers composed it? *The Band Wagon*'s "Beggar Waltz" was written (at least in part) by Arthur Schwartz, but it was apparently not a genuine narrative. "Slaughter" has a plot, and, better, has a composer ready
to expand his style in melody that is born instrumental, not vocal. This
man grows.

On Your Toes' vocal numbers are Rodgers and Hart in the first show we
are conversant with that exemplifies their style. We know "Manhattan,"
from 1925—but we don't know their twenties shows. Just as *Anything
Goes* announces the Cole Porter that the term "Cole Porter" means, *On
Your Toes* gives us our Rodgers and Hart. When Hart begins the verse of
"Too Good For the Average Man" with a reference to Tsarist Russia,
Rodgers matches it with a melody drawn from the first theme of the first
movement of Tchaikofsky's Fifth Symphony. When Hart continues the
verse with a reference to Tudor England, Rodgers puts the melody into
the major, and the line "That's how England grew!" inspires a taste of
clavichord in the accompaniment. For the refrain, Rodgers simply
expands that tiny pasticcio into a minuet in AABA.

One can enjoy this team even without catching their allusions, but
not in "The Three B's," whose jokes take in repertory titles, a stream of

musicians' names (including Trentini; Emma, we presume, the original star of Victor Herbert's *Naughty Marietta*), and a reference to a long-forgotten Kálmán operetta, *Der Zigeunerprimás*, given here in 1914 as *Sári*.

The last time Rodgers composed for Balanchine was "Peter's Journey," an eleven-minute Big Ballet in *Babes In Arms*' second act. The first-act ballet was a performance piece, part of the babes' show. A bargain-basement Egyptian Number, it followed "Johnny One Note" and did little more than churn out the song's refrain in various styles, including Latin rhythm and Pollyanna twitter.

"Peter's Journey," however, is a narrative monster of a what if? daydream. One of the babes, Peter, is a fierce believer in socialist sharing till he wins $500 on a movie theatre's bank night.* Rather than help his friends, he goes off to see the world, his "text" drawn from "Imagine," sung earlier in the act by Wynn Murray and a close-harmony men's quartet that turns up throughout the *Babes In Arms* score. Taking over the song to speculate on his future, Peter begins his journey, and Rodgers gives him an elated travelogue of old and new music. The ballet is roughly in rondo form, with "Imagine" as the first theme and "Sailing, Sailing, Over the Bounding Main" (with a three-note quotation of the "sea" motif from Rimsky-Korsakof's *Scheherazade*) as the second. Episodes cite Waldteufel's waltz "The Skaters," a Scots theme, and "walking" music on the piano, as Peter meets John D. Rockefeller, a mermaid, and movie stars.

Framed by Peter's own vocals of "Imagine," the "Journey" expanded the very content of Big Ballet, forcing the musical to add a new technician to its troupe, the dance arranger who is no mere grunt but a composer in his or her own right—Trude Rittman, Genevieve Pitot, Roger Adams, Luther Henderson, Peter Howard, and even future composers of their own scores John Morris, Laurence Rosenthal, and Marvin Hamlisch. "Slaughter on Tenth Avenue" and "La Princesse Zenobia" might have been Rodgers' busman's holiday fare, tricks of the dancing trade in a dancing show, not to be repeated. But when, on his very next show, he pursued the composition of narrative dance music, Rodgers was quietly affirming the start of a new era.

---

* The Communist or other left cultist who instantly loses his faith when given access to money was a thirties stereotype. Rodgers and Hart offered another example in Egghead, the Harry Langdon role in their Al Jolson film *Hallelujah, I'm a Bum* (1933).

Before this, ballet in musicals was strictly pictorial, like *East Wind*'s "Indo-Chinese Ballet," or very slightly synoptic, like that revolt of sugar-cane cutters in *Parade*. Now, however, ballets could function within the structure of a musical's action—even so essentially that shows would become incoherent if performed without them.

Rodgers' timing couldn't have been smarter, because the revolution that he was to effect with Oscar Hammerstein lay only a few years ahead, and the musical play that they were to invent couldn't have existed without the impressionistic stylization that Agnes de Mille and Jerome Robbins would effect in her *Oklahoma!*, *One Touch of Venus*, *Bloomer Girl*, *Carousel*, *Brigadoon*, and *Paint Your Wagon*, and his *On the Town*, *High Button Shoes*, *The King and I*, and *West Side Story*.

The reader will note a few musical comedies in that list; but it was elemental to the musical-play era that the form's influence was developing musical comedy as well. George Jean Nathan couldn't stand it; when he heard the word "integrated," he reached for his revolver. But it is undeniable that "modernistic" dance became, in succeeding decades, a civilizing force in the musical generally. One might call it The Last Integration: the final breakthrough in the Third Age's voyage from *Lady, Be Good!* to *Chicago*.

I GOT RHYTHM: THE MUSIC OF THE 1930s

Girl Crazy (1930) was an Aarons-Freedley property, with a Gershwin score and the brand-new star of the producers' *Hold Everything!* two years before, Bert Lahr. As so often in those days, it was not the story that inspired songs and fun but the setting: *Girl Crazy* would travel west, where the northeast urban Lahr could play culture shock with the cowboys and cactus. The idea may owe something to a show that opened two months after *Hold Everything!*, Florenz Ziegfeld's *Whoopee*, in which Eddie Cantor took on the frontier.

Two more different comics there never were: Cantor the young fogy (in *Whoopee* a hypochondriac) forever prancing and cringing yet helplessly baiting the bullies; and Lahr the one-man rabble, a paradox of fear and daring. (This was before he adopted his spoof of the snooty.) However, Lahr decided to break his contract with Aarons and Freedley and do George White's aviation musical, *Flying High*. Lahr was replaced on *Girl Crazy* by Willie Howard, who lacked the unique enlightenment of the first-division zany and would have had a hard time carrying *Girl Crazy* without the smashing score. Remember that the Boy Meets Girl in the star-clown vehicle tended to go to capably unimportant players, though here Allen Kearns was paired with the nineteen-year-old Ginger Rogers. Luckily, the second couple paired comic William Kent with the twenty-one-year-old Ethel Merman (in her Broadway debut), and an especially lively pit included a group put together by Red Nichols and featuring Glenn Miller, Jimmy Dorsey, Benny Goodman, and Gene Krupa.

So Howard didn't have to carry the show—or, rather, either of the two shows that *Girl Crazy* represented. Like so many musical comedies of the

1920s and early 1930s, *Girl Crazy* was two different works operating more or less autonomously. One of the two was a book (by Jack McGowan and Guy Bolton) about a New York playboy sent to Custerville, Arizona by a reproving father, only to set up a dude ranch while romancing Custerville's postmistress. The second couple arrive to work in the hero's new saloon, and Willie Howard gets into the plot as Gieber Goldfarb, a cab driver who ferries the hero out to Arizona, for a fare of $742.30. There is little story beyond that: the Boy Meets Girl takes everyone to Mexico for Act Two, when Girl runs off with Other Boy; and Gieber is elected sheriff of Custerville and gets into the various ridiculous disguises without which Guy Bolton felt no musical was complete.

The other half of *Girl Crazy* comprised the music, which for the most part works independently of the story. Besides reprises and finales, there are fourteen separate numbers; nine of them have nothing to do with the action in any real sense. After watching how variously Rodgers and Hart launched their late thirties shows, it is bemusing to see how vaguely, how gradually *Girl Crazy* gets down to business. The opening number, "Bidin' My Time," does a nice job of establishing the lazy emptiness of Custerville in its close-harmony men's quartet. But then a cowboy in fancy duds comes in to announce that he's off to Mexico to bring back a wife, which takes us right into "The Lonesome Cowboy (won't be lonesome now)." Who is this character? A lead? A motivator of a subplot? Neither: he's a cowboy in fancy duds who announces that he's off to Mexico to bring back a wife. After the song and dance, he vanishes from the story.

At least now the action can begin, as the hero enters, dressed pour le sport at Bar Harbor. But the score will never quite tally with the book. The love plot provides virtually the only basis for character numbers—in the Meeting ("Could You Use Me?"), the confirmation ("Embraceable You"), and her torch spot ("But Not For Me"). Otherwise, songs drop in like guests at an open house. When living conditions in Custerville prove too primitive for Ethel Merman and she says, "I wish I was back in the old dump on the Barbary Coast," we are but a joke away from a thoroughly extraneous number called "Barbary Coast." First, the joke: Merman met husband William Kent "at the toughest honky-tonk in the place." How tough was it? Kent says, "It was so tough, why, even the girls wore barbed-wire garters." Merman does a take. "How do *you* know?" she asks, and Kent holds up his palms, saying, "Look at the scars." And with a "Why, you—" look on her face, Merman chases him offstage to clear space for three soubrettes to cue in the big dance number.

It's a good number, of course; the whole *Girl Crazy* score is tuneful and sharp even when it isn't going anywhere in the narrative. We know how songwriters around 1930 hoped to see their titles extracted for hit-parade popularity, but most of *Girl Crazy*'s songs didn't need to be extracted, as they were never truly a part of the story that *Girl Crazy* purported to tell.

For example, Merman's two first-act numbers, back to back in the closing saloon scene, actually make more sense when extracted than they do in the show. Not knowing how they are used on stage, one might assume that "Sam and Delilah" is a canny gloss on the love plot, or that "I Got Rhythm" is Merman's character song. Actually, though Merman sings one A of "Sam and Delilah" to the hero during the first-act finaletto as a bit of advice, the number as a whole is just a performance piece, rather like "The Lorelei" in its saga of a treacherous woman of myth and in its big choral swelling as the music proceeds.

"I Got Rhythm" arguably *is* a sort of character song, Merman's response to Kent's flattery when she catches him setting up a rendezvous with another girl. However, this is an absurd inducement for Merman suddenly to define herself characterologically after a very long first act in which every player above the rank of chorister has been chattering endlessly. If the story needs Merman to communicate her joie de vivre to the audience in musical terminology, why does it arrive so late in the action?

Granted, what we might call the Idealess Musical is bound to go astray in its tunestack, because it doesn't really have characters: so how can it have character songs? Moreover, while it has a plot, the plot dithers and scrambles, foreclosing the possibility of viable plot songs. By comparison, an earlier Gershwin show of 1930, the revised *Strike Up the Band*, has such a rich idea and pursues it so greedily that it cannot bother with equivalents of "The Lonesome Cowboy" or "Barbary Coast." By the last minutes of its first act, *Strike Up the Band* has turned into an operetta whirligig, as opposing forces (in this case, pacifism versus warmongering) battle over an issue of importance to everyone on stage. The finaletto of twenties musicals liked to bring in snatches of music heard earlier in the action, sometimes with new lyrics, using them to punctuate and encapsulate new developments in the spoken script. *Strike Up the Band* is too busy to accommodate this stop-and-start tempo. Its finaletto contains some reprise material, but essentially moves ever forward entirely in song till it reaches its ironic climax, the war-hating war cry of the title song, unveiled for the first time in the show.

Girl Crazy's finaletto is, on the other hand, old-hat in structure (though it does get very dramatic) as the chorus dives into "Broncho Buster," from earlier in the act. On its first appearance it was another of *Girl Crazy*'s many diversions; now it really means something, for Boy is turning into Man. For the first time, the story makes sense on an emotional level, when Boy sings a bit of "Embraceable You." Then, when he grabs Girl's arm to stop her from going off on that jaunt to Mexico, she tells him, "This rough stuff doesn't suit you." Then she adds, "You're a play-boy," cutting nice and deep. "A dancing man!"

And with that she humiliates him to the utmost, shooting her pistol at his feet to make him hop as he never had to in the ballrooms of the east. It's a strangely unpleasant moment for a show that has been taking romance for granted. Most musical comedies of the era manufactured the Boy Loses Girl plot suspense; this show features Girl robbing Boy of his Manhood. As Ginger Rogers exits with Boy's rival—someone we neither know nor care about—Ethel Merman sings to Allen Kearns that aforementioned snippet of "Sam and Delilah." Has something so brutal, so—really—suspenseful actually occured in this farrago? While we puzzle over this unhappy but unquestionably arresting moment, the first-act curtain falls.

The second act returns us to *Girl Crazy*'s two separate entities. The languid second-act opening chorus, "Land of the Gay Caballero," sets the atmosphere correctly. However, to introduce the act's final scene, back in Custerville, the heroine leads the ensemble in the sportive "Cactus Time in Arizona." Wait a minute! Wasn't her heart broken in Mexico? Didn't she learn what a foul character that other guy was and that Boy is true blue? Didn't she confess her sorrow in "But Not For Me"? Worse, Willie Howard then gave his own reading of that ballad, voicing it in impressions of Maurice Chevalier, Eddie Cantor, and others of his catalogue of replica spoofs. Excuse me?

But, as Aarons and Freedley might tell us, Why waste talent? It outweighs storytelling, for Bolton and McGowan do not trouble to bring Boy and Girl together organically. Instead, they employ objective-correlatives: she enters in a frilly outfit and he comes on as a full-fledged cowboy. In other words, she is no longer a threat to his masculinity and he'll at least look aggressive. Good, that's settled. As Willie Howard tells Ginger Rogers, "Marry him, Molly. It is 11:15 now." So the two kids reprise "Embraceable You," and everyone else runs on for "I Got Rhythm." Curtain!

To be fair, *Girl Crazy* is not a representative thirties musical. It is a representative *early* thirties musical. If we can use 1934's *Revenge With Music* as a marker—and only for our convenience, because it was not thought of as a transitional or breakthrough piece when new—musical comedy before 1934 maintains sloppy communications between book and score, and musical comedy after 1934 tends toward musico-dramatic synthesis. Perhaps it was because more books were being written by the show's lyricists, so that the act of composition automatically united script and tunestack in spontaneous generation.

This is why major revivals of thirties musicals favor titles from 1934 on. When, in the 1990s, *Girl Crazy* was singled out for a resuscitation on The Street, those involved were appalled to see how clunky the thing was. It records well: *Girl Crazy* was another of the old shows that Goddard Lieberson thought essential to his library of classic scores on Columbia Records in the 1950s. Still, the load of characters without character songs, the "Lonesome Cowboy" nothing-doing numbers, the narrative inconsistency, and the Dutch comic all erected such barriers to a modern audience's potential for pleasure that *Girl Crazy* could not even be revised. A new show was built on its foundations: *Crazy For You* (1992), whose only period quality was a John Held Jr. feeling about the logo art, of Boy in a white three-piece suit and Girl in western kit with kerchief and boots, the two of them spooning on a star-dazed crescent moon.

Before we see how well the late 1930s reacclimated score to book, let's consider an early thirties show that may well be the most integrated musical of all time. This is Jerome Kern and Otto Harbach's *The Cat and the Fiddle* (1931). One is tempted to discuss this work in tandem with Kern's following title (with Oscar Hammerstein, remember), *Music in the Air*, that other astonishingly well integrated piece. But this would be misleading. Both shows are virtually made of musical scenes, yes—but *Music in the Air* nevertheless reveals a healthy contingent of out-and-out songs within those scenes. *The Cat and the Fiddle* does not. Music and spoken dialogue course through its action in such intricate cooperation that the tunestack is deconstructed. "Songs" appear in fragments that may later burst into hearing without warning, now linked to each other and now in combat.

For instance, *The Cat and the Fiddle*'s most enduring number is the heroine's "She Didn't Say 'Yes.' " Typically in this jigsaw puzzle of a score, the song is never sung straight through even though its lyrics tell a story. Rather, it is unveiled bit by bit, just when its verses can comment on the show's plot. This is especially effective on its third appearance. We are in a producer's apartment—for *The Cat and the Fiddle* is among other things a backstager—and the heroine puts on a phonograph record of the number while the producer is busy offstage. She sings along, and when she reaches the line "She wasn't even sure that *she'd* be good," she grabs her things and runs out.

For another instance, the orchestra turns one set change into a kind of cinematic wipe for the ear by charging into the sound of a solo piano with a havoc of a dissonance in antagonistic rhythm. It's combat, I say: because *The Cat and the Fiddle*'s subject is war. Not *Strike Up the Band*'s and *Johnny Johnson*'s war, but that endemic thirties war of pop versus classical. The hero (Georges Metaxa) is legit; he composes operetta. The heroine (Bettina Hall) is jazz; she composes pop tunes, including "She Didn't Say 'Yes.' " The pair actually play duelling pianos at one point (hers is offstage), and the evening revels in opposing to that touch of violin a raging band of Terminal Swing. Kern hated the noise, but he could write it with expertise, and given Harbach's labored book, it must be the music that filled the oversized Globe (today the Lunt-Fontanne) for very nearly a year at a time when six months was an achievement. It's amazing that the sublime sounds in the Globe's pit were raised by just eighteen players, on twenty-four instruments (and the drums). Robert Russell Bennett's scoring varies from rumbustious to delicate, as does the story, set in contemporary Brussels with a detour to Louvain, where Metaxa's operetta *The Passionate Pilgrim* is being performed.

We see the finale of this work, a highly mannered bit of commedia dell'arte in which Pierrot (Odette Myrtil, in a trouser role) loses Pierrette (Margaret Adams) to Harlequin (Peter Chambers), plays a last sob on his violin (Myrtil was an accomplished fiddler), and falls senseless. Bennett has been serving us with helpings of flute, clarinet, and oboe solos. Now the trombone, the celesta, the marimba! It's like a candy box of music, too lovely to sample; and it's sung in French. "With childlike simplicity," the score directs, another of the commedia characters announces that Pierrot has died, and the reckless lovers celebrate their dalliance with high notes over an orchestral tutti fortissimo as the stage curtains close.

This is perhaps the most atypical event in the entire decade: the farthest one can travel from *Anything Goes*—or, for that matter, *Johnny Johnson*. Some might call this onstage episode "precious," but let's use the neutral word, which, at this time, was "aesthetic." We of today have no term for this kind of thing, with its woman playing a man while playing a violin, and its eerie descending glissando wails from Pierrot and Harlequin as they adore Pierrette, and its general air of *espièglerie*.

Amusingly, the Compère and Commère of this onstage sequence give us an anticipation of the *Cabaret* Emcee's polyglot greeting of the audience in very slightly different wording. They then perform one of Kern's most delicious numbers, "Poor Pierrot." This music belongs to the Late Kern of such ecstatic ballads as "Yesterdays," "Smoke Gets in Your Eyes," and "All the Things You Are." But this commedia thing takes Kern and his public into even rarer territory, so esoteric that it's easy to forget that *The Cat and the Fiddle* as a whole teaches that highstrung art (in the person of Metaxa's composer, Victor Florescu) needs the normalizing assistance of lowslung art (in Hall's composer, Shirley Sheridan) to succeed. The Pierrot episode was thought so central to the *Cat and the Fiddle* experience that an illustration of it was featured on the sheet music. But the brass growls and duo-piano wackadoo heard all through the rest of the score are more elemental to the work's style.

"A musical love story" was the subtitle; what book show in this era isn't, save *The Cradle Will Rock? The Cat and the Fiddle* is more of a musical debate, as "The Breeze Kissed Your Hair" (which eventually turns out to be nothing more than the verse to "One Moment Alone") and "The Night Was Made For Love" vie for dominance with "Hh! Cha Cha!" and the fox-trotting "Try To Forget." "Hh! Cha Cha!" is marked *Moderato*, but there's nothing moderate about its "Beedenbodendoden dodendada Hhchacha," or Odette Myrtil's violin obbligato of *Show Boat's* "Why Do I Love You?" to "Hh! Cha Cha!"'s second chorus.

At least some of *The Cat and the Fiddle* was simply self-contained vocal numbers, or an exhibition dance, or even a cliché Act One Boy Loses Girl suspense curtain. "The Love Parade" was the show's only big choral number, set out in public where bands parade past one with the usual waving midinettes. Kern and Harbach make no attempt to draw the scene into the work thematically; this is a divertissement, a luxurious one with some French lyrics, powerful choral writing (in seven staves of harmony), and another of Kern's harmonic lurches on a dime, from A Flat to E^7 in a single measure. "I Watch the Love Parade (gaily going by)" is the number's title in the published sheet, suggesting the song's lack of pertinence to the narrative. Moreover, the two soloists who lead the chorus are supporting characters of no plot importance (George Meader, Flora LeBreton). It's one of the few times when this extraordinary show does what other shows do. Comparable are the two dance duets of Shirley's brother (Eddie Foy Jr.) and sister-in-law (*On Your Toes'* soubrette, Doris Carson): the couple just starts dancing, or even just comes on stage and starts dancing, rather in the style of Fred and Adele Astaire in about 1921.

As for that first-act finale, we all know where Jerome Kern stands in the war of charm against swing. Not only does Bettina Hall reject Georges Metaxa by going off with that bawdy producer (José Ruben) whom she will eventually run out on to the strains of "She Didn't Say 'Yes' ": Kern himself signifies his absolute mistrust of Hall's pop by going into Operetta With Extreme Prejudice at the moment of the lovers' confrontation.

The scene is the stage of the Louvain theatre where we just saw the finale of *The Passionate Pilgrim*. Much of *The Cat and the Fiddle* cast is there, all aware that the producer slipped a bit of Hall's pop into Metaxa's classical to make it commercial. Metaxa rebukes Hall, and she defies her sensitive Pierrot by singing yet more of her work, the aforementioned "Try To Forget." For all its contemporary feel, it really isn't that jazzy, with its references to "day dreams" and "gay dreams," to "glad dreams" and "mad dreams." Nevertheless, it's bound to offend Metaxa. "Monsieur Chef d'orchestre," Hall cries out, "continuez, s'il vous plaît!" Six strings and saxophone led off as Hall defended herself in fox trot and Metaxa sang a high descant in operetta style, defying her defiance. For a coda, everyone else joined in on wordless vocalizing as Hall crossed the stage to allow the producer to claim her. The heroine is musical comedy—but the music is operetta, as orchestra and singers came to rest on an F major seventh chord, perfectly unresolved, just like *The Cat and the Fiddle's* war of romance and art. And there the first-act curtain fell.

Of course, Hall and Metaxa made it up by show's end, as Ginger Rogers and Allen Kearns did in *Girl Crazy*. In musicals of this time, if Boy but Meet Girl, Boy shall Get Girl. *Carousel, Street Scene, South Pacific*, and *A Tree Grows in Brooklyn* usher in a different time later on. Note, by the way, that while *Girl Crazy* got not only its Lieberson airing but an authentic-reconstruction CD during the *riezumazione, The Cat and the Fiddle* is all but unrecordable. Can a musical be *too* integrated? Over the years, the show has collected nothing but snips. A full-out recording would have to separate the singing from the underscored talking, an all but impossible task.

I paired *Girl Crazy* with *The Cat and the Fiddle* in order to explore the relationship of words to music at the decade's start in works respectively typical and exceptional. Now, from the decade's end, we comparably consider shows by Cole Porter and by Kurt Weill. Ask the latter whom he wants to work with and he'll say, Give me a playwright, because he'll create a new form of music theatre—someone like Maxwell Anderson, for instance. Porter would say, Give me pros who know how it works.

Porter's show is *Leave It To Me!* (1938), based on Sam and Bella Spewack's play of 1932, *Clear All Wires*, about a character type very popular at the time, the scalawag globe-trotting reporter. In this case, "based" means that the Spewacks simply reclaimed their journalist hero, named Buckley Joyce Thomas,* adding in his gold-digger girl friend, Dolly Winslow, and the triangle subplot of Thomas, Dolly, and Thomas' boss. On that much alone the Spewacks could run *Clear All Wires*' farce, especially with twenty-eight speaking parts and the single set of a room in the Hotel Savoy in Moscow, in the good old structure that allows two chambermaids to start the exposition as they make up the room.

One couldn't get a musical out of so little, which is why *Leave It To Me!* is really an original. Vinton Freedley was its producer, and in the style that he helped popularize he ordered up a helping of William Gaxton, Victor Moore, and Sophie Tucker with a Cole Porter score. Gaxton, of course, would be Buckley Joyce Thomas. The debuting Mary Martin, then just shy of twenty-five, would play Dolly, and by expanding another character in

---

* He is presumably a knock-off of Richard Harding Davis, the most glamorous of the war correspondents who excited the nation's worship in the early twentieth century. The joke is that where Davis was genuinely bold and dashing, Thomas is an unscrupulous opportunist.

Clear All Wires, a woman reporter in love with Thomas, the Spewacks found a role for that worrisome Tamara.* But what of Moore and Tucker?

This is where *Leave It To Me!* takes leave of *Clear All Wires*, for the new show's driveline moved from Thomas' finagling to the appointment of Alonzo P. Goodhue (Moore) as the American ambassador to Russia, to Goodhue's homesickness, and to his conspiracy with Thomas (working for his publisher boss, who wants Goodhue's post) to get himself disgraced. Fired, Goodhue could return to his beloved Topeka, Kansas; this in itself constituted one of *Leave It To Me!*'s running gags. It's not merely that Goodhue likes smalltown America: it's that he takes not even momentary interest in a beguiling scene plot that moves from Paris to Moscow (with a stopover in Siberia). Filling out the view is the far more adventurous Mrs. Goodhue (Tucker), accompanied by the five Goodhue daughters, who in a typical musical-comedy conceit appear to be exactly the same age and are always dressed exactly alike.

Reading the *Leave It To Me!* script today, one sees why thirties writers let star personalities rather than narrative logic guide their pens. Goodhue's lines evoke perfectly the middle-American lord of woe that Moore had made into an art form. Even his hesitant timing seems written into his scenes. Consider this blackout joke that ends the episode in the Gare de l'Est in Paris. It's a busy space in the plot, with a couple of star entrances as the Goodhues arrive to take the train to Moscow; and this is where the driveline is revealed. Goodhue makes his deal with Thomas to get discredited. "Leave it to me!" Thomas cries. They shake on it, and suddenly the piercing screech of a train whistle is heard:

GOODHUE: Mrs. Goodhue is calling me.

The Spewacks even managed to create Sophie Tucker lines, drawn from the persona that Tucker had adopted for her variety-show work. Victor Moore had been on Broadway in book shows for thirty-two years; Tucker had done virtually nothing but vaudeville and revue. Yet there

---

* Do we know *for certain* that Tamara and Tamara Geva are two different persons? Has anyone ever seen them both in one room at the same time? Why this sudden explosion of Tamaras in this decade only, when the 1920s got by happily with Marilyn and Helen and the 1940s with Nanette and Joan?

was a Sophie even so: known to the public for addressing certain subjects in a certain way.

A spot in Act One gives her Cole Porter's version of a Sophie Tucker specialty, "Most Gentlemen Don't Like Love." It's classier than the solos that Tucker commissioned for her vaudeville bookings, with allusions to Madam Sappho and Guinevere and Lancelot. But the cynical view of the male's lack of nesting skills is Tucker 101. The Spewacks sneak the number into play with a single takeover line from Sophie, in her signature radiant grandeur: "Time for your story hour, children." After some shtick comedy for the daughters, Sophie moves into her annunciatory style for "And now, as a mother and a woman, a word of advice."

What more do we need to start up a Sophie Tucker Number? After her vocal, Sophie leaves the stage to the dancers, then returns on a trick line. Offstage, she calls out, "Children!" The girls answer, "Yes, mother?," and Sophie strides back into view for the second chorus, adding in a ramp-up of "I told you" to restart the refrain.

Sophie's role is not as well aligned with the plot as Gaxton's and Moore's are. For example, in Act Two we learn that there is a Goodhue Plan, a reference no doubt to the previously footnoted Townshend Plan and a burlesque on world peace programs. Moore and Gaxton get a long comic scene out of it, not unlike a revue sketch. Then it's Sophie's turn, so the two men go off, some women enter, and one hands Tucker her opening with a question about the Goodhue Plan. "Is it a secret?" the chorister asks. Anyone familiar with the Tucker style will visualize her taking stage as she says, "I can't tell you, exactly"; and will hear that uniquely laughing timbre of voice as she goes on, "But roughly . . ."; and see her moving downstage as the chorus moves with her and the traveler closes behind them and she cues the conductor with a "*Very* roughly . . ."

And she launches "To-morrow," a Cole Porter list song in the form of a Sophie Tucker raveup about all the wonderful things that are about to transpire. Note that the number is completely unnecessary to the plot but absolutely necessary to the presence of Sophie Tucker. Note, too, that Porter's lyrics carelessly turn the Goodhue Plan into *Mrs.* Goodhue's panacea. It's a mistake, of course; the song must have been written when Porter was unaware of precisely how it was to fit into the finished script.

However, *Leave It To Me!* is no *Girl Crazy*, and virtually all the rest of the fourteen-number score adheres to plot and character. Sophie's

aria di sortita, "Taking the Steps To Russia," is not typical Tucker, but it
is a superb novelty in jitterbug style, insistently diddled by an ingenious
syncopation that seems to create a downbeat one and a half seconds too
early. This song was Sophie's first in the tunestack, after her star entrance
in that train scene, so she bustles in with porters and luggage following.
"Boys! Boys! Be careful of that caviar!" she calls out, as the public wel-
comes her. When the applause starts to subside, Sophie adds, "They're
just fish eggs, you know," as she returns to character and reporters pelt her
with questions to regain show tempo. The scene builds to the song on a
nice logic: to disprove the charge that America has no culture, Sophie's
bringing some along, and they call it "swing." She's taking *dance* steps to
Russia.

Truth to tell, *Leave It To Me!* has a shockingly good score considering
that it's not one of Porter's great ones. Of course, *Jubilee*, *Kiss Me, Kate*,
and *Out Of This World* have more reach and density. *Leave It To Me!* is
more like *Anything Goes* or *Can-Can*—not much lucidity of character but
marvelous examples of the sort of music that only Porter made. "Vite,
Vite, Vite"—like "Bon Voyage" a choral quodlibet used in the first set
change—has not two but three separate melodies to be combined at the
end; and "Far Away" has that salty Porterian syncopation with which he
often spiked a ballad. Even a charm song so unimportant it wasn't published, "When All's Said and Done," has a sharp lyric. Oddly, it moves
from the specific—Thomas and Dolly's farewell in one—to the general,
as the traveler curtain parts and the full ensemble seizes the piece for
a dance.

One of the show's smartest use of story numbers actually involves three
songs. The first scene is a *droshky*—"practical," as they say, meaning it
moves like a real-life carriage, or at least gives that impression, bouncing
a bit as it faces the audience and its driver "drives." Thomas is riding with
Tamara's character, one Colette Arnaud; they take the opportunity to
establish the context for a song coming later in the act, for it turns out
that Dolly is stranded in Siberia:

THOMAS: She wants one thousand dollars. How much money do I have
   in the bank?
COLETTE: [You're] twenty-three dollars overdrawn.
THOMAS: All right, I'll send her that.

Now they get to the love plot, in "From Now On (no more philand'ring)." It's a rhythm ballad of the Porter kind, with a verse that makes yet another quotation of Kipling's line "A fool there was" and gives us one of Porter's catchiest lyrics ever: "My address is you, dear."

The two have scarcely finished when Goodhue shows up. The Spewacks despatch some fast plotting, and the *droshky* arrives at Colette's hotel, leaving Goodhue alone to suffer further isolation. He can't communicate with the driver or with various passersby, and at last sinks into "I Want To Go Home." It's ideal Victor Moore material: wishfully sad and as suitable for whining as for singing. A dream sequence brings on a Good Humor man, a gas jockey, a peanut vendor, a horseshoe player, and, for a sight gag that must have convulsed audiences in 1938, Sophie Tucker in gingham and a sun bonnet. Then four barbers enter, to back up Goodhue in close harmony, to be sure that the public hears at least one chorus truly sung.

It's a fine scene, almost startling in its fidelity to the narrative; but we worry about Dolly in Siberia. Two scenes later, we catch up with her for the third number in this collection. I imagine all my readers have seen the photograph of "My Heart Belongs To Daddy," set at another train station. A sign reads, in Cyrillic, "Irkutsk," and Mary Martin sits in white fur on an upended trunk, framed by five chorus boys wearing parkas over their chorus-boy suit pants and dress shoes. (One of them is a strangely gaga-looking Gene Kelly.) The song may suggest a Cole Porter party turn. But we do remember Gaxton and Tamara setting it up—and the Spewacks made it clear in the very first scene that Dolly calls the other man in her life, Thomas' boss, "Daddy."

Of course, the very notion of the piece is silly whimsy. How would this character have got all the way to Siberia, and why would she go into a chaste little striptease in the snow? Here *Leave It To Me!* reverts to what we might call Life Before *Show Boat*, yet the number remains a great show-biz moment: because an entire career grew out of the réclame earned in it. It is definitive not only of Mary Martin's charm but of Cole himself, at his bawdiest ("to dine on my fine finnan haddie") in a minor-key rhumba that tingles with heat. Some commentators point to the melismatic turn on "Da-da-ad!" as suggesting a Jewish protégeur because Porter associated the use of minor keys in pop music with Jewish culture. Yes, but the turn, for all its exotic inflection, occurs in one of the song's few measures of *major-key* writing; in any case, Dolly's "daddy," remember, is J. H. Brody, a publishing magnate who doesn't appear to have any Jewish affiliation.

Maxwell Anderson's affiliation was anarchist, though he conceded that anarchy is out of reach and democracy flawed but useful. When the playwright and Kurt Weill decided to get a musical out of Washington Irving's spoof of 1809, *Diedrich Knickerbocker's History of New-York*, they no doubt had in mind the setting of old New Amsterdam in general, using some of Irving's details (such as the town crier, Corlear the trumpeter) and in particular the character of Peter Stuyvesant. Irving's impish book has no plot per se. It is discursive and anecdotal, starting with theories about world creation ("Nor must I omit to mention the great atomic system taught by old Moschus, before the siege of Troy . . .") and eventually reaching Stuyvesant's regime as governor of Dutch Manhattan.

So *Knickerbocker Holiday* (1938) has even less to do with Washington Irving than *Leave It To Me!* has with *Clear All Wires*. In the Porter musical, the Spewacks had only to fit the play's leads into a new plotline for Victor Moore, applying the conventions of late-thirties style. For instance, to get Sophie Tucker onstage in the first embassy scene, the script goes into American Bourgeoise Redecoration shtick:

MRS. GOODHUE: (bustling in, followed by two decorators, pointing right) I want that wall out. (Turning, pointing left) I want a fireplace there. (Turning, pointing upstage) I'd like something Victorian in that corner. A fountain would be nice. (Turning, spotting Mr. Goodhue, pointing at him) And rip out that monstrosity.

Anderson didn't know these jokes; he didn't *get* these jokes. So already we expect the *Knickerbocker Holiday* libretto to defy the handbook of shtick. Like most of the other playwrights Kurt Weill worked with, Anderson wrote too little libretto and too much play, but the show's director, Joshua Logan, had very recently kept *I Married an Angel*'s talky script zipping along—and he was not shy about asking for cuts. At least Anderson adapted easily to the writing of song lyrics. He might clutter his line with too many syllables as a sort of lugubrious Ogden Nash, but his bank of ideas and images was vast.

Besides, Weill and Anderson forged a genuine bond as friends, and in creating musicals, Weill liked an adventure. A *Leave It To Me!* conforms to a model; its authors must address the public's expectations. Weill worked without models, and despite his need for a Broadway success after the inconclusive performance of *Johnson Johnson* and *The Eternal Road*, he didn't write for a public. Weill didn't even write for himself: he just wrote.

Knickerbocker Holiday's plot is simple. Washington Irving (Ray Middleton) provides a frame, conjuring up his New York history:

> IRVING: The Battery, circa 1647. Stone piers along the waterfront, windmills in the distance. Perhaps a ship at anchor behind the rows of houses with their corrugated roofs. And then dawn flushing up over ancient Brooklyn. Little Dutch Maidens washing the steps, a trumpeter coming through.

This evocation of what will turn out to be *Knickerbocker Holiday*'s virtual unit set is no more than twenty seconds of light pounding on the bassoon, cello, and piano as the winds dream up the place in dramatic chords echoed by a two-note theme on the flute. Corlear's trumpet calls merge with the pounding as those Little Dutch Maidens begin what in earlier eras would have been the opening chorus, "Clickety-Clack." It's a dashing little piece, peremptory in its $\frac{2}{4}$ oompah bass, wistful in a romantic B section, and then—this is typical Weill—irresistibly rhythmic as the piccolo imitates the trumpet call and the $\frac{2}{4}$ section returns to a new rhythmic impetus on clarinet and plucked strings.

Anderson is strangely obliging here, keeping the lyrics simple (as befits a group of scrubwomen) but for the rhyme of "pass by you" and "descry you," which does sound a bit studied. Indeed, when Irving reenters the vocal plot to hail with maximum irony the arrival of the corrupt city council, the lyrics take in "dilatoriness," "deliberations," and "impenetrable intransigence." Clearly, we are in for a very rich evening, and the authors, it turns out, can get a song out of anything—even the council, a bunch of Dutch comics in the traditional as well as literal sense, with a Weber and Fields patois. They explain those "deliberations" as the simple paying out of bribe money in "Hush, Hush," which has the distinction of combining the music of a charm song and the verbal content of a Juvenalian satirist.

All that Irving has to do now is bring on his hero (Richard Kollmar) for an establishing song, "There's Nowhere To Go But Up!," put him together with the heroine (Jeanne Madden) for "It Never Was You," then get to the first of the work's explanatory anthems. This is a duet for narrator Irving and his hero, "How Can You Tell an American?," and the answer is: by his fierce resistance to authority. All that lacks now is that authority himself—but first the two sweethearts develop their relationship in the soulful "Will You Remember Me?" *Now* it's time: and Walter Huston walks in as the respelled Pieter Stuyvesant, peg leg and all.

A Novelty Star, Huston was no singer, though he took part in six numbers, including the one hit, "September Song." As a tyrant taking over New Amsterdam, trying to kill the tyrant-hating hero, and even (in "September Song") courting the heroine, Stuyvesant is almost certainly the musical's first headliner role to be thoroughly bad. He's not an anti-hero, one of those lovable scalawags. He's not even a regrettable scalawag. He's Hitler. This is made explicit in "One Touch of Alchemy," Stuyvesant's celebration (with the chorus) of his plan to usher in prosperity in a fascist New Amsterdam. The song's key line refers to "Strength Through Joy," a well-known Nazi slogan.

As I pointed out elsewhere, Anderson intended Stuyvesant as a replica of Franklin Delano Roosevelt. The cronyism and payola of "Hush, Hush" represent Anderson's view of any regime of organized party politics; it's a good thing he didn't collaborate on *I'd Rather Be Right*. The worst thing about that show's cabinet was that they were all a little silly, not least the Secretary of Labor, Frances Perkins. *Knickerbocker Holiday*'s council is made exclusively of conniving, well-off males (one of whom is a Roosevelt ancestor) whose rule guarantees that they flourish and all others suffer. Ultimately, they stand up to Stuyvesant and the two lovers unite, but not before Anderson has amused himself in haranguing and decreeing.

This held the show back from success in its day, and the marvelous score is largely unknown. In fact, what made the work big news in 1938 was not the still obscure composer or even the novelty of the age's second most Important playwright suddenly trying the impertinent fandangoes of musical comedy. The news was Walter Huston. His expansive charm made Stuyvesant bearable, as when joining Jeanne Madden and those Dutch Maidens in the brief "Dutch Dance," in mixed metre of $\frac{2}{4}$ and $\frac{3}{8}$, with the heavy downbeat of wooden clogs. Or when introducing "September Song," specifically crafted for Huston's limited vocal reach, though he did stay the course for two verses and two choruses with no help from anyone. (Jeanne Madden was standing right next to him the whole time, and could easily have helped if he'd needed some.) Or consider Huston's tiny minuet with Madden during "The Scars." Like *Candide*'s "Dear Boy," this is a Syphilis Number, another example of how out of the ordinary this score truly is.

Don't we take "September Song" for granted as another thirties classic like "Time On My Hands" or "All Through the Night"? But where else in this decade do we hear an older man trying to make love to a soubrette, and with genuine purpose? Today, folks respond to the song's romanticism of youth's "waiting game" and the wistful sorrow of the middle-aged.* We're not, of course, surprised at the cagey simplicity of the refrain's start, as it slips from one measure of the tonic major directly into the tonic minor with a sixth in the melody (on "long, long while"), guyed by a solo violin arpeggio, at least in Weill's original charts. We expect this invention of the permanently contemporary from Weill, not only one of the century's genius composers but also, behind that lifelessly myopic stare, a rascal of an ironist. But why is the humorless and unmusical Anderson so keen as well? "September Song" marks the moment when *Knickerbocker Holiday* can wow as *Leave It To Me!* wows: with the utter rightness of composition prepared for the confidence of talent, all tightly locked into the context of people in a story. We love it when Cole Porter writes a Sophie Tucker Number in "Most Gentlemen Don't Like Love," because Porter is giving up nothing of himself while yielding entirely to Sophie: both thus expand as artists. But we love it, too, when Kurt Weill and Maxwell Anderson invent a Walter Huston Number.

An interesting new version of a cliché number—the parted sweethearts' lament—is "We Are Cut in Twain." Anderson loads it with ratiocinative argument ("Oh, life and love are compact of mortifications," the hero advises the heroine) and Weill frames it in a rhumba with the concluding cabaret cymbal crash that fans of Weill's Weimar days would delight in. It's a dazzling piece, strangely speedy (marked "*Vivace assai*") for what in other shows would be her torch song or his sad reprise of the

---

* Ian Marshall Fischer, the impresario of London's Encores!, the Lost Musicals series, has commented that when musical theatre's great ladies of advanced age need an exhibition ballad, the only two that seem appropriate are "Begin the Beguine" and this same "September Song," no doubt because of their imagery of lost power.

big ballad or even that vaguely incestuous "Spring Is Here" for *I Married an Angel*'s two siblings. *Knickerbocker Holiday*'s version of the "parted lovers" genre is very traditional in subject matter; we're just not used to ratiocinative rhumbas in musicals.

"We Are Cut in Twain" is sung in *Knickerbocker Holiday*'s only alternate setting, the town jail, where the hero is incarcerated. This provisions another Latin number, the habanera "Sitting in Jail," Stuyvesant's sardonic baiting of the hero and thematically not unlike *The Boys From Syracuse*'s "Come With Me." Of course, that piece is a grand march in the unique Rodgers manner. He doesn't only have a patent on waltzes: think of "Babes in Arms," "For Jupiter and Greece," and even "Oklahoma." "Sitting in Jail" is endearingly sly, another opportunity for Walter Huston to trouble us with his charm even as he schemes to hang the man who is his rival in love and politics. Anderson wants us to remember that Stuyvesant is a bad guy by profession. This we learn in the second-act opening, Washington Irving's "Ballad of the Robbers." Another ironic piece, it starts with a lengthy flute solo, reminding us that Kurt Weill was not only his own orchestrator but one of Broadway's few innovators in instrumentation.

"Ballad of the Robbers"—note the generic title, redolent of *Die Dreigroschenoper* or *Johnny Johnson*—tells how, shortly after Eden, there were so many crooks and so few honest men that the former rose up and jailed the latter: and called it law. So society is ruled—to quote a play that Anderson co-wrote with Harold Hickerson, *Gods of the Lightning* (1928)—by "brigands in power who fight for more power! Till you die! Till we all die! Till there is no earth!"

Unmistakably, that is the voice of Maxwell Anderson: in melodrama. In musical comedy, he understates a bit. We enjoy his busman's holiday, the playwright vacationing by giving the light stage the weight of disputation. Weill brings the helium. One of the more overtly political numbers, "The One Indispensable Man," a duet for Stuyvesant and the heroine's council-member father, sings of the party bag man. But its vamp consists of a flighty woodwind figure over a bass of four chords in $\frac{4}{4}$: f^7, B^b aug.^{7}, c$\frac{7}{4}$, and c, this quartet outlining an inner-voice melodic line of four notes, A^b, G^b, F, and E^b. It's five seconds of giggle. On top of this, each of the two men starts the chorus on a phrase of "Huh huh huh" nonsense syllables, a musical version of a whispered conspiracy.

Like everything in this brilliant score, it shows what happens when a word man who doesn't know "musicals" and a composer who doesn't write them get together on a "musical comedy"—for, yes, so the show was billed.

But then, the four works highlighted in this chapter show also how quickly the people of the 1930s learned to revise the twenties handbook. *Girl Crazy* is a narrative chaos, but *Leave It To Me!* sort of makes sense. *The Cat and the Fiddle* is a niche-musical, so integrated that it has never been outshone, not even by *Grand Hotel* or *Passion*; and *Knickerbocker Holiday* invents new ways to sing old songs along with its new ones. After the Wall Street Crash, the art got reactionary in sheer survival mode. But writers do like to try out novelties, and when *The Cat and the Fiddle* ends up as one of the decade's biggest money-earners, experimental work is welcomed. *Hellzapoppin* was the longest-running title of the 1930s—but what is the decade's most revived title?

Porgy and Bess.

ALL IN FUN: MUSICAL COMEDY II

In the late twentieth century, English musicals became a Broadway staple. In the 1930s, however, they were all but unknown except for the works of Noël Coward. Yet the late 1930s did see an importation from London, *The Two Bouquets* (1938), an old-fashioned accident-creates-whole-evening's-plot-complications script decorated with new lyrics to Victorian melodies. The wordsmiths were Eleanor and Herbert Farjeon; they had enjoyed success with the concept at home. Here, *The Two Bouquets* languished for 55 performances, and the title gets mention if at all today only because Alfred Drake and Patricia Morison played leads in it ten years before they played leads in *Kiss Me, Kate*, which shares with *The Two Bouquets* the contrivance of flowers delivered to the wrong person.

The Two Bouquets was a tidy little piece, but an American entry called *Knights of Song* (1938) got an elaborate staging, mounted by Laurence Schwab and directed by Oscar Hammerstein. The eponymous knights were Gilbert and Sullivan, and excerpts from *H.M.S. Pinafore*, *The Pirates of Penzance*, and *The Mikado* punctuated this chronicle play, which covered the period from 1878 to 1907, when Gilbert was finally knighted, twenty-four years after his former partner. Nigel Bruce played Gilbert and John Moore was Sullivan, with such eminences as Oscar Wilde, George Bernard Shaw, James McNeil Whistler, and even Queen Victoria taking part. At the pageant's end, the thirteen-year-old Edward VIII turned up— a young version of the king who had abdicated two years before to marry Wallis Simpson. *Knights of Song* lasted only two weeks.

The Master himself returned to Broadway in *Tonight at 8:30* (1936), a devilish notion: three one-act plays, highly varied in tone and setting, the third of which had some music. That's original enough—but Coward in fact got up three separate evenings of these one-acts. In a long English provincial tour starting in 1935, some of the plays were tried in different combinations till the London run settled on a final schedule, omitting a tenth play, *Star Chamber*, that was performed only once.

So one really had to visit the show three times to collect it. It was worth it for the headliners. "Upheld by my stubborn faith in the Star System," Coward said, "I wrote the *To-night at 8:30* [the English spelling] plays as acting, singing, and dancing vehicles for Gertrude Lawrence and myself." A company of nine supported the pair, and some good roles were distributed among the West End cast, virtually all of whom played in New York. For our purpose, only the three titles with music—they are not "musicals" in any real sense—are of interest here. "Shadow Play," a society comedy with a touch of expressionism, unveiled the intense number "Play, Orchestra, Play" and one of Coward's most expansive ballads, "You Were There." On another evening, "Family Album" observed the Featherwayses and their in-laws after the death of the Featherways patriarch, all growing nostalgic at the playing of some old tunes on a music box; amusingly, one of these was a strangely patriotic version of the typical Coward patter song in $\frac{6}{8}$ time (beginning "Harriet married a soldier . . ."). It was really the one-acter called "Red Peppers" that gave the two stars anything vocal to bite on, as a third-division music-hall couple, Lily and George Pepper. We catch them well on in their career both on and off the stage "of the Palace of Varieties in One of the Smaller English Provincial Towns." The Newcastle Empire, say, if such there be.

Coward has thus assigned himself the task of delighting us with what we have to imagine are dreary talents in tiresome material. The chief set piece is "Has Anybody Seen Our Ship?," sung "onstage" by the two stars as sailors on a drunken leave, "the world forgetting by the world forgot." That's a lovely line, though its mate marks a rare descent for this writer into bodily-function humor, "Now we haven't got a penny for the you-know-what."

Of course, that is the kind of thing that one heard in music hall, and the joke of "Red Peppers" generally is that *Tonight at 8:30* is the height of glamour—two of our brightest stars showing off in nine roles each, most of them classy enough for "Shadow Play" 's "The Gayforths' House in

Mayfair"—while "Red Peppers" is socially unspeakable. "It'll never get well if you pick it," Coward calls out to the violinist after a pizzicato. Though *Tonight At 8:30* played New York only 118 times, this was still a rather splendid showing for a twice-difficult sell, for the one-acter anthology has never been popular on Broadway and theatregoers had to take pains simply to learn which bill they were to attend.*

As different from the English as possible would be our all-American Federal Theatre, which sponsored musicals on the national level. Few were seen in New York except those that originated there, but there was *A Hero Is Born* (1937), a rare chance to catch a spectacle at a $1.10 top. This fairy tale did not advertise itself as intended for children—perhaps because the Federal Theatre hoped to break through categorical theatregoing populations to an ecumenism of playgoers. Nevertheless, the piece addressed the so to speak naive community. A huge cast and a truckload of scenery set forth a complex tale of a prince who doesn't believe in the princely things—a flying carpet, seven-league boots, a cap of invisibility, a giant-killing sword. The show is long unheard of, yet two of its authors remain noteworthy, if not for writing. The Theatre Guild's Theresa Helburn authored the book (from a story by Andrew Lang), and a certain A. Lehman Engel composed the music, to Agnes Morgan's lyrics. Engel, without the A., is of course the eventual conductor of *Wonderful Town*, *Li'l Abner*, *Goldilocks*, *Do Re Mi*, and most of Harold Rome's shows, as well as the mentor of a generation of writers in the BMI workshop, which makes him a character in the Ed Kleban "bio," *A Class Act* (2000). Engel had already begun serving as a Broadway musical director with *Johnny Johnson*, but he also entertained composing ambitions. *A Hero Is Born* may have cured him of them, for he always discouraged people from trying to learn anything of it. "I had a terrible time on it," he said, with finality, "and it was a terrible event."

So that's that. The only winner that the Federal Theatre threw off in the musical was *The Swing Mikado* (1939), a huge hit in, first of all, Chicago.

---

* The Saga Continues: not only were feature films spawned by some of these one-acters (most notably David Lean's *Brief Encounter*, to Coward's screenplay drawn from "Still Life"), but a West End musical called *Mr. & Mrs.* (1968) tried to find music in 8:30 titles that Coward had left dry. "Fumed Oak" and, again, "Still Life" were the sources, and John Neville, Honor Blackman, and Hylda Baker appeared in different roles in each half. Mainly the work of John Taylor, *Mr. & Mrs.* suffered from excessive mediocrity and vanished unmourned.

Reset on "A coral island in the Pacific," the piece did not create something new out of something old in the *Swingin' the Dream* mode. *The Swing Mikado* was simply a jived-up *Mikado* with an all-black cast. The critics generally liked the Nanki-Poo (Maurice Cooper), the Ko-Ko (Herman Greene), and the Katisha (Mabel Walker), but felt that the production sagged when playing straight and was vocally weak in many respects.

Good word had traveled from Chicago all the same, and opening night brought out Jock Whitney, Mayor La Guardia, former W.P.A. chief Harry Hopkins, and even his boss, Franklin Delano Roosevelt. This was an astonishing congregation for the Federal Theatre, whose only fame was political controversy. Even so, *The Swing Mikado* was chicken feed next to *The Hot Mikado*, a local commercial entry put on by Michael Todd just three weeks later. Todd had offered to take over the management of the W.P.A. production, but the Federal Theatre was unwilling to give away the glory of its one lovable achievement.

So Todd ran up his own black *Mikado* in high style and with Bill Robinson in the title role. One problem with *The Swing Mikado* was the senior-class-play look of the thing; *The Hot Mikado* was Big Broadway, directed by Hassard Short. Jazzier than its rival and taking more liberties with the original (even if both *Mikados* gave credit for special "swing" orchestrations, to the Federal Theatre's Charles Levy and Todd's Charles L. Cooke), *The Hot Mikado* also had a better cast in toto. Rosa Brown's Katisha changed the marriage-crazed beldame into—so the critics noted—a Harlemized Mae West, tearing into her second-act lament about "the living I" as a throbbing torch number. As for Robinson, he held to the role's extremely delayed entrance (not till midway in Act Two), trucking on at the head of a line of girls, the entire pack in derbies topped with white feathers.

Todd's costuming generally went thus wild. Rosa Brown's outfit, a winged dress with train and a gigantic hat, weighed thirty-five pounds. Unlike *The Swing Mikado*, *The Hot Mikado* did not change the Japanese setting: but the atmosphere was Lenox Avenue on Thursday night, with so much dancing that four of the original's numbers were cut.*

* These were all from the second act: "Brightly Dawns Our Wedding Day," "See How the Fates," "The Criminal Cried"—an important plot number, by the way—and "There Is Beauty in the Bellow of the Blast." By comparison, *The Swing Mikado* dropped two rather turgid numbers, "Comes a Train of Little Ladies" and "I Am So Proud," but failed to see the potential in "Oh, Living I" and omitted it as well.

Critic Wolcott Gibbs thought this invasion of *Mikados* "as remarkable as if *two* dinosaurs suddenly turned up at the Zoo." Their cages faced each other after *The Swing Mikado* abandoned the bad-luck New Yorker Theatre for the Forty-Fourth Street, when it played across from *The Hot Mikado*, at the Broadhurst. Most preferred Todd's upmarket version, but the W.P.A.'s version was the scrappy underdog. Gibbs liked it better on a technicality, "a man's first dinosaur being inevitably more gripping than his second."

Moving now to the odds and ends department, we should at least mention *Right This Way* (1938), a historian's choice footnote because although it lasted but two weeks it threw off two standards, by Sammy Fain and Irving Kahal, "I'll Be Seeing You" and "I Can Dream, Can't I?" More interesting is how casually the show featured a Boy and Girl who have not only Met but are Sleeping Together Though Unmarried. This was unheard of in twenties musicals; part of the Cole Porter thirties effect was a lessening of respect for the received cautions. *Right This Way*'s Boy was operetta stalwart Guy Robertson, but Girl was that confounded Tamara, forever skulking through our pages, refusing to be perceived, categorized. Who *was* Tamara? Who did she hope to be? Russian by birth, she seems like Russia itself, in Winston Churchill's famous definition: "a riddle wrapped in a mystery inside an enigma."

Those who wonder how Ray Henderson and Lew Brown fared without B. G. DeSylva should know that the two survivors broke up after the failure of *Strike Me Pink*, in 1933. With lyricist Jack Yellen, Henderson wrote much of the undistinguished score to the most successful of all the *Ziegfeld Follies*, the 1943 edition, then retired from the stage. Lew Brown's last major credit was the semi-hit *Yokel Boy* (1939), which Brown "conceived," produced, directed, and co-wrote. Considering that the typical DeSylva, Brown, and Henderson show was filled with wisecrackers no matter what the setting, *Yokel Boy* has to be called the very opposite of the style in which the younger Brown flowered. The piece took place in both Lexington, Massachusetts and Hollywood, whither the Girl, Lois January, went in pursuit of an acting career, egged on by newcomer Phil Silvers, as "Punko" Parks. Buddy Ebsen was the Boy, and Mark Plant (*Jubilee*'s Mowgli), as the village blacksmith, got to introduce the first-act finale, "Uncle Sam's Lullaby." After Plant's vocal, the stage was seized by a bizarre modernistic ballet on war preparations. The bucolic mood of

Lexington was maintained, however, by the hillbilly-flavored Canova family, with daughter Judy getting the show's temporary hit, a list song called "Comes Love."

From what little is left of DeSylva, Brown, and Henderson, we move on to the biggest names, such as Rodgers and Hart. One wonders what they thought of *Yokel Boy*, whose plot outline and use of outlandish rustics recalls *America's Sweetheart*. Perhaps Rodgers and Hart were too busy making history with their Balanchine shows to notice *Yokel Boy*—but they must have had a lot of spare time in 1935, when they returned from California and wrote *Jumbo*. Not only did *Jumbo* make no history: it almost doesn't have a score. For *Jumbo* is not a musical, but rather producer Billy Rose's odd idea of reclaiming the gala days of the old Hippodrome with a circus. That's what *Jumbo* is: a circus with a slight storyline and some songs.

This is quite in keeping with the Hippodrome itself, which was built (in 1905) specifically to bring the physical excitement and variety of an amusement park to the stage: opera, rodeo, aquacade, baseball game, war. The generation that grew up during the Second Age often had their first taste of theatre in the Hippodrome, and it was without question one of New York's "sights." (It is on Chip's outdated itinerary in *On the Town*.)

The Hippodrome's greatest days were over by the early-middle 1920s. It was handed over to vaudeville, cinema, and a passion play, then became derelict. Now Billy Rose enters the scene. Rose loved two things above all: *big* and *famous*. The Hippodrome was *big*, and the man who could bring it back to glory would be *famous*. Rose decided to gut the auditorium, turn it into an arena-style "big top" venue, and put on a great old Hippodrome spectacle, but one with a tale of two rival circuses. Boy (Donald Novis) is the son of one of the circus owners, so of course Girl (Gloria Grafton) is the daughter of the other. Jimmy Durante is the star comic in a show without a star, because what really staffed this piece was the array of clowns, aerialists, wire walkers, acrobats, animal acts, and even an elephant, one Big Rosie, in the title role. Circuses also have their own orchestra, and Rose's was Paul Whiteman's ensemble, the most prominent band of the day. This is why Rodgers and Hart were on hand when Rose might easily have hired a second-division team: part of being famous is hiring famous. The tunestack includes three standards, "My Romance," "The Most Beautiful Girl in the World," and "Little Girl Blue." (Are we so used to the last-named that we fail to remark the lovely pun in the title?) Note, all the same, how generic these three lyrics are: because the script, by Ben Hecht and Charles MacArthur, is almost completely lacking in character. Anyway, far more central than anyone above to *Jumbo*'s success was Rose's other "famous" hire, of special-events and revue specialist John Murray Anderson to handle the logistics of staging a circus. The little that was left of the show was directed by George Abbott.

Jimmy Durante had one bit that has become one of theatre lore's most exhausted clichés; but to omit it from any account of *Jumbo* would be irresponsible. Trying to sneak out of a bankrupt circus with Big Rosie herself, Durante had somehow to get past a marshal. "Shh," Durante whispered to his charge. "Not a word, not a word." (This last line is too inspired to be anything but a Durante ad lib.) The marshal ramps up to the joke with a threatening, "Where are you going with that elephant?" He repeats the question till Durante and Big Rosie come to a stop. Durante looks right. Durante looks left. Then, in a tone mixed of incredulity and innocence, Durante replies, "*What . . . elephant?*"

Observing that the libretto was just an anchor for the circus attractions, the critics nevertheless thought *Jumbo* an immense delight. But Rose had spent something like $350,000 at a time when the biggest musicals capitalized themselves at less than half that much, and the running costs were as spectacular as the show. In an odd innovation, Rose decided to call attention to *Jumbo*'s songs by withholding them from the radio, thus presumably to compel music lovers' attendance at the Hippodrome. But surely there was superb PR to be had if the three hits were put into rotation in the culture generally through airplay. There was as well a wonderful instance of the Rodgers waltz in the opening number, "Over and Over Again," sung by Bob Lawrence and a men's chorus of thirty-two and undoubtedly the classiest music that ever accompanied a trapeze act.

As ticket sales drooped, Rose lifted his embargo. (Novis and Grafton recorded two of their numbers, with Whiteman's band.) Still, *Jumbo* closed after five months, deeply in the red. Rose secured an engagement at the Texas Centennial in Fort Worth for the summer of 1936, but a sluggish box office led him to drop the show's entire book and simply run the circus and songs. It still failed. At least Rose had got so much personal réclame that he was now, indeed, big and famous. But the Hippodrome stood empty for three years and was then demolished.

After *Jumbo* came Rodgers and Hart's four Balanchine shows, separated right in the middle by *I'd Rather Be Right*. I saved the fourth of the Balanchines for this chapter because the power of "musical-comedy ballet" had already been secured in the first three, and *The Boys From Syracuse* (1938) uses dance much less imposingly than its predecessors had done. *On Your Toes* is about dance, and *Babes In Arms* and *I Married an Angel* use dance in enticingly narrative ways. But *The Boys From Syracuse*, even with the increasingly obligatory Dream Ballet, looks back to pre-Balanchine days, when people in musicals danced because someone had just sung a song. Besides, *The Boys From Syracuse* is a book musical with a lot of book (by George Abbott)—or, more exactly, a lot of Shakespearean storyline. And this led Rodgers and Hart to create one of the decade's most narrative and characterful scores.

We know how it begins, in that strange first number "interpreted" out of clarinet lines. Most of the company is on stage, but not a single one of the principals: the twins, local boy Ronald Graham and visitor Eddie Albert; their respective slaves, cast with two actors who really resembled each other, Teddy Hart (brother of Lorenz) and *Parade*'s Jimmy Savo; the two women who can't tell the twins apart, Graham's wife (Muriel Angelus) and Hart's wife (Wynn Murray); and Angelus' sister, to mate with Albert, Marcy Westcott.

This may be one reason why the score stands among the most story-oriented in the Rodgers and Hart catalogue. By comparison, *Girl Crazy* hasn't many characters that need musical definition. Nor does it see a great deal of movement within the character relationships; the secondary couple, Ethel Merman and William Kent, can't use a Boy Meets Girl as they're married before they so much as gain the stage. *The Boys From Syracuse* has two love plots and the comics to treat, not to mention a vaguely important background of cops and courtesans who also figure in the music.

So *The Boys From Syracuse*'s tunestack is unusually orderly even for the late 1930s. After the opening came the Hero's Wanting Song, "Dear Old Syracuse," for Albert with a follow-up dance that brings in the chorus girls; then the first of the comedy duets for the servant class, "What Can You Do With a Man?" Now for romance: Angelus' "Falling In Love With Love" and Graham's "The Shortest Day of the Year," whose follow-up dance simply brings on the show's soloists, George Church, Betty Bruce, and Heidi Vosseler. After two ballads, we need something bright: what is called an "up tune." So Westcott and Albert introduce "This Can't Be Love," and we're on the verge of the first-act finale, the insistent "Let Antipholus In." Though it consists of that one line constantly repeated, it is formidably integrated into Shakespeare's mistaken-identity suspense.

Note that there has been no Big Ballet yet—the authors had too much story to traverse. The plot doesn't just inspire songs but seeps into them—in those dialoguing clarinets in "I Had Twins" and the "pacing back and forth" effect in "Let Antipholus In," indicative of a husband locked out of his own house by his wife. There is also the hurdy-gurdy laughter in the music between the vocal lines in the verse of "This Can't Be Love," as if the orchestra itself is mocking the notion of musical-comedy romance. "Falling In Love With Love" mocks that notion, too, but with a rueful wish, and as the scene was built around the household women working at a loom, the music contains a spidery theme suggesting the passage of woof through warp.

For some reason, the show's second-act numbers are less well integrated. Though music and lyrics remain at highest level, the second-act opening, "Ladies of the Evening," is a standard-make intermission-ending song and dance, and the ensuing "He and She," another servants' duet, has nothing to do with the story. Later on, "Sing For Your Supper"—Rodgers and Hart's version of the close-harmony "girl trio"—and Wynn Murray's "Oh, Diogenes" are irrelevant larks.

However, between these two song sets we find a highly central solo, "Big Brother," in which one of the twin slaves wonders where on earth his long-lost sibling can be. It's touching because his brother is in that very place looking for him. Note, too, that Teddy Hart was singing "Big Brother" on lyrics written for him by his own big brother. Perhaps this was why the Big Ballet finally kicked into the show at this very spot; there was just too much magic going on for Balanchine to resist making a dance on it. The number took the form of a choreographed prophecy, as a seer gave the hopeful vassal a crystal-ball look at his brother and the brother's owner.

The Boys From Syracuse ran only 235 performances—a good showing commercially but not worthy of the wildly positive reviews, a few of which noticed the flaws in George Abbott's script but almost all of which raved over the score. Walter Winchell checked in with "breathlessly recommended"; aren't we always told that his word was law? At least, in the longer view the show was a smash, so constantly performed that its scripts and orchestra parts were ever in use and never got the chance to be lost. When Goddard Lieberson recorded the work in his Columbia series in the 1950s, he didn't have to commission new orchestrations, because Hans Spialek's 1938 charts were right on hand. Of course, Lieberson had some unnamed musician design a fifties tough-up. "This Can't Be Love" departs completely from the original in hothouse jazz for clarinet and keyboard, losing the tympani heart poundings that terrorize "Just hear it beat." But the typical Spialek overture is brought back to a place of honor at history's table. Spialek may have invented the structure of the Golden Age overture: a fanfare based on one vocal theme (here, "This Can't Be Love"); an anticipatory lead-in to a solid rhythm number to arrest the ear ("Come With Me"), thence to a full stop; a selection of ballads and charm songs ("Falling in Love With Love," a solid wind band on both "This Can't Be Love" and "Sing For Your Supper"); and a boffo coda (based on a choral line from "I Had Twins") that closes on a last quotation of one outstanding melodic cell (the first line of "This Can't Be Love"). It is the sound of Broadway, and Spialek is its author.

Where was Cole Porter at this time? Rebuked by the relative failure of *Jubilee*, he looked for another commercial success in the *Anything Goes* manner, agreeing to write *Red, Hot and Blue!* (1936) as a kind of sequel: not to *Anything Goes'* storyline but to its teamwork. Vinton Freedley was again to offer Gaxton, Moore, and Merman in a tale in which society met the underworld, in another Lindsay-Crouse book directed by Lindsay, with settings by Donald Oenslager, back at the Alvin. Even the orchestrator was the same, Robert Russell Bennett.

However, it would appear that Gaxton overheard the librettists assuring Merman that her role in the proceedings would be promoted from what it had been in *Anything Goes*—which was, after all, basically the second female lead with an unusually high share of the tunestack. Possibly, all that Lindsay and Crouse meant was that the new show would give Merman more plot time, for now she was to play the romantic lead and actually Get the Guy. But Gaxton may have feared the unleashing of Merman's power, and he bowed out (which left him free to be miscast in *White Horse Inn*), and for some reason Victor Moore did as well. Their replacements were no Gaxton and Moore, but completely different in type. As the Guy, Freedley brought in Bob Hope in what was to be his last Broadway musical (of nine) before he went to Hollywood. Like Gaxton, Hope was famous as a sort of con man—but not yet. On Broadway, from chorus boy to sidekick to leading man, Hope was an essentially ingratiating presence, strangely nice-looking for a comic (in fact, virtually the twin of MGM's romantic comic Robert Montgomery) and a pleasing singer. Gaxton had a certain command, given the styles of the day; but Hope had charm.

Then, too, the whining Moore was replaced by the volcanic Jimmy Durante, which seems particularly odd when the *Red, Hot and Blue!* plot reveals a powerful resemblance to *Of Thee I Sing*, the definitive Gaxton-Moore outing. As in the earlier show, a nationwide contest is held to choose the hero's bride, he rejects the winner, and the Supreme Court hears the case, siding with the hero. Again, Hope was the hero. Merman was "Nails" Duquesne, a former manicurist now turned rich merry widow. Durante was "Policy" Pinkle, a jailbird sprung to help Merman run a lottery to get Hope a wife, specifically his childhood infatuation, a girl who sat on a hot waffle iron and has the mark to prove it. Like *Anything Goes*, *Red, Hot and Blue!* was not about its storyline. Nor was it about its most famous attaching legend, the silly billing dispute between Merman's and Durante's agents that led Freedley to proclaim the two stars above the title in criss-crossing strips, the top-left-to-bottom-right name taking over the bottom-left-to-top-right spot in alternating two-week stays.

No, *Red, Hot and Blue!* was Aarons-Freedley in its worldview, which made it about its stars and its Cole Porter score. Unlike its predecessor, *Jubilee*, it is musically generic. There's the Ethel Merman torch song, which we already know is "Down in the Depths." There's the Merman raveup, "Ridin' High," with the name-dropping patter section and the long held note over the orchestra in the second chorus. There's the list song, "Ours," and the country spoof, "The Ozarks Are Callin' Me Home." And the "Lord, please make me good but not yet" ballad, "You're a Bad Influence on Me."

The show's outstanding hit, "It's De-Lovely," even creates a genre: two verses and five choruses on a couple's courtship, marriage, homelife, and golden-boy firstborn. There had been story songs before, of course, and "Makin' Whoopee" somewhat points in this direction. But the grandiose structure of "It's De-Lovely," its alliterative plays on the titular adjective, and simply the game of Merman and Hope occupying the stage for an epic that plays as a breezy improvisation make the number a one-off.

Amusingly, Porter used "It's De-Lovely" in place of the finaletto to bring down the first-act curtain. Alone together, Merman, Hope, and Durante used the song's coda—that alliterative sequence—to lament their project as a "failure," a "fold-up," a "fade-away," and so on. Now, Durante's act habitually gamed with his unpredictable use of big words and malapropisms. But Red, Hot and Blue! especially made a running gag of it, and Durante chimed in on these f-words with "flacus."

So the orchestra comes to a stop, and Hope asks, "What does that mean?"

Putting on his trademark look of martyred innocence, Durante replied, "Well, don't pin me down."

And, as the audience laughed, Merman sang out just two words more of the number before the plummeting curtain hit the deck.

Had Red, Hot and Blue! enjoyed a score on the Anything Goes level, it might have been with us ever since in various revisions. On the contrary, there wasn't even a movie. (The Betty Hutton film with this title has no connection with the stage show.) Worse, the score's only standard got into the 1956 Anything Goes remake and has been with the stage Anything Goes ever since. Still, a new version of Red, Hot and Blue! has been making the rounds of late, including Goodspeed and Paper Mill. The adaptation is the one, previously mentioned, that slips "Goodbye, Little Dream, Goodbye" into Act Two, assigning it to Merman's character and her rival, in duet. While following the original storyline, the new version helps itself to the usual interpolations, including the relatively unfamiliar "It Ain't Etiquette," "I'm Throwing a Ball Tonight," and "Most Gentlemen Don't Like Love." So far, so good, for these are very much in the Red, Hot and Blue! spirit, and written for the kind of star talent that headlined in Porter at the time. But interpolating standards upends the work's integrity, in effect concertizing a book show. "Just One of Those Things" does not belong in Red, Hot and Blue!'s characterological environment; and the purist risks a heart attack when the verse of "You Do Something To Me" glides into the refrain of "I've Got You Under My Skin."

Doesn't the riesumazione make these faux-scores unnecessary? Encores! and its regional derivations, small companies such as San Francisco's

42nd Street Moon that specialize in modest but faithful revivals, and the growing interest in integral recordings of old shows all suggest the revisal movement should consider the approach that David Ives so successfully adopted with *Pardon My English*: writing a new script around the original story and score.

Porter's *You Never Know* (1938) has also undergone a modern revision that plays here and there. This one, too, includes interpolations; so did the original. A greatly protracted and unhappy tryout led management to the customary "Change everything!" panic, and by the Broadway opening the program revealed that not all the score was Porter's.

We saw this happen with *The New Yorkers*, of course: but that was because no one could write for Jimmy Durante as Durante himself could (though by *Red, Hot and Blue!* Durante was singing Porter and liking it). No, what happened on *You Never Know* was that Porter agreed to work on a genre entirely foreign to his taste and abilities: the typical Shubert Brothers Americanization of a German original. Oddly enough, *You Never Know* is Cole Porter's *Maytime*.

The material started off as a comedy by Siegfried Geyer, *Bei Kerzenlicht* (*By Candlelight*), seen on Broadway as *Candle Light* in 1929, in P. G. Wodehouse's adaptation. Leslie Howard played a prince's valet who passes himself off as his employer to seduce Gertrude Lawrence, who turns out to be a chambermaid also in upwardly mobile disguise. Geyer turned his play into a musical with composer Robert Katscher, retaining the original title. A Shubert must have caught the Viennese premiere, in 1937 at the Deutsche Volkstheater, and bought the rights with the intention of changing—for starters—the score, retaining little more than the title song, with English lyrics by *You Never Know*'s adaptor and director, Rowland Leigh. Couldn't Porter have written his own "By Candlelight"? Indeed, Porter did. His wasn't used, though it's a fine example of Porter expanding his style to encompass a setting and characters he isn't used to.

In fact, *You Never Know* wasn't a job for Porter. The emphasis on class in masquerade sounds like Porter, perhaps. But Porter's view of class does not relish the idea of the butler and maid dressing up; it leads to anarchy. Porter's class is what one is, not what one pretends to. There's masquerade in many of his shows, because it was a basic element in Third Era librettos. It's a plot device, not a genuine social enhancement. Even when a mug and a broad go royal in *DuBarry Was a Lady*, they retain their personal style and mode of expression. *You Never Know* is about something Porter isn't comfortable with: class deception.

The show was, at first, a quiet little comedy with songs, something like Porter's twenties hit *Paris*. But *Paris* had atmosphere aplenty in its star, Irene Bordoni. *You Never Know*'s leads were valet Rex O'Malley, chambermaid Lupe Velez, nobleman Clifton Webb, and noble adulteress Libby Holman, rather a make-do cast. Webb had appeared in Porter's first Broadway credit, *See America First*, a whole twenty-two years earlier. But that wasn't an authentic Porter-style show, either. Worse, this comedy of manners was inflated with a nightclub sequence, with specialty dancers such as June Preisser and Paul and Grace Hartman, and those aforementioned interpolations. It was Porter's least favorite of all his shows and a genuine bomb, though it still lasted two and a half months.

The odd thing is that despite Porter's low morale—he had suffered that permanently debilitating horseback-riding accident the year before—he wrote a fine brace of numbers in his signature genres. Webb and Velez got the list song, "From Alpha to Omega," Webb and Holman presented "What Is That Tune," which like "You're the Top" and other Porter titles launches its refrain on an orchestral theme preceding the vocal, and Webb alone introduced the Sinful Ballad (with a list-song infusion and lots of triplet figures in $\frac{4}{4}$), "At Long Last Love." Toby Wing, some other principals, and that supererogatory Shubert chorus were assigned a number that sounds exactly like something Fred Astaire should have sung in *Gay Divorce*, "For No Rhyme Or Reason," and Libby Holman won a solo in Porter's syncopated style in the title song.

The whole score swings, and a number written to establish Libby Holman, "I'm Going In For Love," is a kind of jazz waltz in which the melody keeps pushing ahead of the accompaniment. The number was cut in tryouts, but revivals reinstate it—and, indeed, despite the work's poor reputation, it has been constantly revived. Perhaps the appeal of the original plan for a small romantic comedy in a single set was what made *You Never Know* a summer-stock repertory item in the post-war years. An inept off-Boadway revival in 1973 similarly used a small cast in a single place of rendezvous. Eleven of the original Porter titles were sung—including his version of "By Candlelight"—and the four interpolations were all by Porter. One of them was "They All Fall in Love," a list song introduced in the 1929 film *The Battle of Paris* by Gertrude Lawrence, so here is a link with the Geyer play that started it all off. The current *You Never Know*, mentioned above, is Paul Lazarus' 1982 edition. As in 1973, six players occupy a single set, but this revision recalls only eight of the original songs, and interpolates *Red, Hot and Blue!*'s "Ridin' High," which is surely too familiar to moonlight in other Porter shows.

Porter recovered from *You Never Know* with one of the Porterest of shows the very next year, as we'll soon see. But what of Arthur Schwartz and Howard Dietz, who virtually held the patent on the new thirties sound in their revues? Now concentrating on book musicals, the two failed to please in *Between the Devil* (1937), which sounds like an English show: Jack Buchanan, Evelyn Laye, and *Three Sisters'* Adele Dixon were the stars. In its original form, the show anticipated the 1953 movie *The Captain's Paradise* (and its musical version, *Oh Captain!* [1958]), as bigamist Buchanan blithely shared himself with English wife Laye and French wife Dixon. Out-of-town audiences were scandalized, so in a rewrite now anticipating the 1940 movie *My Favorite Wife*, Buchanan thought Dixon dead and married Laye in all innocence.

The problem with this subject matter is that unless it is given an emotional foundation—as it is in *My Favorite Wife*—there's no logical way for the story to end. It remains a naughty jest without a punchline. *Between the Devil* all but admitted that: it didn't resolve the narrative's problem, but simply asked the public to imagine an ending of its choice.

Billed as "a gay musical comedy," meaning "guiltlessly sinful," the work certainly enjoyed its wicked ways, bringing the rival wives into a hair-pulling fight to climax Act One. With Buddy Ebsen in Hollywood, sister Vilma danced with Charles Walters, and a male trio called the Tune Twisters introduced "Triplets," which Buchanan got a crack at sixteen years later in the *Band Wagon* film: he, Fred Astaire, and Nanette Fabray all shrimped down as caterwauling infants.* Buchanan sang as well *Between the Devil*'s one standard, "By Myself," which he ceded to Astaire in that same film.

---

* It's worth pointing out that in 1937 three guys could just show up and perform "Triplets" as a diversion, but that by the 1950s logic had so swept the musical on both stage and screen that "Triplets" had to be sung by triplets. Those who had no purpose other than to twist tunes found a welcome on television variety shows, where point numbers observed mimetic realism as much as the male band singers of the 1920s who sang "Can't Help Lovin' Dat Man" and "Looking For a Boy."

Schwartz and Dietz then broke up for no less than twenty-four years, so Schwartz teamed up with Dorothy Fields for a Hollywood spoof starring Ethel Merman and Jimmy Durante, *Stars in Your Eyes* (1939). There was no billing fight on this one: the pair split the top line, with Merman on the left. A third Tamara joins us for this title, Tamara Toumanova, along with Richard Carlson and Mildred Natwick. Here was a rather original idea, a political show that would take its burlesque of the era's isms into musical comedy: what if a movie studio hired an idealistic leftwing playwright—someone of the Group Theatre, say—to bring art and prestige to the next vehicle of an imperious Queen of the Lot? Clifford Odets takes on Joan Crawford!*

I see the potential for something lively; unfortunately, the show's director, Joshua Logan, saw it closing Saturday night (in George S. Kaufman's famous warning about what happens to satire). Logan persuaded producer Dwight Deere Wiman to lose the leftwing stuff and just go Hollywood. What good's that? J. P. McEvoy's book now concentrated on movieland types, so Durante, originally a union organizer, was now Monotone Pictures' troubleshooter, playing a sort-of love plot with gossip columnist Mildred Natwick. The real love plot united Merman not with Carlson's socially-dedicated screenwriter but with Carlson's just-plain screenwriter, as the Boy who sings ballads with Merman's rival, Toumanova.

The staging, at least, had interest, for Jo Mielziner gave Logan one of the first unit sets, a sound stage. Backdrops and furniture could be lowered or pushed on while the lights were still up, a genuine innovation, and Logan all but choreographed his players' entrances and exits during these changes by letting treadmills move them on and off.

Merman always recalled *Stars in Your Eyes* as an undervalued gem. (It ran only 127 performances.) Perhaps she felt that Queen of the Lot gave her a dignity and glamour that her sidekick and goodtime-gal roles had thus far failed to. True, she was dressed to the utmost in Early Technicolor Dream Sequence, and her character, Jeanette Adair, does suggest a certain grandeur after Merman's Wanda Brill, Reno Sweeney, and Nails

---

* Odets did in fact marry Luise Rainer, a different kind of movie star than Crawford but like her a Queen of the Metro lot. Note, too, that in the next generation Arthur Miller marries Marilyn Monroe. Is there something about idealistic leftwing playwrights that we should know?

Duquesne. But Logan directed her in the style to which she was accustomed, that hot-date physical-innuendo plastique that is not all that evolved from the degraded art of thirties burlesque.

Perhaps Merman thought her numbers exalted her, for while Schwartz and Fields came up with a second-rate score, Merman's numbers—the confident "This is It," the wishful "Just a Little Bit More," the rueful "I'll Pay the Check"—did give her some stature. She was so Merman by now that one had to write Merman numbers if one wanted her to sing them; five years later. she walked out of *Sadie Thompson* during rehearsals at least in part (I believe) because the score failed to accommodate her genres. Schwartz and Fields did not make that mistake. They even wrote her a Cole Porter Merman number, "A Lady Needs a Change," complete with a naughty double meaning when the new chauffeur "drives me all day Monday." *Stars in Your Eyes'* most popular moment was Merman's duet with Durante, "It's All Yours," which they interrupted with vaudeville jokes. A telephone rings and someone in the orchestra pit hands it up to Durante. Answering, Durante says, "Hello, is this the meat market? Well, meet my wife at four o'clock!" and hangs up.

For a finale, let us consider three shows of 1939, each by a most prominent source of music: Cole Porter, Rodgers and Hart, and the house favorite, Jerome Kern. This trio of titles reveals the musical in its advanced late-thirties state, for all are musical comedies, the dominant form of the time; all offer the integrated tunestack; and all are "entertainment" shows, with scarcely a political remark anywhere.

Some characteristics are lacking. We see no technical innovation in design, little New Dance. Truth to tell, all three of our authors made their major history at other times. Porter's show, *DuBarry Was a Lady*, epitomizes the star vehicle as a brilliant showcase for Bert Lahr and Ethel Merman; it marks as well a high point of the raunchy tone associated with both stars and their producer, B. G. DeSylva, who collaborated on the book with the man who all but introduced ribaldry into the musical, Herbert Fields. Rodgers and Hart's *Too Many Girls* is a college show complete with a big game, filled by its producer-director, George Abbott, with his customary raids on 4-H clubs, the Boy Scouts, and nursery schools. Jerome Kern's *Very Warm For May* is a backstager in which nothing happens.

It didn't start out that way. Why would Kern and his collaborator, Oscar Hammerstein, waste their time on a harmless piece about a summer theatre this late in their career?* The plan was to merge the backstager with a gangster thriller, as the heroine, May (Grace McDonald) flees the danger by hiding out in summer stock. The company is run by Ogden Quiler (Hiram Sherman), a raving queen of a director, and financed by that thirties stereotype the screwball society dame (Eve Arden). Her grown children (Richard Quine, Frances Mercer) are in the troupe as well. Meanwhile, May's Broadway bigwig brother (Jack Whiting) and father (Donald Brian, New York's first Danilo in *The Merry Widow*) catch up with her, the former to romance Mercer and the latter to recognize Arden as a long-lost love.

The gangsters and some cops are the second-act's plot complications, obscuring the authors' real interest, which is to explore what happens when a visionary guru of the higher drama—that flaming director, screaming, "I want *dimension*!"—is forced to make do with amateurs and crepe paper. To May's scornful brother, who stars in shows he writes and stages, summer stock is "a lot of phonies in slacks and shorts rehearsing around swimming pools and under apple trees." As we then see, he's exactly right—but to the raving director, it's "The Ogden Quiler Progressive Playshop Theatre Guild, Inc." There is plenty of one of Hammerstein's favorite things, satire on theatremaking, as when one of the troupe turns out to have only one talent, accordion playing. "No accordions!" Quiler immediately rules. Can he at least be the prompter? Quiler consents, and then the accordion player stutters out, "Wh-wh-wh-what's the pr-pr-pr-prompter?"

Still, what gave *Very Warm For May* its substance was not its genre bending or theatre spoof but its excellent score. It isn't *Show Boat*–superb or *Cat and the Fiddle*–innovative. Rather, it's simply a wonderful collection of songs and, in addition, Kern's usual grudging exhibition of his finesse in swing. The show's overture starts on a hemiola (three beats played against two beats) outlined by a xylophone, going immediately to the brass section for the stabbing repeated-note triplets of the ballad "In the Heart of the Dark." It's so unexpected from the man who composed "Ol' Man River" that it invariably coaxes gasps and grins from modern listeners.

* *Very Warm For May* was Kern's last new Broadway show. At his death of a cerebral hemorrhage in 1945, he and Hammerstein had already revised *Show Boat* for its 1946 revival, and Kern was about to start work on *Annie Get Your Gun*, with lyricist Dorothy Fields.

Unfortunately, producer Max Gordon was not grinning when he came back from Hollywood business to catch the show on the first booking of its tryout, in Wilmington, Delaware. Gordon fired director Vincente Minnelli and brought in Hassard Short; Albertina Rasch came in as well, to spiff up Harry Losee's choreography. Worse, Gordon demanded a rewrite from Hammerstein, with the complete elimination of the gangsters and less of Quiler's carrying on. Originally, *Very Warm For May* watched the *cadette* of an important theatre family seeking refuge from a life-threatening situation in the bottom of the theatrical profession— where, she discovered, all theatre is equal because theatre in all its forms is everyone's blessing. In its revised state, all that the heroine was running from was the threat of summer school. The lesson about the democracy of theatre went silent, and the second-act tightening of the plot lost its grip in some specialty bits and a selection of Boy Gets Girl conclusions.

The show flopped, throwing its wonderful score into obscurity. "All The Things You Are" became a standard, but not in the form that Kern intended for it, as an elaborate choral movement led by a high-flying coloratura soprano. And the other numbers are not even cabaret caviar today, though they all show the signs of the musical theatre's wizard, as if his melodic cells were to be pestled in a mortar for the blending of spells. Kern builds "In Other Words, Seventeen" on simple diatonic harmony yet keeps accenting the melody on the second or seventh tone, creating simple havoc. For a dance number, "Heaven in My Arms (Music in My Heart)," he creates a syncopated descending phrase that is sung in the verse, then transformed into the accompaniment to the refrain. I tell you, it's magic. Kern spices the second beat of the chorus of "All in Fun" with a $c^\#dim.^7$ chord over D in the bass, setting the word "fun" in ironic quote marks. Indeed, Hammerstein's lyric is one big irony, revealing that one of two platonic pals wishes to take the friendship to loveland.

The entire score has this air of the ageless masters who can write anything because they've already written everything. If, as Kern once said, Irving Berlin was American music, then Kern and Hammerstein were American musical comedy, and in *Very Warm For May* they troubled to emphasize the form's youthful essence. Aside from Donald Brian, Eve Arden (who was in fact only about thirty), and Hiram Sherman (thirty-one), the cast was sons, daughters, and summer-stock kids, and Hammerstein never sounded younger: dancing and dating were his topics here, along with reading forbidden lit from Marx to Hemingway. True, "All the Things You Are" breathes the rarefied air of poetic imagery, with its "promised kiss of springtime" and "moment divine." But Kern had composed a grand line and the lyrics had to match it—and the reason that this number is grand is that it is part of Ogden Quiler's pageant: and Quiler wants dimension. Kern and Hammerstein might easily have given him a spoof of arty music; that's the easy way out. While laughing at Quiler's behavior, they are nevertheless respectful of his ambition, so "All the Things You Are" ratifies the program of a thespian who hopes to get something special out of the forms of musical theatre. The elaborate choral setting with the soprano descant substantiates Quiler's vision, taking what most listeners probably assume is a Boy-and-Girl love duet into a place well beyond convention.

The song has been called Kern's greatest, even the greatest song, period. That praise once went to Kern's "They Didn't Believe Me," from *The Girl From Utah* (1914). *That* one was, indeed, a simple love duet, for Julia Sanderson and *Very Warm For May*'s own Donald Brian; historians loved it for naturalizing the Broadway ballad. "All the Things You Are," however, *idealizes* the ballad, exploring the possibility that even a loon like Quiler might have some good ideas. It is worth remarking that "Heaven in My Arms" is also given the big choral treatment with coloratura soprano (in both cases Hollace Shaw). But "Heaven" is a plot number, built around Jack Whiting and Frances Mercer, and "Heaven" swings. It naturalizes. It is no accident that "Things" is so espressivo and "Heaven" so zingy; Kern and Hammerstein didn't work by accident.

They had one with *Very Warm For May* even so, with a set of horribly deflating notices. In *The New Yorker*, Robert Benchley thought it "lovely to the ear and complimentary to the intelligence," and when the *New York Post*'s idiot Wilella Waldorf called the score "routine" one knew it was of high quality. But the out-of-town revisions must have done great damage, for the plot is termed "flimsy" in the *World-Telegram* and "confusing" and "involved" in *Variety*—a sign that the cuts, additions, and joins had not cohered. Oddly, the show played smartly at Equity Library Theatre in 1985, even without Robert Russell Bennett's orchestration or the lavish décor with which the original distinguished Quiler's chaotic rehearsals from the professionalism that the theatre never fails to rise to. Well, hardly ever. Best of all, Glen Mure's Quiler was encouraged to retrieve the hysteric that the authors conceived, though it is unlikely that Hiram Sherman, or anyone else in 1939 including Danny Kaye, could have played the role with such gay abandon. Mure got every laugh, and so centered what on Broadway in 1939 had played without focus that it was good shocking narration when, late in Act Two, Quiler cried, "To *hell* with the *theatre!*" and walked out of the entertainment.

Those same critics cheered the Rodgers and Hart show, though *Too Many Girls* had none of *Very Warm For May*'s insight and curiosity. What college show does, even one with *Too Many Girls*' novelty of some Latin accenting? There was certainly nothing novel about the recycled *Girl Crazy* jokes concerning tenderfeet in the southwest, and George Marion Jr.'s book told even less story than we just got from Hammerstein: a plutocrat hires four all-American football players as bodyguards for his wild daughter. All matriculate at the father's alma mater, Pottawatomie College in Stopgap, New Mexico. The head bodyguard and the daughter fall in love, she feels manipulated when she learns that he's her father's hireling, so Boy Loses Girl. Love of course overtakes her misgivings; and Boy's three buddies pair off in turn.

Maybe that's what *Very Warm For May* needed: a solid Boy Loses Girl. When Hammerstein dropped the gangster suspense, he was left having to feature two romances that had been intended as slim subplots with no major setbacks to hurdle. *Too Many Girls* has a genuine conflict at its center: the four bodyguards have sworn to keep their relationship with their charge strictly professional, so first the hero, Clint, has to struggle with his attraction to the heroine, Consuelo, and then he has the problem of persuading her of his sincerity. It's a silly musical-comedy thing, true: but within those bounds it makes sense.

Then, too, George Abbott was a great pacer of shows, and *Too Many Girls* seems to have been one of his most limber productions; "swift" and "speed" keep turning up in the reviews. Let us not forget Abbott's mysterious ability to discern top talent that other producers passed up. The lead sweethearts, Richard Kollmar and Marcy Westcott, have left us no legend. But dancer Hal LeRoy, comic Eddie Bracken, and Latin lover Desi Arnaz filled out the athletes' quartet with considerable charm, and appear to have poured a gala chemistry with, respectively, singer Mary Jane Walsh, comic Leila Ernst (later that naive "mouse" in *Pal Joey*), and singer Diosa Costello.

These eight and the dancing corps really *were* the show, for it was the score and the choreography that gave the evening its content; one didn't attend thirties musical comedy for the Boy Meets Girl. One came for the accessories, and in this case they were the singing and dancing—especially the latter. Besides the Pottawatomie anthem, Westcott's wryly comic establishing piece, "My Prince," and ballads for Westcott and Kollmar, the breezy "Love Never Went To College" and the more soulful "I Didn't Know What Time It Was," virtually every title in the tunestack is a dance number. Moreover, except for the four songs just cited, nothing in the score connects with the story in any meaningful way. "Tempt Me Not (get thee behind me, Satin)," " 'Cause We Got Cake," the quodlibet fight song "Look Out," "The Sweethearts of the Team," and the title number are simply songs suitable for the boys and girls of a college show, any college show. And the cognoscente's favorite *Too Many Girls* titles were so extraneous to the narrative that the script could anchor them only on shameless pretext. One of these is a list song on the irritations of Manhattan life, "Give It Back To the Indians," but the other has some timely relevance, if not to *Too Many Girls*, then to the dissemination of show music at this time. "I Like To Recognize the Tune" amiably rebukes showboating swing bands for misguising melody with arrangements—drum solos, variations on the theme, cacophony.

It recalls the controversy over jazz bands in the 1920s, when Jerome Kern took the unprecedented step of banning all recordings of his *Sitting Pretty* (1924) songs, arguably his best set to that time. Rodgers' take was more pragmatic: he wanted his music to catch on in its "pure" state, after which he didn't mind the tampering. In his memoirs, he wrote, "A singer or an orchestra can add a distinctive, personal touch that actually con-tributes to a song's longevity." For his part, Lorenz Hart so enjoyed the verbal structure of the song's release that he wrote more strophes than the show could use, including one of his best couplets in picturing the scene when bandleader Kay Kyser "jazzes *Florodora*," because the beat is so com-pelling that "Mrs. Roosevelt starts to dance with Borah."*

Too Many Girls' 249 performances tell us that its lack of narrative sur-prise didn't hurt it. The story held together well enough to support the song and dance; this was sufficient in an age that preceded the time of the

---

* No, not harmonica player Borrah Minevitch (whom Hart had cited in *On Your Toes'* "The Three B's"), but Senator William E. Borah, one of F.D.R.'s outstanding critics.

Important Musical. George Abbott never asked for "dimension," though his decades in the musical took him to shows with ambitious scores and such themes as working-class poverty, labor relations, and Eugene O'Neillian destiny. In fact, the early George Abbott musicals propose a form that revises Aarons-Freedley with an alternative that also aims only to entertain. In the Abbott plan, instead of star performers and star songwriters, the ingredients are *potential* star performers and *potential* star songwriters. Mr. Abbott takes a chance. No, not on the long-established Rodgers and Hart, with whom he worked exclusively from 1935 through 1940. But later Abbott shows welcome the newcomer. The Aarons-Freedley format gives you, in effect, a series of encores. The Abbott format gives you debuts.

It would not be "Mr. Abbott," then, who would produce and co-author *DuBarry Was a Lady*, but B. G. DeSylva: Bert Lahr, Ethel Merman, and Cole Porter, on the Aarons-Freedley plan. The all-important cultural décor that provides the evening's theme lies in the crazy dream of Louie the nightclub lavatory attendant. That, of course, will be Lahr, who nourishes a hopeless attraction for the club's star (Merman). She loves the Usual Guy (Ronald Graham) who turns up in shows of this kind, unobtrusively used to urge the plot along and just about the one part of the event that we don't care about. Mcguffin Gets Girl: but not till after Lahr prepares for him a mickey finn, accidentally drinks it himself, and passes out. His dream is then enacted for us, as he sees himself as King Louis XV and Merman as his DuBarry back in pre-revolutionary France, with the powdered wigs and buckled shoes. The Usual Guy is now a writer of subversively satiric verse, and the second couple is Charles Walters and Betty Grable.

The last two names have an odd ring together, for Grable hasn't been in this book yet while we've watched Walters spend his twenties in the 1930s trying the typifying forms—theme revue in *The Show Is On*; Cole Porter in *Jubilee* and Rodgers and Hart in *I Married an Angel*; a little Schwartz and Dietz in *Between the Devil*; even a taste of politics in *Parade*. Grable was making her Broadway debut in *DuBarry*, having come east from an inconclusive assault on the movies; a fine personal success in *DuBarry* sent her back in style. Walters, too, would go Hollywood. He had already tried choreography, on *Sing Out the News*, and after two more such outings, in 1941, Walters set up shop in California as a choreographer and dancer, then as director, all at MGM. It's interesting to contemplate that the *Good News* remake (1947) that Walters directed and choreographed (with Robert Alton) may be a demonstration piece made in part of lessons learned from such thirties stage gurus as Hassard Short, Vincente Minnelli, Joshua Logan, Kaufman and Hart, and Vinton Freedley.

If *Very Warm For May* was family fare for grownups and *Too Many Girls* a bit risqué, *DuBarry Was a Lady* could be called burlesque by other means. In their various ways, Cole Porter, Herbert Fields, and Buddy DeSylva had been "opening up" the musical's naughty secrets, making everything overt in *The New Yorkers*, *America's Sweetheart*, *Flying High*. But *DuBarry Was a Lady*'s score itself strikes a bawdy proletarian tone that previous shows hit only intermittently. True, the action, laid in the Club Petite and Louie's dream, makes no place for the fashionable classes or even someone like *Pal Joey*'s mouse. The Club Petite is a dive. And the dream is a mug's idea of the French court, not the real thing. Louie has won the Irish sweepstakes, so he really is (temporarily) in the money. But even as Louis XV, he's still a mug.

So his establishing song, a dos and don'ts of the *comme il faut* called "It Ain't Etiquette," is skewed to discuss the worldview of the late-thirties Lahr, the one who visualizes the limitless freedoms of Park Avenue through the narrow attitudes of Hell's Kitchen. Thus, Louie's idea of a dinner party is "some mean old minx" serving one nothing but "a meatball," and he imagines a White House reception enlivened when the wife of the Chinese ambassador "unfurls after three drinks of anisette." Of course, like all lyricists of the time except Oscar Hammerstein, Porter writes in the voice of Porter rather than the voices of his characters. He observes distinctions in class only—the "ain't," for instance. In fact, "It Ain't Etiquette" captures perfectly Louie's *attitudes*—and the music, a rowdy waltz, is a well-judged match. But would Louie be conversant with "unfurls" and "anisette"?

Considering that *DuBarry* was entirely a Lahr-Merman affair but for the Usual Guy and the Walters-Grable numbers, it's odd that Lahr had only two other songs per se, both duets with Merman. "But in the Morning, No" is a relentless minuet of doubles entendres, from "shooting" to "third parties"; "Friendship," another of Porter's country-cousin struts, is a clever way to round off a "romance" that never existed. Merman, however, had seven numbers. These included Betty Grable's only solo, the second-act opening, "Give Him the Oo-La-La," which Grable had to yield to the star after a few performances in Boston. It is possible that Merman demanded it, but, to be fair, it would have looked strange to thirties audiences if Grable suddenly turned up with such an imposing assignment in the middle of a Merman show.

It must have fit Grable nicely, though, as a user's manual for pretty girls that plays with a kind of worldly innocence. Grable's first-act duet with Walters, "(We'll make) Ev'ry Day a Holiday," is *entirely* innocent, but— paradoxically—the second-act duet is entirely *worldly*. "Well, Did You Evah!" mocks the sangfroid of the truly well-bred, too intent on smooth style and good show to react to anything.*

What amuses about the *DuBarry* score is how much of it is fresh Porter, with his quibbling wordplay and musical shocks, like the jazz that rips into the serene phrases of Merman's first number, "When Love Beckoned (in Fifty-Second Street)," or the speedy tempo of the two ballads, "Do I Love You?" and "It Was Written in the Stars." Yet Porter reverts to the outdated finaletto to close Act One, complete with new music mixed with underscored dialogue and reprises with new lyrics.

Altogether, *DuBarry Was a Lady* was what the 1930s called a smash: 408 performances, good airwave play for the detachable numbers, and a hefty movie sale to MGM. In fact, all of our 1939 trio made it into film. Typically, *Very Warm For May* was made—also by MGM—more or less by the wayside, with a new story involving the show's characters and only "All the Things You Are" retained. Even the show's title was changed: to *Broadway Rhythm*. *Too Many Girls* came out of RKO as a nifty souvenir of the show, with three of the original football heroes (Richard Carlson took over for Richard Kollmar) and seven of the songs. But *DuBarry* could not be filmed in anything like its true form at that time, and was purified with a chaste heroine (Lucille Ball, also in the *Too Many Girls* film) and a midwestern Louie (Red Skelton).

The three shows had to survive in these forms, for none is a featured item of the *riesumazione*; even Encores! failed to deliver on its *DuBarry*

---

* The title was supposedly borrowed from a friend of Porter's who used it as an all-purpose rejoinder. This recalls for us a time when some of the people one met really were well-bred and cultivated expedient verbal ritornellos to avoid awkwardness in the social flow. Kitty Carlisle's—still in use at this writing—is "Darling, it's too divine!"

Was a Lady, with the miscast Robert Morse and Christine Ebersole. One wonders how a modern audience would relate to *Too Many Girls*, with its contentedly irrelevant storyline. Isn't the 1930s a relevant time, after all?

It was the worst of times, perhaps, after the fecund 1920s and before the artistic musical-play 1940s. It was an age of Tamaras and Modernistic Moes. There were few Johnny Johnsons and Larry Foremans, but a lot of *Hellzapoppin*. Still, *Porgy and Bess* holds the decade's center, while Cole Porter plays me a melody that's red, hot, and blue.

INDEX